Accounting in the Developing Countries

Accounting in the Developing Countries

AHMED RIAHI-BELKAOUI

Q

QUORUM BOOKS
Westport, Connecticut • London

Library of Congress Cataloging-in-Publication Data

Riahi-Belkaoui, Ahmed.
Accounting in the developing countries / Ahmed Riahi-Belkaoui.
p. cm.
Includes bibliographical references and index.
ISBN 0–89930–821–X (alk. paper)
1. Accounting—Developing countries. I. Title.
HF5616.5.R53 1994
657'.09172'4—dc20 93–50070

British Library Cataloguing in Publication Data is available.

Library of Congress Catalog Card Number: 93–50070
ISBN: 0–89930–821–X

First published in 1994

Quorum Books, 88 Post Road West, Westport, CT 06881
An imprint of Greenwood Publishing Group, Inc.

Printed in the United States of America

The paper used in this book complies with the Permanent Paper Standard issued by the National Information Standards Organization (Z39.48–1984).

10 9 8 7 6 5 4 3 2 1

Copyright Acknowledgments

The author and publisher gratefully acknowledge permission to quote from the following previously published sources:

Selected excerpts from Lenny Chasteen, "A Taxonomy of Price Change Models," *The Accounting Review* (July 1984), pp. 515–523.

Exhibits 4.2, 4.3, and 4.4, originally Exhibits 1–4, 2–1, and 3–1 from *Service Efforts and Accomplishments Reporting: Its Time Has Come, An Overview*, copyright 1990 by Governmental Accounting Standards Board, 401 Merritt 7, P.O. Box 5116, Norwalk, Connecticut, 06856–5116, U.S.A. Reprinted with permission. Copies of the complete document are available from the GASB.

To My Family, Here and There

Contents

Exhibits

Preface

Developing countries face insurmountable problems in their attempts to achieve progress in their economic development programs. Accounting plays a crucial role in economic development by providing the necessary information to implement the planning process generally relied upon by the developing countries. The development of accounting in these countries becomes an important priority and part of the total development process. The success of economic development is tied to the improvements made in the development and implementation of sound accounting systems at both the micro and macrolevels. This book elaborates on the major aspects of accounting in the developing countries that are generally tied to the development process in general. Chapter 1 discusses the problems and policies generally affecting economic development. Chapter 2 describes the accounting environment in the developing countries. Chapter 3 elaborates on the specific roles of accounting in the planning process and economic development. Chapter 4 covers the techniques used in both project appraisal and evaluation of projects in the developing countries. Finally, Chapter 5 examines the role of state-owned enterprises and privatization in the development context of the developing countries.

The book should be of value to those interested in the role of accounting in the development process of developing countries, including practicing accountants, business executives, accounting teachers and researchers, and students.

Many people helped in the development of this book. I received considerable assistance from the University of Illinois at Chicago students, especially Mei Lee Yu and Arun Hariharan. Assistance from the Department of Accounting provided time and resources to ensure the manuscript was completed on time. I thank Eric Valentine, Katie Chase, and the entire production team at Greenwood Publishing Group for their continuous and intelligent support. Finally to Hedi and Janice, thanks for everything.

Accounting in the Developing Countries

1

The Developing Countries and Economic Development

Developing countries face insurmountable problems in their attempts to achieve progress in their economic development programs. Their efforts led to the rise of a new economic subdiscipline—namely, development economics—to address the various problems and policies affecting economic development. The problems and policies are either domestic—such as growth, poverty and income distribution, unemployment, population growth, education, agricultural transformation and rural development—or international—foreign investment and aid, and new international economic order. These problems and policies are examined in this chapter, in addition to an explication of economic development and its contemporary problems.

THE MEANING OF UNDERDEVELOPMENT

Two-thirds of the world's population subsists on only 20 percent of the world's income. These people live in a state of underdevelopment, forcefully portrayed as follows:

> Underdevelopment is shocking: The squalor, disease, unnecessary deaths, and hopelessness of it all! No man understands if underdevelopment remains for him a mere statistic reflecting low income, poor housing, premature mortality and underemployment. The most empathetic observer can speak objectively about underdevelopment only after undergoing, personally or vicariously, the "shock of underdevelopment." This unique culture shock comes to one as he is initiated to the emotions which prevail in the "culture of poverty." The reverse shock is felt by those living in destitution when a new self-understanding reveals to them that their life is neither human nor inevitable. . . . the prev-

alent emotion of underdevelopment is a sense of personal and societal impotence in the face of disease and death, of confusion and ignorance as one probes to understand change, of servility toward men whose decisions govern the course of events, of hopelessness before hunger and natural catastrophe. Chronic poverty is a cruel kind of hell; and one cannot understand how cruel that hell is merely by gazing upon poverty as an object.[1]

These much less fortunate people live in what are generally characterized as developing countries. Various classifications of these countries exist:

1. The UN classifies these countries in three major groups designed as (a) the "least developed" for the 42 poorest countries, sometimes referred to as the "Fourth World"; (b) the "developing nations" for the 88 non-oil-exporting countries; and (c) the oil-exporting nations for the 13 members of the Organization of Petroleum Exporting Countries (OPEC).
2. The Organization for Economic Cooperation and Development (OECD) classifies these countries into 62 low-income countries (LICs), 73 middle-income countries (MICs), 11 newly industrialized nations (NICs), and 13 members of OPEC.
3. The World Bank, also known as the International Bank for Reconstruction and Development (IBRD), classifies these developed and developing countries into six categories: low income, middle income, upper middle income, high income oil exporters, industrial market economies, and East European nonmarket economies.

Whatever the definition adopted, the developing countries share some common characteristics of underdevelopment generally grouped into the following six broad categories:

1. Low levels of living
2. Low levels of productivity
3. High rates of population growth and dependency burdens
4. High and rising levels of unemployment and underemployment
5. Significant dependence on agricultural production and primary product exports
6. Dominance, dependence, and vulnerability in international relations.[2]

The combination of any number of these categories in a given country creates a state of underdevelopment. It is the result of not only economic but also social forces, not only internal but also external factors, and not only national but also international origins. It calls for each of these nations to formulate appropriate strategies of growth and development at the national level and, as seen later, modification of the international economic order at the international level. The basic objective of these strategies would be to break what Gunnar Myrdal referred to as the phenomenon of "circular and cumulative causation generated by the interactions between low levels of living and low productivity."[3]

These strategies have to take into account the structural diversity of the developing nations as exemplified by the following seven major components:

1. The size of the country (geographic, population, and income)
2. Historical evolution
3. Physical and human resource endowments
4. The relative importance of public and private sectors
5. The nature of the industrial structure
6. The degree of dependence on external economic and political forces
7. The distribution of power and the institutional and political structure within the nation.[4]

ECONOMIC DEVELOPMENT

The Nature of Development Economics

The study of development economics is a relatively new and separate development in the disciplines of economics and political economy. It deals with the economic, social, and institutional tools necessary to bring changes in the levels of living of developing countries.[5]

Basically, development economics addresses the critical questions about the economies of the developing countries, questions that center on finding the best way—economically, socially, and institutionally—of bringing these countries to an acceptable and decent level of living and productivity. It obviously goes beyond simple economics. In fact there is an implicit assumption in development economics about the limited relevance of traditional theory. Myrdal states the case as follows:

> Economic theorists, more than any other social scientists, have long been disposed to arrive at general propositions and then postulate them as valid for every time, place and culture. There is a tendency in contemporary economic theory to follow this path to the extreme. . . . When theories and concepts designed to fit the special conditions of the Western world—and thus containing the implicit assumptions about social reality by which this fitting was accomplished—are used in the study of underdeveloped countries, where they do *not* fit, the consequences are serious.[6]

The developing countries need to go beyond simple economics and adopt strategies that attack not only economic problems but all other problems of the social systems of their nations. That is the objective of development economics. It goes beyond the formal modeling of conventional economics to cover a more exhaustive approach to development. In effect, formal modeling, by itself, is insufficient to provide a clear picture of poverty. Such a model would not be able to describe adequately the complexity of poverty and its application would not be easy given the more difficult task of measuring all the required parameters.[7] This model needs to differ from those adopted in developed countries. A new paradigm of economic development, which differs from those adopted for the economic development of the Western countries, is needed as shown by the following arguments:

1. The capital and cultivable land resources available to the underdeveloped countries are much more limited than was the case during Western economic development.
2. Without comparable resources labour productivity cannot be improved by means similar to those which have been successful in the West.
3. International and domestic demand conditions are such that urban industrialization cannot be expected to grow at a rate which permits the transfer of labour from agriculture into higher productivity urban industrial occupations: at the same time the limited demand conditions also slow down or prevent the adoption of modern agrarian technologies and, hence, prevent the growth of rural income.
4. Urban migration is already in excess of what is economically justified, as shown by the widespread urban unemployment in almost all underdeveloped countries.
5. Social justice and structural conditions in the economy require an improvement in the distribution of income and a growth in the incomes of the lower income groups. But these can be brought about only by increasing employment and work opportunities at higher returns than the market can yield. Since the primary opportunities for the productive use of unskilled labor can be found in rural and agricultural-related activities rather than urban industrial or service employment, the focus of the development effort must be shifted from urban industrialization toward rural transformation. But there are no competitive market processes which can bring about the required change; hence the market must be, in some of its basic functions, replaced by government or community action. Hence the need for a new paradigm for development.[8]

The Meaning of Development

As stated earlier, development is more than an economic process. It involves the economic, social, and institutional process necessary to efficiently eliminate the major evils of underdevelopment: malnutrition, disease, illiteracy, slums, unemployment, and inequality. Besides the creation of self-sustained growth in per capita gross national product (GNP), it involves the requisite modernization of economic, social, and political structures implicit in the achievement of GNP growth. The basic purpose and meaning of development is *depauperization,* which has been defined as follows:

> Depauperization has both economic and noneconomic dimensions and stresses the removal not only of material but equally importantly of social, political and spiritual forms of deprivation. It involves not only equity but more significantly the creation of conditions conducive to continuing improvements in equity. It may require temporary sacrifices in national economic growth and involves major social and institutional changes.[9]

Development calls then for both the elimination of deprivation and the restoration of equity in addition to the achievement of GNP growth. Achieving good growth and effectively distributing the growth is the essence of good development. Development goals focus on the improvement in human life and human happiness. While human life and/or human happiness are universal goals and values sought by every developing country, these universal values that all societies desire and that development claims to foster are life-sustenance, self-esteem, and freedom.[10]

Life sustenance includes people's requirement for food, shelter, healing, or survival. Development's main goal is to provide such life-sustaining goods as food, medicine, adequate shelter, and protection. As Denis Goulet states, "Quite clearly, one of development's most important goals is to prolong man's lives and render those men less 'stunted' by disease, extreme exposure to nature's elements, and defenselessness against enemies."[11]

Self-esteem is every person's sense that he or she has worth, that he or she is respected and is not used as a tool by others for their own purposes. In some societies this self-esteem is expressed by the need for identity, dignity, respect, honor, or recognition. The need for self-esteem is a major drive for achieving development. As Goulet states, "Therefore, the conviction is gaining strength throughout the world that mass poverty cuts societies off from due recognition or esteem. Once deprivation of esteem reaches an intolerable point, people are quite ready to begin desiring material 'development.' "[12]

Freedom from any form of servitude to nature, ignorance, other people, institutions, and beliefs is a fundamental goal of and drive for development. With freedom comes development and a great choice for people in dealing with their environment.

Theories of Economic Development

Three basic schools of thought dominate the economic development literature: an early literature on the stages-of-economic-growth and more recent literature on the structural change models and the international dependency paradigms.

1. The linear stages of economic growth focuses on the importance to development of both the acquisition and use of capital and the historical development of the developed countries. One example is *Rostow's argument* that the advanced countries have passed the stage of "take-off into self-sustaining growth" while the underdeveloped countries are in a "pre-condition" stage, and in need of massive infusion of domestic and foreign savings before growth takes place.[13] A second example is the *Harrod-Domar growth model,* which simply states that the growth of national income will be directly, or positively, related to the savings ratio, and inversely or "negatively" related to the economy's capital/output ratio. Both theories and models did not work effectively for the developing countries because more savings and investments are not sufficient for economic growth. Favorable institutional and attitudinal conditions need to be present before take off can take place. Michael Todaro argues the case as follows:

The Marshall plan worked for Europe because the European countries receiving aid possessed the necessary structural, institutional, and attitudinal conditions (e.g., well-integrated commodity and money markets, highly developed transport facilities, well-trained and educated manpower, the motivation to succeed, an efficient government bureaucracy) to convert new capital effectively into higher levels of output. The Rostow-Harrow-Domar models implicitly assume the existence of the same attitudes and arrangements in underdeveloped nations. Yet in many cases they are lacking, as are complementary factors such as managerial competence, skilled labor, and the ability to plan and administer a wide assortment of development projects.[14]

2. The neoclassical structural change model relies on neoclassical price and resource allocation theory and statistical modeling to describe the structural changes in the developing nations on their way to becoming modern nations. For example, the *two-sector labor theoretical model* of W. Arthur Lewis argues for a labor transfer from a traditional, overpopulated rural subsistence sector to a more productive modern urban industrial sector, and a growth of output and employment in the industrial sector.[15] Another example is the *patterns of development* empirical analysis of Hollis Chenery that identified a shift from agricultural production to industrial production as per capita income rises.[16]

3. Two streams of thought characterize the international dependency models, namely, the neoclassical dependence model and the false paradigm model.

The *neoclassical dependence model* views the world as being dominated by rich countries (the core) at the expense of poor countries (the periphery). In addition, the policies of the core countries have an effect on the peripheral countries because of this dependency situation and most of the time are responsible for the continuing and worsening poverty of their developing nations. The effects are perceived to be negative most of the time given the developed countries' power to control world commodities to their advantages, to dominate the domestic economies of the developing countries through direct foreign investment, to affect the developing economies' trade by exporting unsuitable products, and by dumping cheap products and locking them into exporting primary products with declining revenues. These accusations are well contained into the following observation:

> The very forces which are set in motion by the rapid growth of rich countries—specially the development of even more sophisticated, costly and capital-intensive technologies, and of mortality-reducing health improvements and disease controls—specially a population explosion, rising unemployment and inability to develop their own technological capacities, which may in fact assume that they will not have the time needed for the continued maintenance of current growth rates, let alone their acceleration, so as to result in acceptable levels of development.[17]

A general list of the forces of international dominance and dependence is provided by Todaro.[18]

Immanuel Wallerstein argued forcefully that the core-periphery schema is fundamental, and that the exploited peripheral countries are vital to the functioning of the core countries.[19] Nations, of course, move with development from a peripheral status to either a semicore or core status.

The *false paradigm model* blames the underdevelopment of some of the developing countries on the wrong advice given by well-intentioned advisers sent to help the developing world. These experts resort to sophisticated models, some theoretical and some analytical, which are most of the time inappropriate to resolve the practical problems of underdevelopment.[20]

DOMESTIC PROBLEMS AND POLICIES

There are a number of critical domestic problems that are the main target of development policies in the Third World. In what follows, these problems are described and the economic policies used for their ultimate resolution are explored.

Growth, Poverty, and Income Distribution

The first problem is one of growth, poverty, and income distribution. In effect, one main objective of development is to eliminate poverty and income inequalities. As in some developed economies, the developing economies face the situation where only a small portion of the population constituting the rich class controls a very large share of the national income and resources, influencing the consumption and production patterns toward expensive consumer goods. These income inequalities are aggravated by high levels of "absolute poverty," which is generally measured by the number of people living below a specified minimum level of income. Absolute poverty in the world is widespread, leading World Bank economists Ahluwalia, Carter, and Chenery to conclude that

> almost 40 percent of the population of the developing countries live in absolute poverty defined in terms of income levels that are insufficient to provide adequate nutrition. The bulk of the poor are in the poorer countries: in South Asia, Indonesia and Sub-Saharian Africa. These countries account for two-thirds of the total (world) population and well over three-fourths of the population in poverty. The incidence of poverty is 60 percent or more in countries having the lowest level of real GNP.[21]

Development goals originally focused on maximizing rates of GNP growth and expecting a "trickle down" of the benefits of economic growth to the very poor. Failure of these policies led to a redefining of development goals toward broad-based income growth, with special emphasis on accelerating the growth of incomes of "target" poverty groups. Four policy options are generally advocated in determining a developing economy's distribution of income: (1) to alter the functional distribution of income through policies designed to change relative factor prices, (2) to modify the size distribution through progressive redistribution of asset ownership, (3) to reduce the size distribution at the upper levels through progressive income and wealth taxes, and (4) to affect distribution at the lower levels through direct transfer payments and the public provision of goods and services.[22]

Unemployment

The second domestic problem is that of unemployment. Not only is a very large section of the population unemployed, but unemployment in the developing countries seems to grow faster than employment, mainly due to the phenomenon of labor underutilization. Edgar Edwards distinguishes among the following forms of underutilization of labor: open unemployment; underemployment; the visible active but underutilized as disguised underemployment, hidden unemployment, and prematurely retired; the impaired; and the unproductive.[23] All major economic models of employment determination are advocated in the literature, namely, classical, Keynesian, the output/employment macro model, the price-incentive micro model, and the two-sector labor transfer model. The classical model relies on the forces of supply and demand to set the wage rate and the level of employment. The Keynesian model relies on demand factors such as increases in government expenditures and encouragement of private investments for reducing unemployment. Both the classical and the Keynesian models are considered to be far from relevant to the developing countries. The output/employment macromodel argues that the rate of national output and employment depend upon the rate of savings and investment, lending credence to the "big push" for industrialization in some developing countries. The price-incentive model maintains that the combination of labor and capital will be dictated by the relative factor prices. Cheap labor would lead to labor-intensive production processes. Finally, the two-sector labor transfer of rural-urban migration focuses on the determinants of both demand and supply. Two variations characterize the last model: the Lewis theory of development[24] and the Todaro model.[25] The Lewis model divides the economy in two sectors: (1) a traditional, rural subsistence sector characterized by zero- or low-productivity surplus labor; and (2) a growing urban industrial sector characterized by an influx of labor from the subsistence sector. The Todaro model hypothesizes that migration is due to urban-rural differences in expected rather than actual earnings. All these approaches lead to a consensus position on employment strategy, which would include the following five elements: (1) creating an appropriate rural-urban economic balance; (2) expanding small-scale, labor-intensive industries; (3) eliminating factor-price distortions; (4) choosing appropriate labor-intensive technologies of production; and (5) noting the direct linkage between education and employment.[26]

Another way of reducing unemployment is by creating special trading zones, which are usually intended to attract foreign investors to produce assembly goods for export. The zones are made attractive to investors through offering inducements such as reducing taxes or offering tax holidays, relaxing tariffs and currency-exchange facilities, and allowing administrative advantages, which may include a watering down of union and labor laws.[27] Some groups, however, criticize the concept of special trading zones as merely sweatshops exported by "footloose" multinational companies. For example, the International Confederation of Free Trade Unions, which is the largest organization of democratic labor unions, is concerned by the possible exploitation of workers who are often desperate for jobs, and by the possible isolation of worldwide conventions on labor norms and employee protection drafted under the auspices of the UN International Labor Organization (ILO) in Geneva and ratified by most governments.

Population Growth

The third domestic problem is that of ever-expanding human numbers. All positions on the population debate seem to agree that in the long run "zero population growth" is not only a necessity but also an important means to a better life in the developing countries. The population growth in the developing countries is now accentuated by lower death rates due undoubtedly to the rapid improvement in health conditions. As a result, one may notice that high birth rates are generally associated with national poverty and low per capita income. The question is whether population is a real problem; and whatever the position is in this question, the problem is to find adequate solutions to the population growth. Two extreme positions may be explored. The first claims that population growth is not a real problem but a result of other problems such as underdevelopment, depletion of world resources, and population distribution. The solution advocated is through development programs focusing on improvements in health, nutrition, income, social justice, status of women, and other such general factors. The second position claims that population growth is a real problem requiring deliberate governmental "population policies," which may include providing family-planning services, programs and laws affecting information and education, incentives directed toward fertility behavior, and programs to alter the frequency and age of marital unions.

Advocates of the first position attribute the decline in fertility in some developing countries to their experienced economic development, industrialization, and urbanization, while advocates of the second position point to the intensive population and family-planning programs in these countries for a better explanation of the declining birth rates. One way of solving the debate between both positions is to reach a consensus position based on a population program plus a development position.

Education

The fourth domestic problem pertains to the need for improving the human resources of the developing countries by providing a sound education system.

The general mechanism used is the formal education system, which takes place in schools, uses the traditional academic curriculum, and prepares students to join modern economic lifestyles. There are, however, other types of education most beneficial to the developing countries—namely, *informal education* or learning by doing, which "includes agricultural training, programmes, evening adult literacy classes, radio and mass media campaigns, and vocational training programmes,"[28] and *education for self-reliance* or problem-posing education, which "teaches groups of people to study together and become aware of the political and economic determinants of their poverty."[29]

Given the inadequacy of formal education, various developing countries have experimented with informal education and education for self-reliance. The results are far from conclusive at this time. So the call for education reform beyond the boundaries of formal education continues to stir interest and debate in the developing countries. Education is considered to be the best determinant and hope for a better lifestyle in the developing countries. As stated by Torsten Husen, "the mood has swung from the almost euphonic conception of education as the Great Equalizer to that of education as the Great Sieve that sorts and certifies people for their (predetermined) slot in society."[30] Most calls for an education reform stress the need for a curriculum most beneficial and in accordance with the real needs of each developing country, and more relevant to the development needs.

Agricultural Transformation and Rural Development

The fifth problem pertains to the need for agricultural transformation and rural development. One of the most proven theses in economics relates to the secular decline of the agricultural population and the labor force and agriculture's share of GNP in the course of economic development coupled with a consistent rise in the share of labor in the service sector. Various explanations are given for this structural transformation.

> To some, this structural transformation is simply a consequence of development—of the increase in productivity and incomes in the various sectors of an economy that entails changes in the patterns of consumer demand and the composition of output. Other writers take the position that structural transformation should be viewed not merely as a consequence of development but as a process that should be deliberately fostered by policy measures to accelerate development and to ensure that low income, pre-industrial societies will succeed in realizing their goals of achieving self-sustained economic growth.[31]

In addition to this structural transformation, the performance of Third World agriculture has been relatively poor due mainly to inefficiency and low productivity. Subsistence agriculture on small plots of land and extensive cultivation characterize agriculture in most of the developing countries. These countries need to move from an objective of achieving subsistence to one of agricultural sufficiency. Three stages may be necessary: a first stage of subsistence farming characterized by risk, uncertainty, and survival; a second stage of transition to mixed and diversified farming; and a third stage of specialization and modern commercial farming. To achieve this goal, a strategy of agricultural and rural development is needed. Todaro proposes three necessary conditions for rural development—land reform, supportive policies, and integrated development objectives:

Proposition I: Farm structure and land-tenure patterns need to be adopted to the dual objectives of increasing food production and promoting a wider distribution of the benefits of agrarian progress. . . .
Proposition II: The full benefits of small-scale agricultural development cannot be realized unless government support systems are created that provide the necessary incentives, economic opportunities, and access to needed inputs to enable small cultivators to expand their output and raise their productivity. . . .
Proposition III: Rural development, while dependent primarily on small-farmer agricultural progress, implies much more. It encompasses (a) improvements in "levels of living" including income, employment, education, health and nutrition, housing, and a variety of related social services; (b) a decreasing inequality in the distribution of rural incomes and in urban-rural imbalances on incomes and economic opportunities; and (c) the capacity of the rural sector to sustain and accelerate the pace of these improvements over time.[32]

INTERNATIONAL PROBLEMS AND POLICIES

There are a number of critical international problems that are also the main target of development policies in the developing countries. In what follows, these problems are described and the economic policies used for their ultimate resolution are explored.[33]

International Trade and Development

Developing countries suffer from two main limitations in their trading with developed countries. First, their exports are heavily composed of nonumerical primary products, while their imports include everything from new materials to capital goods, intermediate producer goods, and consumer products. Second, the commodity terms of trade as measured by the ratio between the price of a typical unit of exports and the price of a typical unit of imports are deteriorating. The result shows up in a continuous deficit in the current and capital accounts of their balance of payments. To solve this problem a variety of options are used: export promotion or import-substitution policies; encouragement of private foreign investment, or call for public and private foreign assistance; greater use of the Special Drawing Rights of the International Monetary Fund (IMF); foreign exchange controls or currency devaluation; economic integration with other developing countries in the form of customs unions, free trade areas, or common markets.[34] But above all, the major option is the choice of a trade strategy for development. Should it be an outward- or inward-looking policy? An outward-looking policy results from the classical trade theory and comparative cost-advantage arguments with the implication that free trade will maximize global output by allowing every country to specialize in what it does best. P. P. Streeten states that point as follows: "Outward-looking policies encourage not only free trade but also the free movement of capital, workers, enterprises and students, a welcome to the multinational enterprise, and open system of communications. If it does not imply laissez-faire, it certainly implies *laissez-passer.*"[35]

An inward-looking policy results from the belief that the developing countries should be encouraged to engage in their own style of development and not be constrained by or dependent upon foreign importation, and to learn by doing. Streeten explains this option as follows:

> Inward-looking policies emphasize the need for an indigenous technology, appropriate for the factors available in the country, and for an appropriate range of products. If you restrict trade, the movement of people and communications, if you keep out the multinational enterprise, with its wrong technology, you will evolve your own style of development and you will be stronger, more independent, master of your own fate.[36]

In short, outward-looking is identifiable with export promotion while inward-looking is identifiable with import substitution. These two strategies, when added to the strategies of primary and secondary or manufacturing production, yield a fourfold division: primary outward-looking policies, secondary outward-looking policies, primary inward-looking policies, and secondary inward-looking policies.[37] The choice of any one of these options determines the nature of international trade of each developing country and of its impact on development.

Foreign Investment and Aid

Many developing countries tend to rely on outside financial aid to alleviate the deficits in their current account balances. This aid takes place in the form of either private foreign investment or public development assistance. Both types of aid are examined next.

Private foreign investment is playing a major role in economic development through the activities of the large multinational corporations, whose roles are claimed to be either positive or negative, depending upon which side of the controversy one is on. Adolf Enthoven has successfully summarized the results, both positive and negative, claimed for multinational corporations by the spokespersons for developing countries as follows:

> POSITIVE EFFECTS (Benefits/Advantages): 1. Transfer of capital; 2. transfer of know-how and mannagement; 3. balance-of-payments benefits; 4. increase in competition and lower prices; 5. increase in entrepreneurial spirit; 6. help in training and education;

7. increase in employment; 8. help in infrastructure; 9. improvement of living conditions in developing countries; 10. identification, allocation, management, and efficient use of world material and human and financial resources; 11. greater international unity and interdependency; 12. ensuring a more equal distribution of income and wealth.

NEGATIVE EFFECTS (Costs/Disadvantages): 1. Hampering of balance of payments; export of profits and interest beyond investment; 2. technology too advanced for country and too capital-intensive; 3. limited training and education; 4. input of foreign management to the neglect of local managers; 5. curbing of local enterprises; 6. enforcement of consumption functions (luxury items); 7. uneven distribution of income; 8. affecting employment; restricting transfer of know-how; 9. subordination of companies and countries to the multinational corporations, threatening the sovereignty of the nation-state; 10. hampering of the endogenous socioeconomic development of a nation; 11. distribution of social, political, and cultural patterns in the host country; 12. resentment against foreign penetration, resulting in upsetting the social balance; 13. recession resulting from inability of national industries to compete; 14. loss of national pride and nationalistic spirit.[38]

Public development assistance is as much the subject of a heated debate as private foreign investment. It is viewed by some as essential and beneficial to economic development by supplementing scarce resources and helping the developing countries to achieve more forms of self-sustaining economic growth. Others maintain that foreign aid may have retarded growth through reduced savings and worsened income inequalities.[39] They would even add that countries have strong strategic, political, and economic motivations behind their foreign aid programs. Witness the following statement made by a former U.S. aid official:

> The biggest single misconception about the foreign aid program is that we send money abroad. We don't. Foreign aid consists of American equipment, raw materials, expert services, and food—all provided for specific development projects which we ourselves review and approve. . . . Ninety-three percent of AID [Agency for International Development] funds are spent directly in the United States to pay for these things. Just last year some 4,000 American firms received $1.3 billion in AID funds for products supplied as part of the foreign aid program.[40]

Obviously, a new view of private foreign investment and foreign aid is needed to relieve the ''disillusionment'' on the part of developing countries and ''weariness'' on the part of developed countries. Some useful suggestions have been made in what is known as the ''New International Economic Order'' proposal.

New International Economic Order

Faced with their bleak situation, the developing countries began asking for a ''New International Economic Order'' (NIEO). In fact, the UN General Assembly, in a special session convened in April 1974 following the petroleum crisis, concluded its deliberations by committing itself

> to work urgently for the establishment of a new international economic order based on equity, sovereign equality, common interest and cooperation among all states, irrespective of their economic and social systems, which shall correct inequalities and redress in existing injustices, make it possible to eliminate the widening gap between the developed and the developing countries and ensure steadily accelerating economic and social development and peace and justice for present and future generations.

Before this declaration the United Nation began a series of programs and targets toward achieving this NIEO. Examples include launching the first UN Development Decade, the Alliance for Progress in 1961, the Yaunde Convention in 1967, and the second UN Development Decade of the 1970s. The developing countries used their newfound political and economic leverage to demand a new structure of international economic relations and a new set of rules affecting trade, industrialization, transfer of technology, and foreign assistance. A list of NIEO demands includes the following:

1. Attaining UN Official Developing Assistance targets
2. Providing technical assistance for developing countries
3. Renegotiating the debts of developing countries
4. Undertaking special measures to assist land-locked, least-developed, and island developing countries
5. Using disarmament funds for development
6. Improving the terms and conditions of trade for developing countries: tariff and nontariff barriers, general systems of preference, duties and taxes on imports, invisible trade
7. Adopting an integrated approach to commodities: the integrated program, buffer stocks, producers' associations, indexation
8. Developing an international food program
9. Adjusting the economic policies of developed countries to facilitate expanding and diversifying the exports of developing countries
10. Improving and intensifying trade relations between countries having different social and economic systems
11. Strengthening economic and technical cooperation among developing countries
12. Reforming the international monetary system: using special drawing rights for development assistance and as the central reserve asset of the international monetary system, promoting stable rates of exchange and protection from the effects of inflation
13. Assuring adequate participation by developing countries in World Bank and IMF decision making
14. Increasing the transfer of resources through the World Bank and IMF
15. Negotiating the redeployment of industrial productive capacities to developing countries

16. Regulating and supervising the activities of transnational enterprises and eliminating restrictive business practices
17. Improving the competitiveness of natural resources and ending their waste
18. Providing equitable access to the resources of the seabed and the ocean floor
19. Achieving a more equitable distribution of income and raising the level of employment
20. Providing health services, education, higher cultural standards, and qualification for the work force, and assuring the well-being of children and the integration of women in development
21. Assuring the economic sovereignty of states: natural resources, foreign property, choice of economic systems
22. Compensating for adverse effects on the resources of states, territories, and people of foreign occupation, alien and colonial domination, or apartheid
23. Establishing a system of consultations at global, regional, and sectoral levels with the aim of promoting industrial development
24. Restructuring the economic and social sections of the United Nations.[41]

THE PROCESS OF DEVELOPMENT

The process of development entails a process of economic growth expressed in terms of its components of capital accumulation, growth in population, and technological progress. It is best expressed by Simon Kuznets: "A country's economic growth may be defined as a long-term rise in capacity to supply increasingly diverse economic goods to its population, this growing capacity based on advanced technology and the institutional and ideological demands that it demands."[42]

In fact, Kuznets presents six characteristics of modern economic growth in each developed country based on the conventional measures.

1. High rates of growth of per capita product and of population.
2. High rates of rise in productivity of all inputs, including labor.
3. High rates of structural transformation of the economy away from agriculture to non-agricultural pursuits, away from industry to services, and away from personal enterprise to impersonal enterprise.
4. High rates of social and ideological change, including urbanization and secularization as the components of the process of modernization.
5. Higher access of the developing countries to the markets and raw materials in the rest of the world.
6. The limited spread of economic growth to only a third of the world's population.[43]

These characteristics are significantly interrelated. It is expressed by Kuznets as follows:

With the rather stable ratio of labor force to total population, a high rate of increase in per capita product means a high rate of increase in product per worker; and, with average hours of work declining, it means still higher growth rates in product per man-hour. Even if we allow for the impressive accumulation of capital, in its widest sense, the growth rate of productivity is high, and indeed, mirrors the great rise in per capita pure consumption. Since the latter reflects the realized effects of advancing technology, rapid changes in production structure are inevitable—given the differential impact of technological innovations on the several production sectors, the differing income elasticity of domestic demand for various consumer goods, and the changing comparative advantage in foreign trade. As already indicated, advancing technology changes the scale of production plants and the character of the economic enterprise units. Consequently, effective participation in the modern economic system by the labor force necessitates rapid changes in its location and structure, in the relations among occupational status groups, and even in the relations between labor force and total population (the last, however, within narrow overall limits). Thus, not only are high aggregate growth rates associated with rapid changes in economic structure, but the latter are also associated with rapid changes in other aspects of society—in family formation, in urbanization, in man's views on his role and the measure of his achievement in society.[44]

The interdependence of growth characteristics signals to developing countries the need for a multidimensional approach to development with a stable, but flexible, political and social framework that can accommodate the fundamental societal changes generated by development; a positive attitude toward the role of technological innovations and research for development; and a just relationship with rich nations that minimizes dependence and maximizes self-reliance and equity. In addition, the developing countries need to be sensitive to the emerging economic global issues that may hinder their development. One first issue is the global interdependence that places the developing countries in a situation of dependence on the rich countries, especially on four key issues: energy and resource balances, the global food-population equation, the crisis of the developing countries' debt, and the demand for a restructuring of the international economic order.[45] Each of these issues places the destiny of the developing countries and the success of their development strategies at the doorsteps of the developing nations. The cooperation of the developing countries becomes a key element for the success of the development of poor countries.

CONCLUSIONS

This chapter elaborated on the domestic and international problems faced by the developing countries as well as on the process of economic development. Concerted strategies are obviously needed in each of the developing countries to deal with these problems and direct the process of economic development to successful paths. The situation demands the input not only of the population of each developing country but also the input and the resources of the developed world. Morality, compassion, and a sense of justice call for an international effort to bring the developing countries to a more acceptable level of economic development, which can bring prosperity and better quality of life to their populations.

NOTES

1. Dennis Goulet, *The Cruel Choice: A New Concept in the Theory of Development* (New York: Atheneum, 1971), p. 23.
2. Michael P. Todaro, *Economic Development in the Third World* (New York: Longman, 1985), p. 28.
3. Gunnar Myrdal, *Asian Drama* (New York: Pantheon, 1968), Appendix 2.
4. Todaro, *Economic Development,* p. 24.
5. Ibid., p. 17.
6. Myrdal, *Asian Drama,* pp. 16–17.
7. Keith Griffin and Azizur Rahman Khan, ''Poverty in the Third World: Ugly Facts and Fancy Models,'' *World Development* 6, 3 (1978), pp. 301–302.
8. Louis Feber, ''On the Paradigm for Economic Development,'' *World Development* 2, 1 (1974), pp. 6–7.
9. Irma Adelman, ''Development Economics: A Reassessment of Goals,'' *American Economic Review* (May 1975), p. 306.
10. Goulet, *The Cruel Choice,* pp. 87–95.
11. Ibid., p. 88.
12. Ibid., p. 90.
13. W. W. Rostow, *The Stages of Economic Growth: A Non-Communist Manifesto* (London: Cambridge University Press, 1960).
14. Todaro, *Economic Development in the Third World,* pp. 66–67.
15. W. A. Lewis, ''Economic Development with Unlimited Supplies of Labor,'' Manchester School, 1954; and J. C. H. Fei and G. Ranis, *Development of the Labor Surplus Economy: Theory and Policy* (Homewood, Ill.: Irwin, 1964).
16. Hollis Chenery, *Structural Changes and Development Policy* (Baltimore: Johns Hopkins University Press, 1979).
17. Hans W. Singer, ''Dualism Revisited: A New Approach to the Problems of Dual Society in Developing Countries,'' *Journal of Development Studies* 7, 1 (1970).
18. Todaro, *Economic Development,* pp. 81–82.
19. Immanuel Wallerstein, *The Capitalist World Economy* (Cambridge: Cambridge University Press, 1979).
20. Todaro, *Economic Development,* p. 80.
21. M. S. Ahluwalia, N. Carter, and H. Chenery, ''Growth and Poverty in Developing Countries,'' *Journal of Developing Economics* 6 (September 1979), p. 306.
22. Todaro, *Economic Development,* pp. 146–149.
23. Edgar O. Edwards, *Employment in Developing Countries: Report on a Ford Foundation Study* (New York: Columbia University Press, 1974), pp. 10–11.
24. Lewis, ''Economic Development with Unlimited Supplies of Labor.'' The model was formalized and extented in J. C. H. Fei and G. Ramis, ''A Theory of Economic Development,'' *American Economic Review* 51, 3 (1961).
25. Michael P. Todaro, ''A Model of Labor Migration and Urban Unemployment in Less Developed Countries,'' *American Economic Review* 59, 1, (1969), pp. 138–48.

26. Todaro, *Economic Development,* pp. 244–45.

27. David Fonguet, "Special Trade Zones Increase Despite Cities," *Chicago Tribune* (November 17, 1983), sect. 2, pp. 2–3.

28. John Simmons, "Education for Development, Reconsidered," *World Development* (1979), p. 1006.

29. Ibid.

30. Torsten Husen, "Problems of Securing Equal Access to Higher Education: The Dilemma between Equality and Excellence," *Higher Education* 5 (1976), p. 411.

31. Bruce F. Jonston, "Agricultural and Structural Transformation in Developing Countries: A Survey of Research," *Journal of Economic Literature* 8, 2 (1970), p. 374.

32. Todaro, *Economic Development,* pp. 278–80.

33. Ahmed Belkaoui, *International Accounting* (Westport, Conn.: Quorum Books, 1985), p. 320

34. Felipe Pazos, "Regional Integration of Trade among Less Developed Countries: A Survey of Research," *Journal of Economic Literature,* 8, 2 (1970), p. 374.

35. P. P. Streeten, "Trade Strategies for Development: Some Themes for the Seventies," *World Development* 1, 6 (June 1973), p. 1.

36. Ibid., p. 2.

37. Ibid.

38. Adolf J. H. Enthoven, "Social and Political Impact of Multinationals on Third World Countries (and its Accounting Implications)" (Dallas: Center for International Accounting Development, The University of Texas at Dallas, 1976), p. 2.

39. K. Griffin and J. L. Enos, "Foreign Assistance: Objectives and Consequences," *Economic Development and Cultural Change* (April 1970), pp. 313–327.

40. W. S. Gand, "Foreign Aid: What It Is, How It Works, Why We Provide It," *Department of State Bulletin* 59, 1537 (1968).

41. A thorough description of each of these demands and the history of its organization is provided in E. Laszlo, R. Balser, Jr., E. Eisenberg, and V. Raman, *The Objectives of the New International Economic Order* (New York: Pergamon Press, 1978).

42. Simon Kuznets, "Modern Economic Growth: Findings and Reflections," *American Economic Review* (June 1973), pp. 248–249.

43. Ibid.

44. Ibid., p. 250.

45. Todaro, *Economic Development,* pp. 539–540.

SELECTED READINGS

Chenery, Hollis. *Structural Changes and Development Policy.* Baltimore: John Hopkins University Press, 1979.

Fei, J. C. H. and G. Ranis. *Development of the Labor Surplus Economy: Theory and Policy.* Homewood, Ill.: Irwin, 1964.

Goulet, Dennis. *The Cruel Choice: A New Concept in the Theory of Development.* New York: Atheneum, 1971.

Kuznets, Simon. "Modern Economic Growth: Findings and Reflections." *American Economic Review* (June 1973), pp. 247–259.

Lazlo, E., Robert Balser, Jr., Elliot Eisenberg, and Ventaka Ramen. *The Objectives of the New International Economic Order.* New York: Pergamon Press, 1978.

Myrdal, Gunnar. *Asian Drama.* New York: Pantheon, 1968.

Rostow, W. W. *The Stages of Economic Growth: A Non-Communist Manifesto.* London: Cambridge University Press, 1960.

Singer, Hans. "Dualism Revisited: A New Approach to the Problems of Dual Society in Developing Countries." *Journal of Development Studies* 7, 1 (1970).

Todaro, Michael P. *Economic Development in the Third World.* New York: Longman, 1985.

Wallerstein, Immanuel. *The Capitalist World Economy.* Cambridge: Cambridge University Press, 1979.

2

Accounting in the Developing Countries

The developing countries face difficult problems in their attempts to achieve progress in their economic development programs. Their efforts led to the use of the new economic subdiscipline of development economics, in order to address the various problems and policies affecting economic development. These problems and policies are either domestic (such as growth, poverty and income distribution, unemployment, population growth, education, agricultural transformation, and rural development) or international (such as international trade or development, foreign investment aid, and a new international economic and political order).

Accounting plays a crucial role in economic development too by providing the right information necessary to implement the above-mentioned policies. This role is particularly important in development planning in general and project appraisal in particular. Accordingly, the theories of international accounting as they affect the developing countries, the standard-setting strategies for the developing countries, and the actors involved in international standard setting are also explored, before an examination of accounting education in the developing countries.

THE STATE OF ACCOUNTING IN THE DEVELOPING COUNTRIES

Factors Hampering Accounting Development

History has shown that the rate of growth and the development of a nation's economy in both private and public sectors are tied to a certain extent to the adequacy of the accounting system and the accounting development process in that country. As the developing countries suffer from relatively low growth rates, we may safely say that action in the development accounting process is urgently needed in the developing countries. There are in effect serious challenges facing accounting in the developing countries. George M. Scott feels that the accounting information in these nations is deficient, irrelevant, unreliable, and often lacking credibility.[1] He suggests that this rudimentary level of accounting is a result of some of the environmental factors of each particular nation. For example, the presence of a class elite controlling major domestic firms may have an adverse effect on accounting development because it inhibits the growth of private capital markets. As this elite has a strong prerogative on inside information, there is no tradition of providing adequate financial information to the public to facilitate decision making. Another phenomenon perceived as detrimental to the growth of an accounting tradition is the lack of identification with governmental policies. This leads to an attitude of noncooperation with and even hostility to the government, often reflected by the common practice of tax evasion. It is appropriate, however, to note that the natural erosion of the elite class system and the consequent social mobility has created in some of these countries a new atmosphere more favorable to economic and accounting development.

The insignificant role played by accounting as a source of relevant information for decision making is described by R. Dominguez of the InterAmerican Development Bank:

> Many sectors do not properly recognize the part that accounting has to play in enterprise management, and they have not made appropriate use of it. Among entrepreneurs and managers, including those from the public sector, there is insufficient awareness of the value of accounting and of the information it may provide as an instrument of administrative and financial control. Business ownership, even of large-scale enterprises, is often concentrated among a few individuals. There may be no capital market; if there is one, its field of action is quite limited. This system of broadly based ownership faces a variety of difficulties, and the climate of trust and confidence needed to make it viable is, for several reasons, nonexistent. Lacking broadly based investment by numerous minority shareholders, the need for the protection afforded by the regulation of enterprises of this kind has not been felt, and this extends even to the accounting aspects. Business affairs are frequently conducted in secrecy. Rather than relying on their clients' financial statements—in which they have little confidence—financial institutions emphasize other factors in their credit investigations, such as reputation and personal knowledge of the owners of the borrowing enterprises and substantial security pledged in the form of personal property.
>
> Financial accounting is often limited to the deficient recording of transactions; it is rudimentary and not kept up to date. It is maintained solely for the purpose of satisfying the formalities required by law and the tax authorities. The information provided by such records is consequently of little value in assessing the performance of an enterprise. Accounting methods and practices are usually outdated, even anachronistic, and there is no consistency in their application.[2]

A historical perspective of the economic growth of nations bears witness to the thesis that the rate of growth and the development of a nation's economy in all sectors depend heavily on the adequacy of the accounting information system.[3] It becomes then not only a matter of economic self-interest but a moral obligation to support the development of accounting in the developing countries.[4] The support is needed because of the difficult state of accounting development in those countries. Various factors are hampering the accounting discipline and profession in the developing countries. An example of the accountancy problems in Africa is shown in Exhibit 2.1. Other factors exist:

1. The supply of accountants is not meeting the demand created by economic growth. See, for example, the supply of accountants in Africa as shown in Exhibit 2.2. Factors hampering the increase in the existing supply of accountants include:

- An inadequate number of competent teachers.
- Inadequate programs at educational institutions.
- The absence of a carefully laid-out accountancy development plan based on an inventory of existing and projected supplies and demands.
- A lack of effective coordination between educational institutions, on one hand, and public and private practice, on the other, which prevented gearing the training and supply of accountants to meet the country's needs.[5]

2. Corruption is another problem facing accountants in the developing countries. Corruption may be bureaucratic or administrative, syndicated or criminal, and political,[6] all linked, respectively, to government employees, organized crime, and elected officials. This corruption is not exclusive to the government. As noted by Leonore Briones:

> There are two parties to corruption: The government sector and the private sector. The latter is the corruptee and the former is the corrupter. Oftentimes they reverse roles. Historically, efforts to eliminate corruption have always been directed towards public servants. . . . In order to be effective, efforts to discipline the government should also be directed towards the private sector.[7]

Accounting in the developing countries is failing in the containment of corruption.[8] [9]

3. J. B. Ghartey identified six deficiencies in the accounting systems of developing countries that may thwart development and provide a breeding ground for political instability:[10]

1. *Lack of meaning and direction for accountability* due to confusing discussions on accountability, amorphous, imprecise and illusive definitions, unclear or totally unknown methodology and techniques, and absence of generally accepted accounting standards to guide, regulate, and harmonize accounting practice.

Exhibit 2.1
Accountancy Problems in Africa

	Too few			Poor quality		
Country	FQA a/	Accounting technicians	Public sector accountants	FQA a/	Accounting technicians	Public sector accountants
North Africa						
Algeria	x		x		x	x
Egypt	x		x	x	x	x
Morocco	x	x	x			x
Tunisia	x	x	x			x
West Africa						
Benin	x	x	x	x	x	x
Burkina Faso	x	x	x	x		
Cameroon	x	x	x	x	x	x
Chad	x	x	x	x	x	x
Côte d'Ivoire	x	x	x			x
Gambia	x	x	x		x	x
Ghana	x	x	x	x	x	x
Guinea	x	x	x			
Liberia	x	x	x	x	x	x
Mali		x	x			
Mauritania		x		x		
Niger		x	x			
Nigeria			x	x	x	x
Senegal		x	x			
Sierra Leone	x	x	x		x	x
Togo		x	x	x		
Zaire	x	x	x	x	x	x
East Africa						
Burundi	x	x	x	x	x	x
Ethiopia	x	x	x	x	x	x
Kenya				x	x	
Madagascar	x	x	x		x	x
Mauritius						
Rwanda	x	x	x	x	x	x
Uganda	x	x	x		x	x
Southern Africa						
Angola	x	x	x	x	x	x
Botswana		x	x		x	
Lesotho			x			x
Malawi	x	x	x		x	x
Namibia		x	x		x	
Swaziland	x	x	x		x	
United Republic of Tanzania			x		x	x
Zambia	x	x	x		x	x
Zimbabwe		x	x			

a/ Fully qualified accountant.

Source: United Nations Center on Transnational Corporations, *International Accounting and Reporting Issues: 1990 Review* (New York: United Nations, 1991), p. 196. Reprinted with permission.

Inadequate programmes			Other constraints		
FQA a/	Accounting technicians	Inappropriate education	Socio-political	Not enough nationals	Legal/ regulatory framework
x	x	x	x		x
x	x	x			x
x	x	x			x
x	x	x			x
x	x	x	x		x
x		x			x
x	x	x			x
x	x	x	x	x	x
x	x	x	x		x
x	x	x		x	x
x	x	x	x		x
x	x	x	x	x	x
x		x			x
x		x		x	x
x		x			x
x	x	x			x
			x	x	x
x	x	x	x		x
			x		x
x	x	x	x	x	
x	x	x	x		x
x	x	x	x	x	x
		x			
x	x		x		x
x	x	x			x
x	x	x	x		x
x	x	x	x		x
x	x	x	x		x
				x	
	x			x	
	x	x			
x		x			
x	x	x			
	x			x	

Exhibit 2.2
Supply of Accountants and Structure of the Accounting Profession

Country	Accounting body	Qualifying examination: National	Qualifying examination: Non-local	Private sector: Fully qualified accountants	Private sector: Accounting technicians	Private sector: Bookkeepers	Public sector: Fully qualified accountants	Public sector: Accounting technicians	Public sector: Bookkeepers
North Africa									
Algeria	x	x		56	1 250	..	..	10 000	20 000
Egypt	x	x		9 900	..	..	100	..	..
Morocco	x		x	135	5 000	4 000	35	2 500	16 000
Tunisia	x	x		120	2 000	3 500	..	800	1 000
West Africa									
Benin	x		x	73	61	34	75	190	199
Burkina Faso			x	15	80	600	90	120	350
Cameroon			x	55	450	1 400	25	450	700
Chad				..	4	..	..	..	..
Côte d'Ivoire	..		x	25	..	..	..	..	..
Gambia	x		x	9	30	..	9	..	..
Ghana	x	x		504	..	..	86	..	..
Guinea	x		x	5	8	..	..	..	..
Liberia			x	12	19	..	..	..	..
Mali	x		x	29	100	66	6	152	34
Mauritania	x		x	61	165	425	52	110	160
Niger			x	19	75	50	109	473	372
Nigeria	x	x		3 280	..	..	827	..	..
Senegal	x		x	38	..	..	..	..	..
Sierra Leone	x		x	43	133	450	17	49	300
Togo			x	989	1 868	2 637	86	162	4 734
Zaire			x	15	45	..	..	..	..

East Africa									
Burundi			x	5	..	..	1	..	..
Ethiopia			x	14	..	..	3	..	..
Kenya	x	x		1 520	13 000	30 000	87	19 000	20 000
Madagascar	x		x	38	20	..	..	34	..
Mauritius	x		x	175	465	2 000	25	335	1 000
Rwanda	x		x	46	55	340	15	150	150
Uganda			x	35	..	..	10	..	..
Southern Africa									
Angola			x	..	..	..	..	..	..
Botswana	x		x	130	115	300	125	155	470
Lesotho	x		x	54	35	87	11	16	72
Malawi	x		x	120	..	..	39	100	2 001
Namibia	x		x	65	..	..	10	..	..
Swaziland	x		x	48	40	..	6	16	..
United Republic of Tanzania	x	x		949	2 154	6 008	..	..	..
Zambia	x		x	450	..	..	..	..	..
Zimbabwe	x	x		526	150	..	..	..	..

Note: These numbers should not be interpreted as precise figures. They serve only as an indication of an order of magnitude — that is, whether the country has 10 accountants, 100 or 1,000. Two dots (..) indicate that data are not available.

Source: United Nations Center on Transnational Corporations, *International Accounting and Reporting Issues: 1990 Review* (New York: United Nations, 1991), p. 177. Reprinted with permission.

2. *Untimely and unreliable information systems,* due to obsolete or deficient procedures for collecting and processing information, inaccurate and incomplete accounting data used for budgets and plans, late final accounts, delayed budgetary and financial audits, and contributing to financial mismanagement, embezzlement, fraud, incompetence and inefficiency.
3. *Unnecessary bureaucracy* and red tape leading to delays and corruption.
4. *Inadequate or non-existent institutional linkages,* leading to ad hoc measures, and neglect of the role of government accounting in its stewardship function for public reports and expenditure.
5. *Diffusion of current and capital items in government budgets* resulting in a failure to use the budget as a potent management tool.
6. *Failure or inability to employ or retain qualified and competent accounting and management personnel* leading to absence of estimates and/or budgets; inadequate, unreliable and untimely management and accounting information systems; ineffective management and accounting information systems; ineffective systems of internal check and control; poor auditing; improper organization; and inability to obtain data necessary for policy and project formulation, implementation, review and evaluation.[11]

Efforts to establish accountability and stewardship in some developing countries have been largely unsuccessful. A good example is the case of some of the poor African developing countries where a combination of political, economic, and social factors render the accountability and stewardship endeavor a difficult goal. Witness the following comment regarding the African situation:

> Past and current efforts to ensure effective stewardship and accountability of politicians and public officers have included violent changes of governments, establishment of committees of inquiries (or military tribunals) to probe misdeeds of public officers and others, and frequent declarations and pledges of soldiers and politicians to institute accountability to alleviate misery and poverty. However, these efforts have achieved minimal success mainly because they have focused on attempting to rectify the past mistakes and malpractices of individuals instead of concentrating on combating systemic and/or institutional factors in the environment that create, sustain, and/or exacerbate economic malaise. These environmental factors that exacerbate inadequate accountability and stewardship and hence misery and underdevelopment include deficiencies in accounting systems, conceptual and operational difficulties of accountability, government monopoly of power, bureaucratic secrecy, conflicts in perspectives and inadequate institutional linkages, technological obsolescence and inadequate surveillance systems, poverty and lack of motivation, cultural factors, and crisis management.[12]

Failure to Achieve Accountability

Accountability requires the assignment of responsibility for the user and safe custody and control of human, material, and financial resources to all levels of public- and private-sector managements in the developing countries. Constraints to the realization of sound accounting and accountability abound in the developing countries.[13]

Achieving accountability in the developing countries is extremely important. Ghartey identified ten operational guidelines for achieving accountability:[14]

1. *Exemplary leadership* with sensitive, responsive, and accountable officers promoting the congruence of their actions with the value preference of the community.
2. *Public debate* to take into account the interpretation of perceptions of the public.
3. *Co-ordination* with effective avenues for the redress of grievances.
4. *Autonomy* where the government policy affecting public organizations is implemented with strict propriety through the institutions' boards, or other comparable statutory boards, and frequent direct intervention of the government in the day-to-day management is avoided.
5. *Explicitness and clarity* of the standards of performance and evaluation.
6. *Legitimacy and acceptance* of the purpose, aims and means of achieving accountability.
7. *Negotiation* to insure the acceptance of the levels of responsibility and authority associated with them.
8. *Educational campaigns and publicity* as to how public officers and private individuals are expected to achieve accountability.
9. *Feedback and evaluation* through effective monitoring and reporting.
10. *Adaptation and recycling* of the accountability system.[15]

Elements Influencing the Development of Accounting

A general and rather ethnocentric view of the development of accounting in the developed countries is a result of transfers of knowledge, skills, and manpower from the developed countries. Four explanations are generally given to explain why and how countries have adopted the accounting systems of other countries:[16]

- The first explanation is the "void theory," which suggests that the absence of an organized body of knowledge in one country leads ultimately to the imitation of the systems of another country.[17]
- The second explanation is the "direct-investment theory," which suggests that foreign direct investors can easily impose the accounting requirements of their countries in the recipient country.[18]
- The third explanation is the "dependency theory," which suggests that former colonies find themselves bound and/or attached to the systems of the former colonizers.[19] [20]
- The fourth explanation is the "bandwagon effect," whereby seemingly independent countries opt to follow the lead of another group of countries.

As a result, the comparative accounting literature includes various attempts to classify the patterns in the world of accounting into different historical "zones of accounting influence." A general explanation for these zones is that the accounting objectives, standards, policies, and techniques result from the environmental factors in each country, and if "these environmental factors differ significantly between countries, then it would be expected that the major accounting concepts and practices in use in various countries also differ."[21]

Attempts have been made to identify the environmental conditions likely to affect the determination of national accounting principles.[22] In general, these attempts have assumed that cultural, social, as well as economic factors may explain the differences in accounting principles and techniques between the various countries. A more general model of the elements influencing the development of accounting is shown in Exhibit 2.3. It shows reporting and disclosure adequacy of a given country as being influenced by its political, economic, and demographic environments.[23]

The degree of political freedom in a country is important to the development of accounting in general and reporting and disclosures in particular. When people cannot choose the members of government or influence government policies, they are less likely to be able to create an accounting profession based on the principle of full and fair disclosure. Political repression involves a general loss of freedom, which may hinder to some extent the development of the accounting profession. There is likely to be a negative relationship between accounting freedom to report and disclose and political freedom. As Exhibit 2.3 shows, the degree of political freedom in a given country is assumed to depend on the degree of political rights, civil liberties, and type of political system. Violations of political rights and civil liberties associated with various forms of political structure restrict political freedom in general and may act as a hindrance to the tradition of a full and fair disclosure.

The economic environment is also important to the development of accounting in general and reporting and disclosure in particular. Economic development consists of economic growth and various structural and social changes. One of these structural and social changes is the need for financial and reporting devices to measure the performance of each sector of the economy in terms of efficiency and productivity. H. D. Lowe notes that, from a historical point of view, accounting development is an evolutionary process dependent upon and interwoven with economic development.[24] Similarly, Elliot, Larrea, and Rivera state that the "social function of accounting, to measure and to communicate economic data, cannot be considered simply as the effect of economic development, but should bc considered a valuable tool for promoting the development process."[25] However, economic development may be achieved by various forms of economic policies, depending on the type of economic system chosen, the level and growth rate of income, the extent of government intervention and expenditures, and the level of exports. Each of these factors may imply a specific impact on accounting development.

Exhibit 2.3
Model of Accounting Development

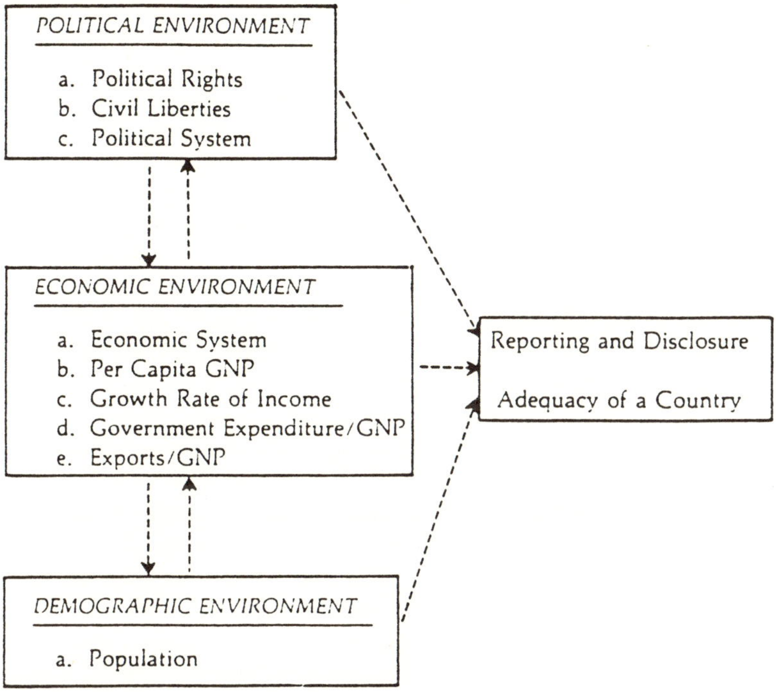

Ceteris paribus, a capitalist system may be more favorable to accounting development than other economic systems. In a capitalist economic system the survival of private enterprises depends not only on the production of goods and services but adequate information to various interest groups from investors and creditors to the capital market in general. In a similar vein, M. A. Quereshi draws attention to the relationship among financial accounting, capital formation, and economic development:

> The choice is based on the idea that financial reporting, capital markets, and capital formation interrelate. Capital formation, a strategic formation in economic development, is closely dependent upon financial mechanisms and institutions. Studies by such eminent monetarists such as Kuznets, Goldsmith, and McKinnon provide a convincing evidence of the parallel between the development of capital markets and economic growth. The development and proper functioning of capital markets in turn is intimately related to the availability of financial information which is provided by the accounting function of reporting.[26]

In addition, the higher the level and growth of income, the higher the political and economic freedom, and as suggested in the preceding arguments, the better the adequacy of reporting and disclosure. This may apply to any economic system, since economic growth in some socialist countries has often been followed by an effort to liberalize the regimes.

Furthermore, the higher the level of government expenditures, the higher the level of government intervention and the better the adequacy of reporting and disclosure. Government intervention is dictated by a need to provide economic security to all classes of society and takes the form of industry and opportunity creation. Because government is assumed to be accountable to all people, its intervention may be followed by an effort to report and disclose and may be favorable to the development of an accounting profession and a reporting and disclosure tradition. This is applicable to any economic system. In the United States, a capitalist economic system, governmental agencies all employ accounting as a tool to accomplish the regulatory mandate placed upon them by Congress. The socialist countries have developed unique accounting systems and procedures in the furtherance of their own centrally managed economies. Finally, the role of governments in developing accounting principles and providing legal authority is assumed to result in a higher reliability of financial disclosures in the developing countries. As stated by B. L. Jaggi, the "interference by governments may be essential to ensure higher reliability (which is vital for the expansion of industries in these countries), for creating public confidence and trust in corporations, for creating an atmosphere where industrialization can progress, and for making economic and social decisions."[27]

Finally, the higher the level of exports, the higher the need for better reporting and disclosure. Free trade policies in general and export promotion in particular increase the cooperation with other countries, the flows of human and physical capital, and the need for comparable reporting and disclosure adequacy. For example, J. Kraayenhof argues that the international flow of capital for financing and participation creates more interest in the soundness of financial presentations and the intelligibility of the explanatory notes.[28]

The number of people in a given country could also be important to the development of accounting. The larger the population, the higher the number of people interested in the profession who feel the need for a well-developed accounting profession and the need for full and fair disclosure. For example, India, Egypt, and Pakistan, which are usually classified as developing countries, have developed accounting professions and also well-developed systems for accounting education.

CONCEPTS OF INTERNATIONAL ACCOUNTING AND THE DEVELOPING COUNTRIES

International accounting has tended to mean different things to different people, and this has colored the extant theories of international accounting. Various authors find themselves proposing various definitions of international accounting and henceforth of international accounting theories. I. L. Fantl suggests three concepts of international accounting: a universal system, a descriptive and informative approach including all the methods and standards of all countries, and accounting practices of foreign subsidiaries and parent companies.[29] The same classification was used by Quereshi et al. for establishing a framework for viewing the different concepts of international accounting.[30] Weirich, Avery, and Anderson's classification included world accounting, international accounting, and accounting for parent companies and foreign subsidiaries.[31]

The concept of "universal" or "world accounting" is by far the largest in scope. It directs international accounting to the formulation and study of a universally accepted set of accounting principles. It aims for an internationally complete standardization of accounting principles. The definition of Weirich et al. is:

> *World Accounting.* In the framework of this concept, international accounting is considered to be a universal system that would be adopted in all countries. A worldwide set of generally accepted accounting principles (GAAP), such as the set maintained in the United States, would be established. Practices and principles would be developed which were applicable to all countries. This concept would be the ultimate goal of an international accounting system.[32]

While very commendable, this goal is unlikely to be reached in the near future and may be safely characterized as highly idealistic by some and even utopian by others. Pessimistic attitudes are based on the many obstacles to a complete standardization of accounting principles.

The concept of "comparative" or "international accounting" directs international accounting to a study and understanding of national differences in accounting. It involves awareness of the international diversity in corporate accounting and reporting practices, understanding of the accounting principles and practices of individual countries, and ability to assess the impact of diverse accounting practices on financial reporting. There is a general consensus in accounting literature that the term "international accounting" refers to "comparative accounting principles." Weirich et al. define the term as follows:

> *International Accounting.* A second major concept of the term international accounting involves a descriptive and informative approach. Under this concept, international accounting includes all varieties of principles, methods and standards of accounting of *all* countries. This concept includes a set of generally accepted accounting principles established for each country, thereby requiring the accountant to be multiple principle conscious when studying international accounting. . . . No universal or perfect set of principles would be expected to be established. A collection of all principles, methods and standards would be considered as the international accounting system. These variations result because of differing geographic, social, economic, political and legal influences.[33]

The concept of "*parent-foreign subsidiary* accounting" or "accounting for foreign *subsidiaries*" is by far the oldest and narrowest in scope. It reduces international accounting to the process of consolidating the accounts of the parent company and its subsidiaries and translating foreign currency into local currency. Weirich et al. provide the following definition:

> *Accounting for Foreign Subsidiaries.* The third major concept that may be applied to "international accounting" refers to the accounting practices of a parent company and a foreign subsidiary. A reference to a particular country or domicile is needed under the concept for effective internal financial reporting. The accountant is concerned mainly with the translation and adjustment of the subsidiary's financial statement. Different accounting problems arise and different accounting principles are to be followed depending upon which country is used as a reference for translation and adjustment purposes.[34]

The advent of new international accounting books on the market expanded the framework to include new notions of international accounting. As a result, an exhaustive list of the international accounting concepts and theories was provided by F. E. Amenkhienan to include the following: (1) universal or world theory, (2) multinational theory, (3) comparative theory, (4) international transactions theory, and (5) translation theory.[35] These theories imply, respectively:

> (1) a universal concept being nurtured by the pragmatists who believe that the solutions to the problems raised in internal reporting lie in worldwide uniformity in accounting; (2) a multinational concept which suggests that international accounting includes all the varieties of principles, standards, and practices of all countries; (3) a comparative concept which suggests an analytical classification of national accounting systems as has been done in the other social sciences such as economics, politics and law; (4) an international concept built around accounting information needed in international trade and international investment decisions; and (5) a translational concept which is used to characterize accounting for parent companies and foreign subsidiaries.[36]

Each of these theories provides some grounds for the development of a conceptual framework for international accounting. While these arguments can be made for the desirability of one theory over the others, the first three—universal, multinational, and comparative—have generated better followings than the other two. The debate lies between those favoring uniformity leading to a universal theory, those favoring standardization leading to a multinational theory, and those favoring analysis of different national accounting systems leading to a comparative theory. The position of the developing world is divided along three lines, with some countries taking an open approach to the North and favoring either uniformity or standardization, and some favoring a separate distinct system.

STANDARD-SETTING STRATEGIES FOR THE DEVELOPING COUNTRIES

The developing countries are characterized by relatively inadequate and unreliable accounting systems and generally new and untested standard-setting institutions. Theory development and academic and professional accounting research add to the economic, social, political, and institutional problems that may be acting as deterrents to an effective standard setting. In spite of these limitations, the development of basic accounting systems and procedures and the process of standard setting have accelerated as evidenced by the increasing number of professional organizations, standard-setting books, and academic accounting associations as well as by the increasing membership of these groups in international standard-setting bodies.

The standard-setting process in the developing countries has not followed a unique strategy proper to these countries and their context. In fact, four strategies may be identified: the evolutionary approach, development through transfer of accounting technology, adoption of international accounting standards, and development of accounting standards based on analysis of accounting principles and practices in the advanced nations against the backdrop of their underlying investment.[37] These strategies are reviewed below.

The Evolutionary Approach

The evolutionary approach consists of an isolationist approach to standard setting whereby the developing country develops its own standard without any outside interferences or influences. The particular developing country defines its own specific accounting objectives and needs and proceeds to meet them by developing its own techniques, concepts, institutions, profession, and education in isolation. The particular country may feel its context to be unique enough to justify this drastic approach of standard setting. The learning process in this approach has to come from local rather than international experiences. It assumes the foreign partners will adapt to its own idiosyncratic rules and may have to if they want to continue to trade with the country and/or maintain operations. Naturally, it may create an additional cost to the foreign partners who may feel the conditions onerous enough to justify complete cooperation. In addition, the absence of an adequate local accounting technology may hamper not only the local firms but also the foreign firms operating in the country.

The Transfer of Technology Approach

Development through transfer of accounting technology may result from either the operations and activities of international accounting firms, multinationals, and academicians practicing in the developing countries, or the various international treaties and cooperative arrangements calling for exchanges of information and technology. Adolf Enthoven, for example, describes the benefits of U.S. accounting assistance to the developing world as follows:

> U.S. accounting and accountants have already had a positive effect on accounting systems, procedures and training in many developing economies. For example, the affiliates of U.S. MNEs [multinational enterprises] have developed sound financial management systems. Other U.S. companies have entered into joint ventures with foreign companies or have set up their own organizations in these countries for the production and sale of goods and services. Good financial and managerial accounting methods have accompanied these investments. Many U.S. CPA [certified public accounting] firms have either established corresponding relationships with foreign firms or set up branch offices abroad. Although much of value has been accomplished by U.S. accountants in CPA firms and in industry developing economies, such activities have generally been directed toward certain companies or to serve CPA firm clients. More might be done; however, I recognize that this task isn't the first priority of accountants in public practice and industry.[38]

Because most developing countries may not have given formal attention to the formation and implementation of a strategy that facilitates the transfer of accounting technology, or the development of an indigenous accounting profession, Belverd Needles, Jr., proposed a conceptual framework by which a country may formulate a strategy for the international transfer of accounting technology as part of its overall economic plan.[39] Basically, national goals combine with the social, political, and economic environment and general resources and constraint to influence the overall economic plan. The economic plan itself contains as a subplan a strategy for the transfer of accounting technology, composed of objectives for the accounting technology transfer, strategy, channels of transfer, and levels of accounting technology. The three types of technology—individual, organizational, and independent professional—are defined as follows:

T_1 level of technical accounting knowledge possessed by individuals;

T_2 level of sophistication of accounting techniques used by government and business organizations; and

T_3 level of advancement of an independent accounting profession.[40]

While the mere transfer of accounting technology may appear to be a direct benefit to the developing countries, there is the cost associated with the transfer of the wrong or inapplicable technology, the lack of appropriate infrastructure for the correct application of the technology, the increased dependence on outside experts, the lack of incentives for developing local standards, and the horrible loss of pride by some culture groups. These costs ought to be compared with the benefits of technology transfer by each of the developing countries. It is a strategic decision that is an integral part of the overall economic plan as suggested earlier. The whole process of development ought to include not only economic growth strategies but accounting growth strategies, and therein lies the question of the desirability of accounting technology transfer by the developing countries.

The Adoption of International Accounting Standards

The strategy available to the developing countries consists of joining the International Accounting Standards Committee (IASC) or some of the other international standards bodies identified earlier and adopting "wholesale" their pronouncements. The rationale behind such strategy may be to reduce the setup and production costs of accounting standards, join the international harmonization drive, facilitate the growth of foreign investment that may be needed, enable its profession to emulate well-established professional standards of behavior and conduct, and legitimize its status as a full-fledged member of the international community. In fact, some of the developing countries give more credence to the IASC and other standards than do some of the developed countries that have a dominant influence in the preparation of such standards.

The question is whether the benefits described as accruing to the developing countries from the mere adoption of the international accounting standards may be outweighed by the misspecifying of costs. Indeed, the international standards for accounting for various transactions occurring in the advanced countries may be totally irrelevant to some of the developing countries, as these transactions have little chance of occurring or may be occurring in a fashion more specific to the context of the developing countries. The particular situations occurring in the developing countries call for specific and local standard setting. In addition, the institutional and market factors of these countries are different enough in some contexts to justify a more "situationist" approach to standard setting. Amenkhienan makes the same point as follows:

> The case against the adoption of international standards by developing nations as an alternative to developing their own local standards is a conclusive one. Accounting in each country should develop in a manner relevant to the needs and objectives of that country. The situational variables should determine the patterns of development.[41]

This situationist strategy has also been labeled as the zero-based option, or what George Scott refers to as "fresh start" because its use established international standards as a basis toward a better fitting with the particular economic development context of the developing country. Scott elaborates as follows: "The major alternative is to effect a relatively clean break with accounting tradition in developing nations and to attempt to develop accounting with a 'fresh start' on the basis of the standards of accounting education, practices and professionalism that are embodied in economic evaluation accounting."[42]

The Situationist Strategy

The situationist strategy was also labeled as "the development of accounting standards based on an analysis of accounting principles and practices in the advanced nations against the backdrop of their underlying environments."[43] Basically, it calls for a consideration of the diagnostic factors that determine the development of accounting in the developing countries. A standard meeting the constraints imposed by these factors can be deemed relevant and useful to the developing countries. The total of these standards constitutes the system of reporting and disclosure of the developing country. The factors influencing it may be represented as being influenced by cultural linguistics, political and civil rights, economic and demographic characteristics, and the legal and tax environment of the country in question. In other words, based on cultural relativism, linguistics relativism, political and civil relativism, economic and demographic relativism, and legal and tax relativism, the accounting concepts and the reporting and disclosure systems in any given country rest on the varying aspects of that country.

HARMONIZATION OF ACCOUNTING STANDARDS AND THE DEVELOPING COUNTRIES

Three models of harmonization are identified in the literature as follows:

> (1) the *Absolute Uniformity Model,* which describes a situation in which there is one set of accounting methods and reports regardless of differences in circumstances or user needs; (2) the *Circumstantial Uniformity Model,* which describes a situation in which different accounting methods and reports can be used for different economic facts under different circumstances; and (3) the *Purposive Uniformity Model,* which considers the uses of accounting information as determinants of appropriate accounting methods and standards.[44]

Harmonization has for a long time been erroneously associated with complete standardization. It is in effect different from standardization. John Wilson presents this useful distinction:

> The term harmonization as opposed to standardization implies a reconciliation of different points of view. This is a more practical and conciliatory approach than standardization, particularly when standardization means that the procedures of one country should be adopted by all others. Harmonization becomes a matter of better communication, of information in a form that can be interpreted and understood internationally.[45]

This definition of harmonization is more realistic and has a greater likelihood of being accepted than standardization. Every host country has its sets of rules, philosophies, and objectives at the national level aimed at protecting or controlling the national resources. This aspect of nationalism gives rise to particular rules and measures that ultimately affect a country's accounting system. Harmonization consists of recognizing these national idiosyncracies and attempting to reconcile them with other countries' objectives as a first step. The second step is to correct or eliminate some of these barriers in order to achieve an acceptable degree of harmonization.

Merits of Harmonization

There are various advantages to harmonization. The most-often-cited favorable arguments include the following: First, for many countries, there are still no adequate codified standards of accounting and auditing. Internationally accepted standards not only would eliminate the set-up costs for those countries but would allow them to immediately be part of the mainstream of accepted international accounting standards. Some of this work is already being accomplished by the major accounting firms in their international practice. For example, E. W. Macrae states: "Each of these firms of course has only been able to set and enforce the standards for its own organization, but combined, they determine the standards followed in a substantial portion of international audit engagements."[46]

Second, the growing internationalization of the world's economies and the increasing interdependency of nations in terms of international trade and investment flows act as a major argument for some form of internationally accepted standards of accounting and auditing. Such internationalization will also facilitate international transactions, pricing, and resource allocation decisions and may render the international financial markets more efficient.

Third, the need for companies to raise outside capital given the insufficiency of retained earnings to finance projects and the availability of foreign loans has increased the need for accounting harmonization. In effect, supplies of capital, here and abroad, tend to rely on financial reports to make the best investment and loan decisions and tend to show preference for comparable reporting.

Limits to Harmonization

Current trends seem to indicate that there is little chance of ever achieving international harmonization. The following arguments are usually advanced to justify this pessimistic attitude: First, tax collections in all countries are one of the greatest sources of demand for accounting services. Because tax-collection systems vary internationally, it can be easily expected that there will be a move to diversity in the accounting principles and system used internationally. As an emphasis Lee Seidler states: "Since tax collection systems vary widely between countries, and since governments show little sign of desiring to harmonize tax systems (except in the collection of maximum amounts from multinational corporations), there is little reason to expect that this barrier to international accounting harmonization will disappear."[47]

Second, accounting policies are known to be fashioned sometimes to achieve either political or economic goals compatible with the economic or political system espoused by a given country. Since there is little hope of having a single political or economic system internationally, it can be expected that the differences in political and economic systems will continue to act as a barrier to international accounting harmonization.

Third, some of the obstacles to international harmonization are created by accountants themselves through national strict licensing requirements. An extreme example occurred in 1976, when the French profession required foreign accountants practicing in France to sit for an oral examination. As a result of the French experience, the European Economic Community (EEC; now European Community, EC) then became involved with the qualifications of auditors. The first published version of the draft Eight Directive created several restraints on the ability of foreign accountants to practice in the EEC member countries. Consider the following paragraphs from the first version of the draft of the Eight Directive:

> The partners, members, persons responsible for management, administration direction or supervision of such professional companies or associations who do not personally fulfill the Directive (i.e., non-EEC qualified accountants) shall exercise no influence over the statutory audits carried out under the auspices of such approved professional companies or associations.

The law shall, in particular, ensure:

- that the above-mentioned persons may not participate in the appointment or removal of auditors and that they may not issue to the latter any instructions regarding the carrying out of audits; . . .
- that the confidentiality of audit reports produced by the auditors and all documents relating thereto are protected and that these are withheld from the knowledge of the above-mentioned persons.

Harmonization has been considered as misguided insofar as developing countries are concerned; given that accounting principles used in the developing countries are generally adopted from developed countries,[48, 49, 50] and harmonizing may be just a way of legitimizing worldwide values that may not be appropriate to the developing countries.[51] Witness the following comments:

> The point is that most developing countries had little chance to evolve accounting systems which truly reflected the needs and circumstances of their own societies. Their existing systems are largely extensions of those of developed countries. In this light the benefits of their being more deeply integrated into systems that predominantly suit developed countries becomes questionable. For the third world, international harmonization may do more harm than good if it preempts the possibility of changing the old, inap-

propriate systems and evolving new ones which are better suited to their development needs.[52]

As with any other method developed by people to assist their efforts to make their environment a better place, accounting should develop in response to the needs of particular environments; accounting has not evolved in the industrialized world as an absolute science, however, but as a response to the economic and social factors prevailing in those parts of the world. This is the form of accounting that was imposed on LDCs [Less Developed Countries]. Information produced on the basis of such practice is not likely to give the correct signals to the governments of LDCs, nor is it likely to be relevant for their decision models or to the overall problem of economic development. How can it be when it was developed in accordance with the environmental needs of a different part of the world, as well as a society with different socioeconomic needs?[53]

There is serious danger that accountants will continue to propound techniques which evolved under circumstances which no longer exist and which are irrelevant or even positively harmful.[54]

In most developing countries, the role of the state in economic development is extremely important. The private sector owes its existence to its contribution to the economic development of the developing countries. There is then a need for the private sector to report the data that provide the most information about its contribution to the specific economic development of specific developing countries. Harmonization is far from being the solution in this case. As stated by J. M. Samuels and J. C. Oliga:

In the developing countries, the private sector must justify its existence; it must satisfy the government that it is contributing to economic development. The accounting reports required, therefore, from both the public and private sectors are not necessarily those that would just satisfy shareholders and bankers. The point here is that accounting professions in developing countries should try to assist in designing reporting systems that are the most useful for economic decision making within the country, rather than trying to persuade the country to adopt systems which are needed for international trade and business. It is possible the two can be developed simultaneously, but the latter should not be seen as a substitute for the former.[55]

ACTORS INVOLVED IN THE HARMONIZATION PROCESS

International Federation of Accounting Committee (IFAC)

Various international organizations preceded the creation of IFAC. First, the International Congress of Accounts (ICA) was founded in 1904 with the general objective of increasing interaction and exchange of ideas between accountants of different countries. Second, in 1972 the ICA founded the International Coordination Committee for the Accounting Profession (ICCAP) with the objectives to conduct specific studies of professional accounting ethics, education and training, and the structure of regional accounting organizations. Third, the

ICCAP dissolved in 1976 to be reconstituted as the International Federation of Accounting Committee. The goals of IFAC are best expressed by the following 12-point program to guide its efforts:

1. Develop statements that would serve as guidelines for international auditing practices.
2. Establish a suggested minimum code of ethics to which it is hoped that member bodies would subscribe and which could be further refined as appropriate.
3. Determine the requirements and develop programs for the professional education and training of accountants.
4. Evaluate, develop, and report on financial managements and other management accounting techniques and procedures.
5. Collect, analyze, research and disseminate information on the management of public accounting practices to assist practitioners in conducting their practices more effectively.
6. Undertake other studies of value to accountants such as, possibly, a study of the legal liabilities of auditors.
7. Foster closer relations with users of financial statements, including preparers, trade unions, financial institutions, industry, government, and others.
8. Maintain close relations with regional bodies and explore the potential for establishing other regional bodies as well as for assisting in their organization and development, as appropriate. Assign appropriate projects to existing regional bodies.
9. Establish regular communication among the members of IFAC and with other interested organizations through the medium of a newsletter.
10. Organize and promote the exchange of technical information, educational materials, and professional publications and other literature emanating from other bodies.
11. Organize and conduct an International Congress of Accountants approximately every five years.
12. Seek to expand the membership of IFAC.[56]

IFAC's governing bodies consist of an assembly comprising one representative designated as such by each member of the IFAC, and a council comprising 15 representatives of member bodies from 15 countries. The agenda of IFAC is set by the following seven standing committees: education, ethics, international auditing practices, international congresses, management accounting, planning, and regional organizations. The International Auditing Practices Committee (IAPC) of IFAC is the most active and most important.

International Accounting Standards Committee (IASC)

IASC was founded in 1973 with the following objectives contained in its constitution:

a. to formulate and publish in the public interest accounting standards to be observed in the presentation of financial statements and to promote their worldwide acceptance and observance;

b. to work generally for the improvement and harmonization of regulations, accounting standards and procedures relating to the presentation of financial statements.[57]

This translates into a goal of developing a common international approach to standards setting in accounting aimed at worldwide harmonization and improvement of accounting principles used in the preparation of financial statements for the benefit of the public.

IASC has an operating structure composed of the IASC board, the consultative group, and various steering committees. Its procedure of exposure and comment is as follows:

a. After discussion, the IASC Board selects a topic that is felt to need an International Accounting Standards, and assigns it to a Steering Committee. All IASC member bodies are invited to submit material for consideration.

b. The Steering Committee, assisted by the IASC Secretariat, considers the issues involved and presents a point outline on the subject of the Board.

c. The Steering Committee receives the comments of the Board and prepares a preliminary draft on the proposed standard.

d. Following review by the Board, the draft is circulated to all member bodies for their comments.

e. The Steering Committee prepares a revised draft, which, after approval by at least two-thirds of the Board, is published as an Exposure Draft. Comments are invited from all interested parties.

f. At each stage in the considerations of drafts, member bodies refer for guidance to the appropriate accounting research committees in their own organizations.

g. At the end of an exposure period (usually six months) comments are submitted to IASC and are considered by the Steering Committee responsible for the project.

h. The Steering Committee then submits a revised draft to the Board for approval as an International Accounting Standard.

i. The issue of a Standard requires approval by at least three-quarters of the Board, after which the approved text of the Standard is sent to all member bodies for translation and publication.[58]

The success of IASC's efforts naturally rests on acceptance of the standards by member countries and recognition and support internationally. Noncompliance with international standards has been attributed to the following reasons by Sir Henry Benson, the founder of IASC:

Some countries take the view that they cannot require compliance locally until they are satisfied that the standards are internationally acceptable. Some see local legislation as an obstacle to the introduction of international standards. Some accounting bodies do not have the power to discipline over their members, and cannot therefore impose compliance with either national or international standards. Some countries have not yet overcome stubborn local resistance from the business community.[59]

Besides these obstacles there is definite evidence that effort toward harmonization is not equally shared by all members of IASC. T. R. Douglas summarized the situation as follows:

Some accountancy bodies have declared to their members that international accounting standards are to be accorded the same status as domestic accounting standards. Each IAS is accompanied by an explanation of the relationship between the international standard and any domestic standard dealing with the same subject. Other accountancy bodies have issued statements declaring support for the concept of international accounting standards and strongly encouraging their members to accept them. Some of these bodies indicate the extent to which an international standard differs from the related domestic standard. They often offer to review, or encourage the relevant body to review, the basis of the domestic standard, with the objective of eliminating any differences.

There are some member countries, however, that have not yet presented any format statement of the status of IASs to the members of the accountancy profession.[60]

The United Nations

The United Nations became interested in accounting and the need for improved corporate reporting when the Group of Eminent Persons appointed to study the impact of multinational corporations advocated the formulation of an international, comparable system of standardized accounting and reporting.[61] It also recommended the creation of a Group of Experts on International Standards of Accounting and Reporting. The group was created in 1976 with the following objectives:

a. To review the existing practice of reporting by transnational corporations and reporting requirements in different countries;
b. To identify gaps in information in existing corporate reporting and to examine the feasibility of various proposals for improved reporting;
c. To recommend a list of minimum items, together with their definitions, that should be included in reports by transnational corporations and their affiliates, taking into account the recommendations of various groups concerned with the subject matter.[62]

As a result the group issued a report that included a 34-page list of recommended items to be disclosed by the ''enterprise as a whole,'' that is, consolidated data; and by individual member companies, including the parent company. Following issuance of the report an Intergovernmental Working Group of Experts on International Standards of Accounting and Reporting was formed with the objective of contributing to the harmonization of accounting standards. It does not function as a standards-setting body; its mandate is to review and discuss accounting and reporting standards. The group will consider, among other issues, whether the United Nations should promulgate accounting standards. Needless to say, this effort by the United Nations has created mixed international reactions. Most of the concerned institutions have expressed the feeling that accounting standards at the domestic or the international level are best set in the private sector. The same institutions are united in their support for the work of IASC and national accountancy groups.

The developing countries are mostly supportive of the UN actions. While the UN standards efforts are mainly targeting multinationals, there is a greater likelihood that eventually they would be expanded to all the companies in the world. The consequences of such actions are as follows:

> Should international accounting standards ever be adopted as a resolution by the UN, enforcement will require actions of either national standard-setting bodies or national governments to carry the force of law. Adoption by the UN certainly would change the political standing of the standards proposed (at a minimum, legitimize them), but it would not mean direct or immediate implementation.[63]

It is obvious that the success of the UN efforts rests on cooperation from all concerned parties. This assessment is also made as follows:

> The success of the United Nations' efforts in the field of international standards of accounting and reporting depends on the readiness of governments, professional accountancy bodies, transnational corporation management, and bodies representing business, labour and other groups to cooperate in these efforts. Governments will need to review their existing reporting requirements, identify gaps, participate in the formulation of international standards, and eventually amend their national laws and regulations to implement these standards. The transnational corporations need to review their reporting systems as well as their policies on information disclosure. Many corporations already publish fairly comprehensive data and, if others agreed to improve their reporting to this level, considerable progress could be made towards standardized reporting. With respect to the accounting profession, a reexamination of established standards, especially in the light of the international standards published by bodies such as the International Accounting Standards Committee, may be necessary.[64]

The Organization for Economic Cooperation and Development

The OECD is an organization whose members include 24 relatively industrialized noncommunist countries in Europe, Asia, North America, and Australia. A Declaration on International Investment and Multinational Enterprises was issued in 1976, including an annex entitled "Guidelines for Multinational Enterprises," a section of which is subtitled "Disclosure of Information."[65] The major elements suggested to be disclosed are listed below:

Enterprises should publish within reasonable time limits, on a regular basis, but at least annually, financial statements and other pertinent information relating to the enterprise as a whole comprising in particular:

- the structure of the enterprise, showing the name and location of the parent company, its main affiliates, its percentage ownership, direct and indirect, in these affiliates, including shareholdings between them;
- the geographical areas . . . where operations are carried out and the principal activities carried on therein by the parent company and the main affiliates;
- the operating results and sales by geographical area and the sales in the major lines of business for the enterprise as a whole;
- significant new capital investment by geographical area and, as far as practicable, by major lines of business for the enterprise as a whole;
- a statement of the sources and uses of funds by the enterprise as a whole;
- the average number of employees in each geographic area;
- research and development expenditure for the enterprise as a whole;
- the policies followed in respect of intra-group pricing;
- the accounting policies, including, those on consolidation, observed in compiling the published information.[66]

The European Economic Community/European Community

The EEC/EC has also been active in achieving regional harmonization of accounting principles through a series of directives that, within the treaty of Rome, are not as binding as regulations. The directive anticipates given results but the mode and means of implementation are left to the member countries. The EEC/EC is in fact the first supranational body to have an important authority in the area of financial reporting and disclosure. Its influence is so pervasive that its directives are perceived to have important effects on non-EEC/EC-based multinationals operating in the community. Particularly relevant to international accounting are the fourth, fifth, and seventh directives.

The Fourth Directive

The fourth directive, formally adopted in 1978, deals with the annual financial statements of public and private companies, other than banks and insurance companies.[67] Its purposes have been summarized as follows:

1. Coordinating national laws for the protection of members and third parties relating to the publication, presentation, and content of annual accounts and reports of limited-liability companies, and the accounting principles used in their preparation.
2. Establishing in the EEC minimum equivalent legal requirements for disclosure of financial information to the public by companies which are in competition with one another.
3. Establishing the principle that annual accounts should give a true and fair view of a company's assets and liabilities, and of its financial position and profit or loss

4. Providing the fullest possible information about limited companies to shareholders and third parties (with some relief to smaller companies).[68]

The major aspects relevant to international accounting were Articles 1 and 2 on types of companies covered by the directive and the general reporting requirements; Articles 3–27 on the format of annual reports; Articles 28–39 on the valuation rules; Articles 44–50 on publication requirements; and Articles 51–52 on the procedural, statutory changes in national laws required for compliance.

The Fifth Directive

The proposed fifth directive, revised in 1984, deals with the structure, management, and external audits of limited-liability corporations. In the revised draft, the directive proposes to require a company that employs more than 1,000 workers in the EEC/EC (or is part of a group of companies that employs more than 1,000 workers in the EEC/EC) to allow the employees to participate in the company's decision-making structure. In addition, the proposal specifies certain rules concerning annual meetings of shareholders, the adoption of the company's annual financial statements, and the appointment, compensation, and duties of the company's auditors.

The Seventh Directive

The seventh directive, issued in June 1983, addresses the issues of consolidated financial statements and offers some guidelines for more standardization of accounting reporting. Countries in EEC/EC member countries and non-EEC/EC corporations with subsidiaries in a member country are required to file consolidated financial statements in that country. However, each of the ten EEC/EC countries has five years to pass legislation to implement the directive, and annual reports do not have to conform until 1990.

Other Actors

The preceding sections identify the most important actors involved in the harmonization drive. Various other national, regional, and international groups are emerging as active in the same drive. They include basically the following.

1. ASEAN Federation of Accountants (AFA)
2. African Accounting Council (AAC)
3. Union Europeenne des Experts Comptables Economiques et Financiers (UEC)
4. Association Interamericana de Contabilidad (AIC)
5. Confederation of Asian and Pacific Accountants (CAPA)
6. Nordic Federation of Accountants (NFA)
7. Association of Accountancy Bodies in West Africa (ABWA)

8. American Accounting Association (AAA)
9. Canadian Association of Academic Accountants (CAAA)
10. European Accounting Association (EAA)
11. Japan Accounting Association (JAA)
12. Association of University Instructors in Accounting (AUIA)
13. Financial Analysts Federations (FAF)
14. Financial Executives Institute (FEI)
15. Arab Society of Certified Accountants (ASCA)

Given the proliferation of actors involved or willing to be involved in the harmonization drive, one would expect some interrelationships among these bodies and cross-representation in an attempt to exercise some influence in the international accounting arena. Only the future will tell whether this is a situation favorable or unfavorable to the harmonization drive.

The developing countries appear to be more highly represented in the global groups like IASC, IFAC, and the UN, in order to be able to extract more data from the multinational corporations. Witness the following comment about some of the technical papers produced by the UN Intergovernmental Working Group of Experts on International Standards of Accounting and Reporting:

> The most notable position of the papers is the extension of requirements to include data that heretofore were excluded from annual reports. These data are primarily oriented toward employment information and technology transfers. This focus appears to be a response to the desires of the developing nations to extract data from the multinational enterprises (MNEs) which they do not feel powerful enough to extract via national controls. Economic development and assisting and "protecting" employees of MNEs are other goals of the UN effort.[69]

ACCOUNTING EDUCATION IN DEVELOPING COUNTRIES

Accounting Education Problems in the Developing Countries

Investment in education in general is a must for the developing countries. It is multidimensional with different perceptions for different parties: "earnings at the *individual level,* expenditure at the *state level,* disequilibrium at the *system level,* and finally perpetuating inequity *at the national level.*"[70] Some would view it as the fourth dimension of a country's foreign policy following diplomacy, defense, and trade.[71] The creation and nurturing of educational institutions at all levels is instrumental to the success of all economic development programs. Education and training in the developing countries take place in five different forms:

(a) *Academic,* mostly within university departments of economics and commerce (business administration), (b) *Institutional,* at the institutional [illegible]s, polytechnical institutes or other administrative centers. It also covers foreign postal (correspondence) courses; (c) *Technical,* mostly for middle and lower levels, whereby programs are given orally and/or by correspondence; (d) *In-House* training and articleship; (e) *Vocational and other centers,* e.g., management institutes.[72]

Given the importance of the role of accounting in development planning in general and project appraisal in particular, accounting education in the developing countries appears to have a major importance. There is obviously a need for systematic accounting education in connection with technical-assistance programs to give a better chance for development planning to be effectively implemented.

The actual situation of accounting education in the developing countries is far from compatible with what should be required for an effective implementation of development planning. There are various accounting practice problems and accounting education problems that need to be effectively handled before accounting education in the developing countries could be considered adequate in its role of facilitating economic development. A survey of experts gives a rough ordering of the relative importance of the major accounting practice and education problems and their causes in the developing countries and shows that many of the most important accounting problems are believed to result from important causes deeply rooted in accounting education.[73] A list of these problems and their extremely important contributing problems are presented as Exhibits 2.4 through 2.7.

Enthoven listed the following main weaknesses of accounting education and training as portrayed by developing countries' accounting practitioners and educators:

- Accounting is still taught as if it was a technical skill instead of as an intellectual discipline.
- Special fields of accounting, for example, farm accounting, bank accounting and industrial development accounting, for which a great need may exist may not be taught at all.
- Attention to operational and managerial auditing tends to be limited.
- Generally no clearing house for information and publication exists.
- An upgrading of teachers—the development of adequate staff and better pay for teachers—is needed.
- Teaching aids, for example, texts, labs and projectors, tend to be deficient, and not enough funds are budgeted for them.
- Workshops are needed for accounting educators, practitioners and students.
- Interests in activities, such as conferences and seminars that expose students, staff and practitioners to developments in accounting may be limited, and accounting training may lack content and motivation.

Exhibit 2.4
Evaluation of Importance of Accounting Practice Problems

	Importance of Problems				
	Total Responses	*International Organizations Canada & U.S.A.*	*Far East*	*Latin America*	*Mediterranean and Africa*
Shortage of qualified accountants at all levels and in all areas of accounting.	Extreme	Extreme	Moderate	Extreme	Extreme
Accounting information is either not available in the proper form, or is received by users too late to be useful.	Extreme	Extreme	Extreme	Extreme	NI
Accounting information is not utilized advantageously for internal management purposes.	Extreme	Extreme	Extreme	Extreme	Extreme
Lack of adequate financial reporting and auditing standards.	Extreme	Moderate	Extreme	Extreme	NI
Lack of strong national associations of accountants.	Extreme	Extreme	Extreme	NI	NI
Lack of adequate accounting in government agencies and government owned businesses.	Extreme	Extreme	Extreme	Extreme	Extreme
Accountants and the accounting profession have significnatly lower status than other professions.	Moderate	Moderate	Moderate	Moderate	NI
The lack of legislation relating to accounting and auditing standards and procedures.	Moderate	Less Important	Extreme	Moderate	Extreme
Accounting practices are viewed and utilized primarily as a means for helping companies evade taxes and manipulate financial reporting.	Moderate	Extreme	Extreme	NI	NI
Accounting practice tends to be procedures oriented.	Moderate	Moderate	Moderate	Moderate	NI
Accountants and accounting do little to improve government tax collection.	Moderate	Moderate	Moderate	Moderate	NI
Some accountants try to apply concepts and techniques imported from advanced nations regardless of their suitability for the local conditions and immediate needs.	Moderate	Moderate	Moderate	NI	NI
Lack of adequate inflation accounting, currency translation techniques and financial disclosure requirements.	Moderate	Moderate	Extreme	Extreme	Moderate
Conflict between national and international accounting firms.	Less Important	Moderate	Less Important	Moderate	Less Important

Source: Committee on Accounting in Developing Countries, 1973–75, "Report of the Committee on Accounting in Developing Countries," *The Accounting Review,* Supplement to Volume XLXI, p. 203. Reprinted with permission.

- Most governments take a limited interest in accounting training and upgrading.
- Educational institutions, in conjunction with governmental agencies, may have to assess the number of accountants needed and their educational requirements.[74]

To improve accounting education in the developing countries and eliminate some of the problems identified earlier, some foreign support is needed—not

Exhibit 2.5
Evaluation of Importance of Accounting Education Problems

	Importance of Problems				
	Total Responses	*Interna-tional Organiza-tions Canada & U.S.A.*	*Far East*	*Latin America*	*Medi-terranean and Africa*
Locally-authored textbooks are inadequate.	Extreme	Extreme	Moderate	Extreme	NI
Inadequate teaching of accounting subjects at the college level.	Extreme	Extreme	Extreme	Extreme	Extreme
Lack of qualified accounting instructors at the college level.	Extreme	Extreme	Extreme	Extreme	Extreme
Lack of professional development opportunities for accounting educators and practitioners.	Extreme	Extreme	Moderate	Extreme	Extreme
Inadequate accounting education for managers and prospective managers.	Extreme	Extreme	Extreme	Extreme	Moderate
Inadequacy of translated accounting textbooks for the local environment.	Moderate	Moderate	Moderate	NI	Moderate
Lack of translated accounting literature of advanced nations.	Moderate	Moderate	Moderate	Moderate	Moderate
Poorly organized college educational accounting programs and curricula.	Moderate	Moderate	Extreme	Extreme	NI
A bookkeeping and procedural approach to accounting education with very limited emphasis on the theoretical grounds of accounting discipline.	Moderate	Extreme	Moderate	Extreme	NI
Inadequate accounting libraries and other educational resources in colleges and universities.	Moderate	Moderate	Moderate	Moderate	Moderate
Lack of an educational program tailored to qualifying examinations for entrance to the profession.	Moderate	Moderate	Moderate	Moderate	NI
Lack of inadequate distinction between financial, managerial and tax accounting nature and role in college accounting curricula.	Moderate	Moderate	Moderate	Moderate	NI

Source: Committee on Accounting in Developing Countries, 1973–75, "Report of the Committee on Accounting in Developing Countries," *The Accounting Review,* Supplement to Volume XLXI, p. 204. Reprinted with permission.

only as a matter of economic interest to the developed countries, but also as a moral obligation. In this regard, a report to the U.S. Congress by former Comptroller General Elmer Staats, *Training and Related Efforts Needed to Improve Financial Management in the Third World,* states:

The absence of effective financial management is a major obstacle to the optimum use of resources, both internal and external, that are available to improve the standard of living in Third World countries. Effective financial management is essential because anything less dissipates available resources and thwarts development. To improve financial management developing countries must:

1. Develop effective accounting and auditing practices.
2. Insure the presence of skilled personnel to effectively run their financial management systems.

Exhibit 2.6
Extremely Important Accounting Practice Problems and Their Extremely Important Contributing Problems

01 *Shortage of Qualified Accountants at All Levels and in All Areas of Accounting & Practices*
Extremely Important reason:
01.1 Inadequate college educational training of accountants
03 *Accounting Information is Either Not Available Or Is Not Available in the Proper Form, Or Is Received By Users Too Late to Be Useful.*
Extremely Important reasons:
03.1 Educational training lacks the emphasis on managerial accounting and on developing accounting systems.
03.2 Accounting information systems are poorly organized and under-developed for managerial accounting and on developing accounting systems.
03.2 Accounting information systems are poorly organized and under-developed for managerial purposes.
04 *The Failure to Utilize Accounting Information Advantageously for Internal Management Purposes*
Extremely Important reasons:
04.1 Managers lack general training and education about the nature and role of accounting information for managerial functions.
04.2 Accounting reports are not adequate for use by management because of improper form or because they are received by the user too late to be useful.
06 *Lack of Legislation Relating to Accounting and Auditing Standards and Procedures*
Extremely Important reason:
06.2 The accounting profession has not been united and forceful in developing and enforcing reporting and auditing standards beyond the legal minimum.
08 *Lack of Strong National Associations of Accountants*
Extremely Important reason:
None
10 *Lack of Adequate Accounting in Government Agencies and Government-Owned Businesses*
Extremely Important reasons:
10.1 Accountants' educational training does not emphasize the role of accounting in planning and control of social goals and achievement or the differences between governmental, quasi-governmental, and private enterprise accounting.
10.2 Engineers and economists who are managing state-owned enterprises lack appreciation of management accounting and lack understanding of the often complex government accounting systems.
NOTE: The two and three digit numbers above represent, respectively, the number of the primary problem and of the contributing problem in the second round questionnaire. For example, problem number 06 was the sixth primary accounting practice problem listed, and 06.2 was listed second as a contributing problem for the sixth primary problem.

Source: Committee on Accounting in Developing Countries, 1973–75, "Report of the Committee on Accounting in Developing Countries," *The Accounting Review,* Supplement to Volume XLXI, pp. 204–205. Reprinted with permission.

3. Develop a comprehensive and up-to-date training program at both the national and regional level. . . .
4. Increase their commitment to the realization of an effective training development program.[75]

Exhibit 2.7
Extremely Important Accounting Education Problems and Their Extremely Important Contributing Problems

---

01 *Locally-Authored Accounting Textbooks Are Inadequate*
Extremely Important reason:
01.4 The accountants most qualified to write texts are too busy with other concerns.
05 *Inadequate Teaching of Accounting Subjects at the College Level*
Extremely Important reason:
05.1 Accounting instructors often occupy several other positions in companies, government, and public accounting firms for the purpose of suplementing their low teaching salaries and they do not have time for adequate class preparation.
06 *Lack of Qualified Accounting Instructors at the College Level*
Extremely important reasons:
06.1 There is a general shortage of qualified accountants and educators.
06.4 College teaching careers are not adequately rewarded financially and this has discouraged many qualified individuals from teaching careers.
09 *Lack of Professional Development Opportunities for Accounting Educators and Practitioners.*
Extremely Important reasons:
None
10 *Inadequate Accounting Education for Managers and Prospective Managers*
Extremely Important reason:
10.1 The accounting education of the engineers and scientists who become managers is limited to the bookkeeping aspects of accounting, or they receive no accounting training at all.
NOTE: The two and three digit numbers above represent, respectively, the number of the primary problem and the contributing problem in the second round questionnaire. For example, problem 06 was the sixth primary accounting education problem listed, and 06.4 was listed fourth as a contributing problem for the sixth primary problem.

Source: Committee on Accounting in Developing Countries, 1973–75, "Report of the Committee on Accounting in Developing Countries," *The Accounting Review,* Supplement to Volume XLXI, p. 205. Reprinted with permission.

Various programs have been recommended for adoption by the developing countries. One noteworthy example is a distinct body of knowledge, called "economic development accountancy," which is recommended as the way to cater effectively to the needs of socioeconomic development. "Economic development accounting can be described as the application of existing and potential accounting systems, techniques, procedures and data to enhance economic development within a nation and among nations."[76] It is a concept more compatible with the requirement of development planning and of accounting for economic analysis, planning, and policies. It is intended to serve both micro- and macrosocioeconomic decisions. Accounting education through informal teaching is another solution used in some of the developing countries. For example, the redeeming features of informal teaching programs in accounting in Pakistan are described as follows:

1. The only Open University of Pakistan (Allama Iqbal Open University) was set up in Islamabad in 1975. Since the literacy rate in Pakistan has averaged around 24 percent, it is a big challenge to reach the masses in all provinces and other places, so that they can get broad education. However, besides accomplishing the goal of banishing poverty in Pakistan, the country has prepared special programs through the above university, whereby accounting education consists of tutorials, lesson notes, and other guidelines. Through informal education, therefore, correspondence courses are continuing.
2. Some private colleges exist, and some are being set up for accounting education.
3. Professional institutes of the country, namely, the Institute of Bankers in Pakistan, The Institute of Cost and Management Accountants of Pakistan, the Institute of Chartered Accountants of Pakistan, and the Institute of Marketing Management have also extended the educational frontiers in the subject of accounting through corresponding courses.[77]

Concrete key proposals for the development of accounting education were also made by IFAC.[78] IFAC also addressed the required levels of education and training.[79] Accounting education in the developing countries shall proceed at the technical level in secondary, commercial, and technical or vocational schools where students are trained to apply the fundamentals of accounting rules and procedures; the intermediate level in colleges and universities leading to an undergraduate and/or graduate degree in accounting; and professional education conducted by professional bodies to insure that a required standard of technical knowledge and skill has been met. Each of the levels requires the existence of an efficient educational infrastructure. One way of creating such an infrastructure may be through the creation of regional training centers for accounting education and development. The following list is an example of the set of aims and objectives for an African regional training center for accounting education and development:

a. Serve as a central resource pool for promoting accounting development and providing for training needs in Africa;
b. Locate, channel and co-ordinate funds and resources to be utilized for the benefit of accounting development in Africa;
c. Provide advanced accounting education and training for accounting professionals and educators;
d. Conduct research in accounting and related fields with emphasis on Africa;
e. Develop appropriate instructional materials, set up model courses, devise teaching methods; compile and translate available accounting educational materials and disseminate them; sponsor programmes for writing texts with special relevance for Africa; stimulate the activities of national and regional accounting association activities;
f. Develop accreditation standards for curricula and education and training institutions and assist with the implementation and maintenance of such standards;

g. Provide professional continuing education for accountants;

h. Liaise with accounting practitioners, educators and established institutions to develop accounting practice and education;

i. Assist countries already possessing accountancy bodies with professional training and development;

j. Serve as a clearing-house for information on the activities of the local accountancy bodies. Develop cooperation and interchange of ideas between African accountants and professional bodies, and the international accounting community at large;

k. Encourage and assist countries without professional bodies;

l. Promote the development, adaptation and harmonization of accounting standards, practices to suit the African environment;

m. Encourage and assist countries without standard-setting bodies to establish such institutions;

n. Assist Governments in establishing enforcement mechanisms for accounting standards.[80]

In fact IFAC issued seven education-oriented guidelines: Prequalification Education and Training, Continuing Professional Education, Test of Professional Competence, The Core of Knowledge, Professional Subjects (which specifies the core of knowledge of professional accountants), Practical Experience in Specifics, Code of Knowledge for Supportive Subjects, and Education and Training Requirements for Accounting Technicians.[81]

Proposals for Accounting Education in the Developing Countries

Different models of accounting education are used in the world. The following elements exist in each of the models:

1. Entry level—the requirement to enter the educational process that will lead eventually to qualification as an accountant. Entry level usually occurs upon graduation from a secondary school.
2. General education—the curricula in the areas of arts, sciences, and other topics that provide a foundation for professional study. General education may be obtained at both the secondary school level and the university level.
3. Professional education—the curriculum in accounting and auditing and in closely related professional topics that may be obtained in a variety of ways: at the university level from professional associations or through business schools or institutes.
4. Practical experience—the amount and type of on-the-job training required to become a qualified accountant.
5. Test(s) of professional competence—a qualifying examination or examinations taken prior to qualification to demonstrate a minimum level of knowledge and skill.[82]

Exhibit 2.8
Models of Accounting Education

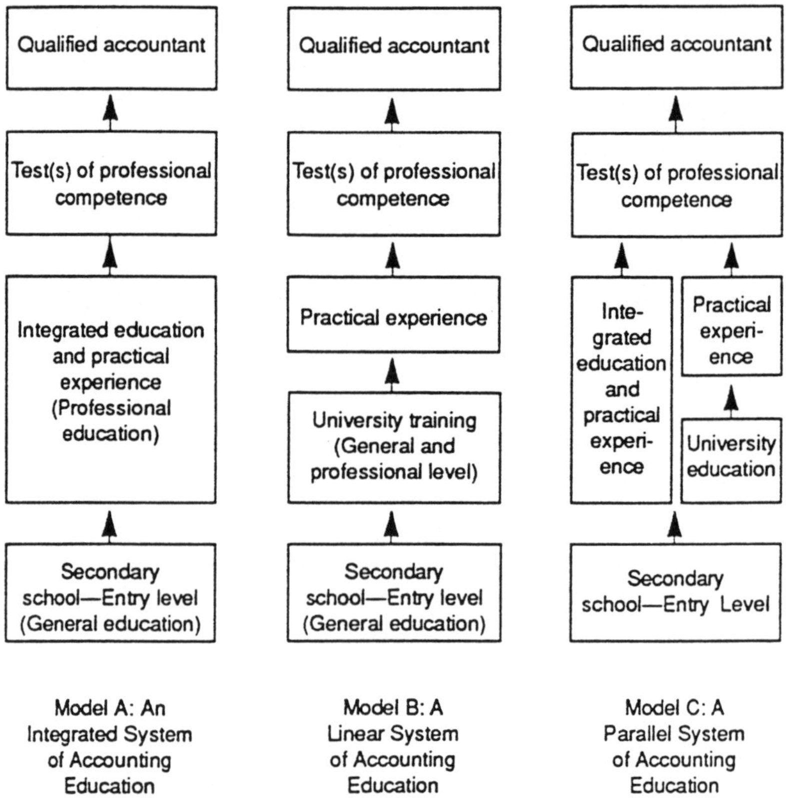

Source: Belverd E. Needles, Jr., "Standards for International Accounting Education: A Consideration of the Issues," in *Comparative International Accounting Standards* (Champaign: University of Illinois, Center for International Education and Research in Accounting, 1990), p. 7. Reprinted with permission.

A combination of each of these five elements leads to three models, identified as the integrated system, the linear system, and the parallel system.[83] They are illustrated in Exhibit 2.8. While these models can serve as a general structure for accounting education in the developing countries, they do not address the specific elements needed in the developing countries. Three proposals for accounting education in the developing countries have been suggested. They are examined next.

First Proposal: Economic Development Accountancy

One proposal for accounting education in the developing countries was advanced by the Committee on International Accounting Operations and Education of the American Accounting Association (herein after referred to as the Committee) in its 1976–78 report.[84] Referred to as Economic Development Accountancy, it is described as the application of existing and potential accounting systems, techniques, procedures, and data to enhance economic development within a nation and among nations.[85] The main objective of accounting education is therefore the economic development of the country. The objective of Economic Development Accountancy is to support micro- and macrosocioeconomic decisions more effectively using the various branches of accounting. Its implementation starts with a comprehensive inventory of the quantity and quality of accountants, manpower availabilities, and the various educational developments in accountancy areas. This ''stocktaking'' is expected to involve:

a. The present status of the developments in the various branches of accountancy, including the institutional, education and training, legal, research, and other professional aspects. These developments must be seen in the context of socioeconomic policies and needs;
b. The assumed requirements at the end of five years, preferably tying in with five-year economic plans (where these exist);
c. The needs in 10 to 20 years, based on long range plans that have been drawn up in the various countries.[86]

Following the stocktaking an Accounting Development plan may be instituted to serve as a blueprint for accounting education.

Second Proposal: Economic Evaluation Accounting

A second proposal for accounting development and education in the developing countries was advanced by George Scott and is referred to as Economic Evaluation Accounting.[87] It is described as structuring the accounting system in order to provide information that will facilitate the economic evaluation of enterprises' activities by management, investors, and the government. The main objective of accounting is economic development. The objective of Economic Evaluation Accounting is to provide information that has maximum economic utility for users in developing nations. This utility depends on the requirement that accounting be based on general economic principles of both a micro- or macronature rather than on business practices, accounting conventions, tax or other narrowly conceived legislation, or some other basis that may serve the narrow needs and interests of certain interest groups.[88] The parts constitute Economic Evaluation Accounting. The first part deals with the various factions—external financial reporting, internal financial reporting, and business advisory services to management—that accounting is intended to fulfill in developing nations. The second part deals with the following four characteristics that need to be present so that accounting is able to fulfill its functions: current value measurement, education of accountants, legislative control and regulation of accounting, and professional accounting.[89]

The implementation of Economic Evaluation Accounting requires both a liberal arts-based curriculum and a "fresh start" approach. Scott elaborates on both requirements as follows:

> During the initial stages of education, a liberal education seems essential for accountants in developing nations to enable them to view accounting and business enterprises in proper perspective as parts of the total social and economic fabric. Narrowly educated accountants are not inclined to observe nuances and implications in accounting in formation nor to be critical of outmoded business and accounting practices.[90]
>
> This writer is convinced that the "fresh start" alternative is the better one. When accounting development began in advanced nations, sophisticated management and accounting systems techniques and knowledge were not in existence; therefore, accounting in these nations only slowly acquired higher standards and advanced techniques. Advanced management techniques now exist and are available and relevant to many companies in developing nations; hence, accounting in these companies should acquire a high state of sophistication rapidly in order to provide the information necessary for utilization of advanced management techniques. Thus, there is good reason why accounting in developing nations should not follow the slow and tortuous routes to accounting development that have characterized accounting in industrialized nations.[91]

Third Proposal: Two-Tiered Accounting Education Approach

The third proposal for accounting education in the developing countries was advanced by Manuel A. Tipgos and is referred to as the Two-Tiered Accounting Education model.[92] Before presenting this model, Tipgos presented various criticisms of the Economic Development Accounting (EDA) and the Economic Evaluation Accounting (EEvA) models. A first criticism is related to the assumption in both models that the objective of accounting in the developing countries is the economic development of these countries. The assumption is viewed as myopic from a planning standpoint because it ignores the inner dream or goal of educated individuals to attain professional status comparable with that of other professionals in society.[93] A second criticism is related to the implementation and timing of output. As shown in Exhibit 2.9, both models create a lengthy lead time between input (beginning of implementation) and output (first group of graduate) of 12 to 17 years that could aggravate the accounting manpower problem and jeopardize development plans of the developing countries.[94] Given these limitations, Tipgos proposed a comprehensive plan for improving accounting in the developing countries based on the following four general propositions:

> First, economic development in a given country is the result of a concerted and coordinated effort of all the social institutions in the country, and accounting is first one of these institutions, irrespective of the importance of its contribution. Second, the accounting profession in developing countries has certain higher-level goals regardless of its stage of sophistication; therefore, its development should *not* be exclusively tied to or dependent upon the socioeconomic development of the country. Third, because of the interdependence of accounting education and accounting practice, any plan to improve

Exhibit 2.9
Estimated Lead Time Between Input and Output of EDA and EEvA

	EDA		*EEvA*	
(In Years)	*Minimum*	*Maximum*	*Minimum*	*Maximum*
Initial contact and decision to go ahead	2	3	2	3
Budget approval	2	3	2	3
*Construction of facilities	3	5	3	5
Stock-taking of existing accounting knowledge (applicable to EDA; assumed to be done simultaneously with construction of facilities. See above)	—	—	n/a	n/a
Formulation of Accounting Development Plan (EDA only)	2	2	n/a	n/a
Recruitment of faculty and students (For EDA, assumed to be done simultaneously with formulation of Accounting Development Plan. See above)	—	—	2	3
Training the students	4	5	4	5
Allowance for delays	2	3	2	3
Total	15	22	15	22
Notes: *If physical facilities are available; lead time is reduced to	12	17	12	17.

Source: Manuel A. Tipgos, "A Comprehensive Model for Improving Accounting Education in Developing Countries," *Advances in International Accounting* 1 (1987), p. 389. Reprinted with permission.

accounting in developing countries must provide for a simultaneous improvement of both these sectors of the accounting profession. And, fourth, any form of assistance, present or future, should be offered and implemented on the basis of the first three propositions.[95]

The comprehensive plan calls for a focus on both professional and paraprofessional training, and a two-tiered Accounting Education Approach. The two-tiered accounting education system in accounting (TES), described in Exhibit 2.10, shows the focus on an initial stage leading a subprofessional certification, and a final stage leading to full professional status. The advantages of the TES model are formulated as follows:

1. TES gives everyone who wants to work in accounting and who has the aptitude for it an opportunity to proceed toward this goal, at least for the first two to three years.

Exhibit 2.10
Two-Tiered Education System (TES)

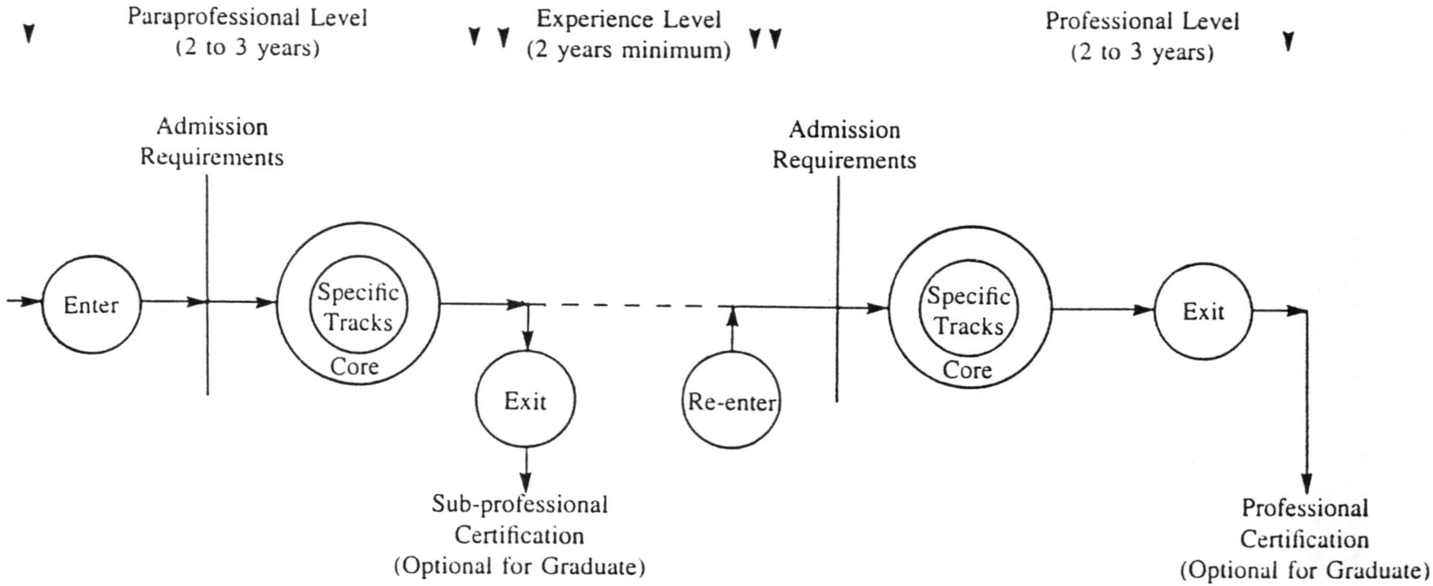

Source: Manuel A. Tipgos, "A Comprehensive Model for Improving Accounting Education in Developing Countries," *Advances in International Accounting* 1 (1987), p. 398. Reprinted with permission.

Exhibit 2.11
Comparison of Models

	AAA MODEL—EDA	SCOTT MODEL—EEvA	COMPREHENSIVE MODEL—TES
Model Identification	Economic Development Accounting	Economic Evaluation Accounting	Two-tiered Education System
Overall Purpose or Objective	Economic development of the developing country	Economic development of the developing country	To be defined by accountants in the particular developing country.
Fundamental Assumption	1. Application of existing and potential accounting systems, techniques, procedures, and data for economic development 2. To integrate branches of accounting to serve a micro and macro socioeconomic decisions effectively. 3. Linkage of model to educational module required for economic development which demand: (a) A conceptual socio-economic foundation of accounting education and training. (b) Specialization in various areas of accounting (c) Closer linkage between institutional, professional, and educational programs. (d) Greater focus on forecasting techniques both internal and external.	Maximum economic utility of accounting for users; based soley on general economic principles of both macro and micro. Two essential parts: 1. To deal with both internal and external policy reporting for private and public enterprises. 2. Key elements needed to perform its functions: (a) current value measurement (b) education of accountants (c) legislative control and regulation of accounting (d) professional accounting	1. Economic development is a concerted and coordinated effort of all social institutions; accounting is one of these institutions. 2. The accounting profession in developing countries has certain higher level aspirations not just economic development of the country. 3. Any plan to improve accounting in developing countries must provide for improvement in both accounting education and practice. 4. Any form of assistance to improve accounting must be offered and implemented based on the three propositions above.
Comprehensiveness of the Model	Provides for long-term accounting manpower needs of developing countries; no provision for short-term needs of economic development.	Focus on long-term needs; no provision for short-term accounting manpower requirements of economic development.	Provides for both short-term and long-term accounting manpower needs of economic development.

Exhibit 2.11 *(continued)*

	AAA MODEL—EDA	SCOTT MODEL—EEvA	COMPREHENSIVE MODEL—TES
Implementation and related matters	Implementation is dependent upon the successful completion of two important requirements: 1. Inventory or "stock-taking" of quality of accountants, available manpower, and educational functional development in accounting areas. 2. Develop an Accounting Development Plan to serve as blueprint for implementing the model.	1. Requires a liberal arts-based curriculum. 2. Uses the "fresh start" approach based on the standards of accounting education, practices and professionalism set forth in EEvA. 3. Establish small programs for a few carefully selected students, and gradually expand as demand increases.	1. Requires definition of objectives of accounting. Identify subobjectives. 2. Requires an inventory of accounting infrastructure and to identify the existing accounting influence. 3. Implement the paraprofessional level of model; can be superimposed on existing 2-year or diploma programs common in certain developing countries. 4. Implement the professional level of model. The objectives of accounting and inventory of accounting infrastructure is necessary for implementation.
Specialization	Specialization, where necessary, to service specific needs of development.	Specialization to serve specific needs of development.	Specialization through specific tracks to serve student preferences and specific demands of development. Subprofessional and professional certification available.
*Output Availability	Significant lead time between input and output of the model (conservatively 12 to 17 years).	Significant lead time between input and output of the model (conservatively 12 to 17 years).	Short lead time between input and output of the model (output of paraprofessional level may be available in 2 to 3 years).
*Expected Output	Adequately trained output.	Better output. Better control of output due to "fresh start" approach.	Adequately trained output.

Notes:
*Provided by the author for comparative purposes.

Source: Manuel A. Tipgos, "A Comprehensive Model for Improving Accounting Education in Developing Countries," *Advances in International Accounting* 1 (1987), pp. 400–402. Reprinted with permission.

2. Since no one is allowed to continue to the next level without seeking employment in either private or public enterprises for a specified number of years, the country is supplied with the needed paraprofessional accounting manpower for its development.
3. TES introduces into the accounting educational system a practical experience requirement at [a] professional accounting level, a requirement which is not common in developing countries.
4. TES gives those with high aptitude and professional promise the opportunity to vie for professional status, as well as gives the accounting profession the opportunity to grow, to mature, and to reach a status comparable with that of other professions.
5. The system would filter out those who are not prepared or who are not willing to go back to pursue a professional certification. This avoids the ineffective and inefficient use of resources at the second level which would result if this level were not subject to stringent requirements.
6. The system will produce better prepared professionals, and at the same time, because of the stringent admission requirements, an oversupply of professional accountants will be avoided.[96]

A comparison of the three models in Exhibit 2.11, shows a clear superiority of the TES model for the developing countries.

CONCLUSIONS

This chapter elaborated on the state of accounting in the developing countries with particular emphasis on the institutional and education issues affecting the developing countries. Proposals are made for the choice of standard-setting strategies, the wants of harmonization, and the choice of accounting education strategies facing the developing countries.

NOTES

1. George M. Scott, *Accounting and the Developing Nations* (Seattle: University of Washington, Graduate School of Business Administration, 1970).

2. Society for International Development, *The Role of Accounting in Economic Development,* International Seminar (Washington, D.C.: Society for International Development, 1976), pp. 13–15.

3. Thomas W. Lelievre and Clara C. Lelievre, "Accounting in the Third World," *The Woman CPA* (October 1977), pp. 3–5.

4. Adolf J. H. Enthoven, "U.S. Accounting and the Third World," *Journal of Accountancy* (June 1983), p. 110.

5. Ibid., p. 115.

6. Leonore M. Briones, "On Containing Graft and Corruption," *International Journal of Government Auditing* (April 1987), pp. 13–14.

7. Ibid., p. 13.

8. Felix Pomeranz, "Accountants and Third World Corruption," *Advances in International Accounting* 4 (1991), pp. 263–274.

9. Ahmed Riahi-Belkaoui, *Morality in Accounting* (Westport, Conn.: Greenwood Press, 1992).

10. J. B. Ghartey, *Crisis Accountability and Development in the Third World* (Brookfield, Vt.: Gower, 1987), p. 63.

11. Ibid., pp. 63–65.

12. J. B. Ghartey, ''Accountability, the Threshold of Political Instability, Underdevelopment, and Misery: The Case of Africa,'' *International Journal of Accounting Education and Research* 21, 1 (Fall 1985), p. 157.

13. International Federation of Accountants, *Proceedings: Asia and Pacific Conference on Accounting Education for Development* (New York: International Federation of Accountants, 1984), pp. 2–3.

14. Ghartey, *Crisis Accountability,* p. 106

15. Ibid., pp. 106–108.

16. R. S. Olusegan Wallace, ''Accounting in the Developing Countries,'' *Research in Third World Accounting* 1 (1990), pp. 3–54.

17. T. L. Wilkinson, ''United States Accounting as Viewed by Accountants of Other Countries,'' *International Journal of Accounting Education and Research* 1 (1965), pp. 3–14.

18. Ibid., p. 12.

19. L. J. Seidler, *The Function of Accounting in Economic Development: Turkey as a Case Study* (New York: Praeger, 1967).

20. P. Walton, ''The Export of British Accounting Legislation to Commonwealth Countries,'' *Accounting and Business Research* 16 (1986), pp. 353–357.

21. Werner G. Frank, ''An Empirical Analysis of International Accounting Principles,'' *Journal of Accounting Research* (Autumn 1979), p. 593.

22. F.D.S. Choi and G. G. Mueller, *An Introduction to Multinational Accounting* (Englewood Cliffs, N.J.: Prentice-Hall, 1978).

23. Ahmed Belkaoui, ''Economic Political and Civil Indicators and Reporting and Disclosure Adequacy: An Empirical Investigation,'' *Journal of Accounting and Public Policy* (Winter 1983).

24. H. D. Lowe, ''Accounting Aid for Development Countries,'' *Accounting Review* (April 1967), p. 360.

25. E. L. Elliot, J. Larrea, and J. M. Rivera, ''Accounting Aid to Developing Countries: Some Additional Considerations,'' *Accounting Review* (October 1968), p. 764.

26. Mahmood A. Quereshi, ''Economic Development, Social Justice and Financial Reporting: Pakistan's Experience with Private Enterprise,'' *Management International Review* (1975), p. 71.

27. B. L. Jaggi, ''The Impact of the Cultural Environment on Financial Disclosure,'' *International Journal of Accounting, Education and Research* (Spring 1975), p. 84.

28. J. Kraayenhof, ''International Challenges in Accounting,'' *Journal of Accountancy* (January 1963), p. 36.

29. I. L. Fantl, ''The Dilemma of International Accounting,'' *New Jersey CPA* (Spring 1968), pp. 3–8.

30. Mahmood Quereshi, ''Pragmatic and Academic Bases of International Accounting,'' *Management International Review* 2 (1979), pp. 61–68; T. R. Weirich, C. G. Avery, and H. R. Anderson, ''International Accounting: Varying Definitions,'' *International Journal of Accounting Education and Research* (Fall 1971), pp. 79–87.

31. Weirich, Avery, and Anderson, ''International Accounting.''

32. Ibid., p. 79.

33. Ibid.
34. Ibid.
35. F. E. Amenkhienan, *Accounting in the Developing Countries: A Framework for Standard Setting* (Ann Arbor, Mich.: UMI Research Press, 1986), p. 20.
36. Ibid.
37. Ibid., pp. 22–26.
38. Enthoven, "U.S. Accounting and the Third World," p. 112
39. B. E. Needles, Jr., "Implementing a Framework for the International Transfer of Accounting Technology," *International Journal of Accounting Education and Research* (Fall 1976), p. 51.
40. Ibid.
41. Amenkhienan, *Accounting in the Developing Countries,* p. 24.
42. Scott, *Accounting and the Developing Nations,* p. 12.
43. Ibid., p. 25.
44. D. D. Alhashim, "International Dimensions of Accounting and Implications for Developing Nations," *Management International Review* (4th quarter 1982), p. 5.
45. John A. Wilson, "The Need for Standardization of International Accounting," *Touche Ross Tempo* (Winter 1969), p. 40.
46. E. W. Macrae, "Implements to a Free International Market in Accounting and the Effects on International Accounting Firms," in John C. Burton, ed. *The International World of Accounting: Challenge and Opportunities* (New York: Arthur Young, 1981), p. 50.
47. Lee J. Seidler, "Technical Issues in International Accounting," in Fredericks D. S. Choi, ed. *Multinational Accounting: A Research Framework for the Eighties* (Ann Arbor, Mich.: UMI Research Press, 1981), p. 41.
48. Lal. C. Jagetia, and Evaristus C. Nwadike, "Accounting Systems in Developing Nations: The Nigerian Experience," *International Journal of Accounting* 18, 2 (Spring 1983), pp. 69–82.
49. T. L. Wilkinson, "United States Accounts as Viewed by Accountants of Other Countries," *International Journal of Accounting* (Fall 1965), pp. 11–12.
50. R. J. Briston, "The Evolution of Accounting in Developing Countries," *International Journal of Accounting* (Fall 1978), pp. 105–20.
51. J. M. Samuels, and J. C. Oliga, "Accounting Standards in Developing Countries," *International Journal of Accounting* (Fall 1982) pp. 69–89.
52. Ibid., p. 72.
53. Mfandaidza R. Hove, "Accounting Practices in Developing Countries Colonialism's Legacy of Inappropriate Technologies," *International Journal of Accounting* 22 (1986), p. 56.
54. Briston, "The Evolution of Accounting," p. 105.
55. Samuels and Oliga, "Accounting Standards," p. 80.
56. Joseph P. Cummings, and Michael N. Chetkovich, "World Accounting Enters a New Era," *The Journal of Accountancy* (April 1978), p. 52.
57. IASC, *Objectives and Procedures* (London: IASC, January 1983), par. 8.
58. Ibid., par. 27.
59. Sir Henry Benson, "The Story of International Accounting Standards," *Accountancy* (July 1976), p. 34.
60. T. R. Douglas, "International Accounting Standards," *CA Magazine* (October 1977), pp. 49–50.
61. *The Impact of Multinational Corporations on Development and on International Relations* (UN Publications, Sales No. E. 74, II.A.5[v]), p. 95.

62. Group of Experts on International Accounting Standards of Accounting and Reporting, *International Standards of Accounting and Reporting for Transnational Corporations* (New York: United Nations, 1977), p. 17.

63. Lane A. Daley, and Gerhard G. Mueller, ''Accounting in the Arena of World Politics,'' *Journal of Accountancy* (February 1982), p. 5.

64. Klaus A. Sahlgren, ''The Work of Non-Accountant International Bodies: The United Nations,'' in W. J. Brennan, ed., *The Internationalization of the Accounting Profession* (Toronto: Canadian Institute of Chartered Accountants, 1979), p. 71.

65. OECD, *International Investment and Multinational Enterprises* (Paris: 1976), pp. 14–16.

66. OECD, ''Declaration on International Investment and Multinational Enterprises,'' *The OECD Observer* (July/August 1976), p. 14.

67. Commission of the European Communities, *Amended Proposal for a Fourth Council Directive for Co-Ordination of a National Legislation Regarding the Annual Accounts of Limited Liability Companies* (Brussels, 1974).

68. *The Fourth Directive* (London: Deloitte, Haskins, & Sells, 1978), p. 1.

69. Daley and Mueller, ''Accounting in the Arena of World Politics,'' p. 5.

70. M. G. Kanbur, *Education for Development in the South Pacific* (Fiji: University of the South Pacific, 1985).

71. P. G. Altbach, *Higher Education in the Third World* (Hong Kong: Manuzen Asia, 1982).

72. Committee on International Accounting Operations and Education, 1976–78, *Accounting Education and the Third World* (Sarasota, Fla: American Accounting Association, 1978), p. 83.

73. Committee on Accounting in the Developing Countries, ''Report of the Committee on Accounting in the Developing Countries,'' *The Accounting Review,* Supplement (1975).

74. Enthoven, ''U.S. Accounting and the Third World,'' p. 112.

75. Elmer Staats, *Training and Related Efforts Needed to Improve Financial Management in the Third World,* ID 79–46 (Washington, D.C: General Accounting Office, 1979), p. 1.

76. A. J. H. Enthoven, *Accountancy and Economic Development Policy* (Amsterdam: North Holland, 1973), p. 168.

77. Khawaja Amjad Saeed, ''Accounting Education in Different Social-Economic Environments: A Case Study from Pakistan,'' in Kyojiro Someya, ed., *Accounting Education and Research to Promote International Understanding* (Westport, Conn.: Greenwood Press, 1988), p. 285.

78. International Federation of Accountants, *Proceedings: Asia and Pacific Conference,* pp. 4–5.

79. International Federation of Accountants, *International Education Guidelines* (IEG7: ''Education and Training Requirements for Accounting Techniques'') (New York: IFAC, February 1982 to October 1986).

80. United Nations Center on Transnational Corporations, *International Accounting and Reporting Issues: 1989 Review* (New York: United Nations, 1990), pp. 101–102.

81. Belverd E. Needles, Jr., ''Standards for International Accounting Education: A Consideration of the Issues,'' in *Comparative International Accounting Standards* (Center for International Education and Research in Accounting, University of Illinois, 1990), pp. 4–5.

82. Ibid., pp. 6–7.
83. Ibid., p. 7.
84. Committee on International Accounting Operations and Education, p. 50.
85. Ibid., p. 20.
86. Ibid., p. 88.
87. Scott, *Accounting and the Developing Nations,* p. 145.
88. Ibid., p. 150.
89. Ibid.,
90. Ibid., p. 154.
91. Ibid., p. 168.
92. Manuel A. Tipgos, "A Comprehensive Model for Improving Accounting Education in Developing Countries," *Advances in International Accounting* 1 (1987), pp. 383–404.
93. Ibid., p. 387.
94. Ibid., p. 388.
95. Ibid., pp. 391–392.
96. Ibid., pp. 396–397.

SELECTED READINGS

Altbach, P. G. *Higher Education in the Third World.* Hong Kong: Manuzen Asia, 1982.

Amenkhienan, F. E. *Accounting in the Developing Countries: A Framework for Standard Setting.* Ann Arbor, Mich.: UMI Research Press, 1986.

Briston, R. J. "The Evolution of Accounting in Developing Countries." *International Journal of Accounting* (Fall 1978).

Committee on Accounting in the Developing Countries. "Report of the Committee on Accounting in the Developing Countries." *The Accounting Review,* Supplement (1979).

Committee on International Accounting Operations and Education, 1976–78. *Accounting Education and the Third World.* Sarasota, Fla.: American Accounting Association, 1978.

Enthoven, A. J. H. *Accountancy and Economic Development Policy.* Amsterdam: North Holland, 1973.

———. *Accounting Education—Its Importance and Requirements.* Center for International Accounting Development, University of Texas at Dallas, 1982.

Ghartey, J. B. "Accountability, the Threshold of Political Instability, Underdevelopment, and Misery: The Case of Africa." *International Journal of Accounting Education and Research* (Fall 1985).

———. *Crisis Accountability and Development in the Third World.* Brookfield, Vt.: Gower, 1987.

International Federation of Accountants. *Proceedings: Asia and Pacific Conference on Accounting Education for Development.* New York: International Federation of Accountants, 1984.

Lelievre, Thomas and Clara C. Lelievre. "Accounting in the Third World." *The Woman CPA* (October 1977), pp. 3–5.

Riahi-Belkaoui, Ahmed. *Morality in Accounting.* Westport Conn.: Greenwood Press, 1992.

Scott, George M. *Accounting and the Developing Nations.* Seattle: University of Washington, Graduate School of Business Administration, 1970.

Staats, Elmer. *Training and Related Efforts Needed to Improve Financial Management in the Third World.* Washington, D.C.: General Accounting Office, 1979.

Tipgos, Manuel A. ''A Comprehensive Model for Improving Accounting Education in Developing Countries.'' *Advances in International Accounting* 1 (1987), pp. 383–404.

3

Accounting and Economic Development

Economic development requires in large part a well-established and monitored planning process. The planning process relies on the provision of relevant macro and micro information for a better deliberation of the activities required and the necessary standards of performance. Accounting appears to serve an important role in the provision of this information, resulting in a crucial role in the promotion of economic development. Accordingly, this chapter elaborates on the role of accounting in economic development. First the role of the planning process in economic development is presented, followed by a description of the role of social indicators and accounting.

DEVELOPMENT PLANNING

The Developing Economies

The development economies form a third element in a world power structure dominated by the technologically more advanced nations of the Atlantic bloc and the former European Communist bloc. This third element has been seen for a long time as the ''commonwealth of poverty,'' in spite of its niche and complex cultures, its immense human resources, and its possession of much of the world's metallic minerals, water power, oil and coal, timber, and potential cropland. This Third World is also seen as ''a universe of radical scarcity. Defining and determining every dimension of men's relationships to each other . . . the inadequacy of the means of livelihood is the first and distinguishing truth of this area.''[1]

In effect, for much of the Third World real GNP per capita is under $200, the daily intake of calories is under 2,200, and the daily intake of animal protein is under 15 grams. Added to this poverty is a legacy of warped economics facing continuous environmental difficulties—poor soils, erratic climates, floods and droughts, and diseases. This is particularly serious given that the economies of the Third World are plagued by two distortions: a grossly inflated agricultural sector and an overexpanding tertiary sector. In general, these countries are characterized by low per capita real income, limited stock of capital goods, dominance of subsistence agriculture, and relatively low levels of education and wealth. The rate of economic growth in these economies appears to be dependent on the rate of capital formation, the incremental capital output ratio, technological change, the growth of the labor force, and a favorable social and political environment.

To escape from this vicious cycle of underdevelopment, the Third World countries have begun searching for a new economic and social identity. In fact, since acquiring their independence, most developing economies have begun major efforts to improve their economic situations. Economic development is now the primary goal in the developing economies. It is understood to include both economic growth and social and institutional changes. The strategies adopted to spur economic development in the developing economies have been either of the kind putting a primacy on economic growth or of the kind emphasizing socioeconomic development.

Barriers and Impediments to Economic Development

There seems to be a consensus on the factors contributing to the economic problems of the developing countries, which include rapid population growth, resource limitations, and inefficiency in resource use.

Rapid population growth is an important concern for the developing countries. It has been further stimulated by improvements in health care and the eradication of major epidemic diseases. This improvement in health care has averted the doom predictions, known as the iron law of population growth, as envisioned by Malthus. Population growth remains serious, however, leading economists to talk about the ''critical minimum effort'' needed to increase capital quickly enough so that the increase in output exceeds the increase in population.

With respect to resource limitations, economic development must rest on an adequate presence of financial and physical capital, social-overhead capital, and human capital. Physical capital in terms of natural resources endowment is important for economic development, but its presence has never been an absolute precondition for economic growth. It needs to be complemented with an adequate supply of financial, social-overhead, and human capital.

Financial capital plays a vital role in economic development by spurring investment. It may be generated internally through the savings of households and firms if a healthy banking climate is maintained in the country. In most cases, the developing countries have to rely on external funding of their major projects.

The social-overhead capital of a country is also known as the infrastructure of the economy. It is composed of the system of supporting services, such as transportation and communications, necessary to an efficient conduct of the economy. Consequently, a dependable social-overhead capital is vital to the economic development of the developing countries.

Human capital, in the form of a well-developed, healthy, educated, and efficient work force, is often missing in the developing countries. A precondition to economic development is a high-quality system of education, training, and health.

The developing countries are also plagued by an inefficient use of resources, both in terms of allocative efficiency and X-efficiency. Allocative efficiency results from the use of a nation's resources to make the wrong products. X-efficiency, to use a term introduced by Professor Harvey Liebenstein,[2] arises wherever resources are used poorly even in making the right products. The source of X-efficiency may be inadequate education, poor health, traditions, institutions, habitual ways of producing, custom, or cultural attitudes. The presence of X-efficiency in the developing countries is evident in the enormous differences in productivity from country to country, in particular in industries using the same technology.

It is generally believed that entrepreneurship is a vital ingredient for economic development. The lack of entrepreneurship in most developing countries is generally seen as one of the major ingredients for a maintained economic growth. Entrepreneurship is "a combination of the following attributes: imagination, daring, willingness to take risks, a sense of timing, and an ability to recognize profitable opportunities, all driven by a love of money, power, or some other such goal, which together combine to make up the quality of business leadership."[3] Moreover, the lack of entrepreneurship, political stability, and political freedom and civil liberties may act as a major barrier to economic growth. Instability may discourage local and foreign direct investment because of the constant fear of nationalization, harassment, and a poor business climate.

Approaches to Development

Two major approaches have been applied to development in the developing countries.[4] The first strategy aimed at a high push to be achieved by a high rate of growth and industrialization, leading to a high rate of growth in per capita income. This view was reinforced by the works of S. Harrod and A. Domar, which transformed development into a process of growth resting on a few quantifiable variables,[5] and by W. W. Rostow's theory of stages of economic growth and the idea of a take-off.[6] The process of economic development consisted of transforming the underdeveloped societies from an ascriptive, particularistic, and functionally diffuse pattern to a pattern characterized by achievement, universalism, and functional specificity.[7] As stated by Nasir Islam and Georges Henault, an "underdeveloped society thus suffers from a lack of social and geographic mobility, a lack of division of labour, emphasizes status rather than achievement, and consequently leads to low productivity."[8] This first strategy called for a direct involvement of the government in achieving industrialization and urbanization and in maintaining a high rate of sustained economic growth through the "planning" process.

Planning is seen as the essential ingredient of any development policy. At the microlevel, the "technology gap" was to be reduced by a transfer of relevant techniques and procedures taken from Western countries. All projects were to be conducted systematically using "development administration" as a way of designing, implementing, and evaluating policies and programs leading to socioeconomic changes. It relied on what is known in UN technical assistance circles as MMT (modern management technology), which refers to techniques such as linear programming, CPM, PERT, queuing theory, long-range planning and forecasting network analysis, modeling, and cost-benefit analysis. The total impact of this first strategy is far from perfect. For example, Islam and Henault state:

> In our opinion, the net overall result of this gigantic effort of international and foreign-aid giving agencies in the area of administrative development was over-bureaucratization, excessive controls and regulation of the economy, proliferation of bureaucratic structures, increase in the size of bureaucracies, and excessive concentration of power in the hands of the administrative elites. The impact of these factors on development at best remains questionable. In fact, the balance may tip toward the negative rather than the positive side.[9]

The second strategy is usually traced back to the institutional school of C. E. Ayres, Thorstein Veblen, and Gunnar Myrdal, with their emphasis on the social and institutional preconditions for progress. Here the growth models of the first strategy were replaced by a new ideology of development. The main elements of this new ideology are supposed to include need orientation; endogenous, self-reliant, ecologically sound motives; and be based on agricultural transformation.[10] The approach moves from a largely economic perspective to a wider, all encompassing, socioeconomic one aimed at the fulfillment of all basic needs: adequate nutrition, health, clean water, and shelter. The advocates of this second strategy are generally influenced by the center-periphery thesis in dependency theory, which holds that underdevelopment is a function of one society's dependence on another. This explains their constant demands for a new international economic order based on both a global redistribution of economic surpluses and major changes in the productive relations within the periphery sector.[11] In fact, a major cause of discontent in the center-periphery thesis (also known as the North-South controversy) is the price of commodities, which the periphery countries consider to be unfairly low and unstable.

The second strategy views development in terms of the fulfillment of basic needs, which have been eloquently defined as follows:

> The concepts of basic needs bring to any development strategy a heightened concern with meeting the consumption needs of the whole population, particularly in the areas of education and health, but also in nutrition, housing, water supply, and sanitation. In formulating policies aimed at reducing poverty, a good deal of attention has generally been paid to restructuring the patterns of production and income so that they benefit the poor. But similar attention has not been devoted to their needs for public services.[12]

The concept of basic needs was justified by the failure of the three types of justification used for the emphasis on a country's economic growth as the principal performance indicator. First, income did not automatically trickle down to the poor; second, governments did not always take steps to reduce poverty; third, a period of inequality is not needed in the early stages of development.[13] The concept of basic needs is also perceived as a positive concept and has a broad appeal, politically and intellectually.

The performance of developing countries in meeting basic needs varies from one country to another. Frances Stewart used life expectancy as the single most significant indicator of performance on basic needs.[14] She compared achievement in life expectancy with what may have been predicted on the basis of a country's level of income per capita as a way of classifying countries' performance. Three types of economies turned out to be notably successful: the rapidly growing, market-oriented economies; the centrally planned economies; and the "misled" economies with welfare intervention. The less successful cases are evident in three categories of developing economies: the very poor economies, the economies with rapid growth but without substantial poverty reduction, and the economies with moderate growth and moderate poverty impact. It is accepted, however, that most developing countries have made some progress in meeting basic needs, such as education, basic health, nutrition, water and sanitation, and shelter.

But is it possible that policies aimed at providing the poor and neglected with basic goods and services are the cause for a sacrifice of productive investments and economic growth? Proponents of the basic needs approach argue on the basis of theoretical and empirical evidence that providing for basic needs can improve growth performance. In short, "investing in people may be a good way to both eliminate the worst aspects of poverty and to increase the growth rate of output."[15]

The Planning Process

Development planning involves a coordinated governmental intervention in the direction of the economy of a nation through the setting of national economic targets, and the implementation of these targets. It involves primarily setting an economic plan that specifies quantitative economic targets, but also monitoring economic activities toward reaching specified goals. The definition of economic planning is subject to different interpretations. For example, four types of planning are viewed in a 1951 UN publication as follows:

> First, . . . it [planning] refers only to the making of public expenditures, extending over from one to say ten years. Second, it refers sometimes to the setting of production targets, whether for private or for public enterprises, in terms of the input of manpower, of capital, or of other scarce resources, or use in terms of output. Thirdly, the word may be used to describe a statement which sets targets for the economy as a whole, purporting to allocate all scarce resources among the various branches of the economy. And fourthly, the word is sometimes used to describe the means which the government uses to try to enforce upon private enterprise the targets which have been previously determined.[16]

The economic planning route chosen by most developing countries in the context of a mixed economy is motivated by several variables. The most important variable is related to the market-failure argument. The imperfection of structure and operations of markets in the developing countries, with the results of distorted prices and inequities, renders the market concept an inefficient tool for economic development in these countries. Here is a great argument for the explicit market-failure theme for planning in the developing countries:

> Governments can not, and should not, take a merely passive role in the process of industrial expansion. Planning has become an essential and integral part of industrial development programmes, for market forces, by themselves, cannot overcome the deep-seated structural rigidities in the economies of developing countries. . . . Today the need for some degree of economic planning is universally recognized. It is, of course, an integral part of the economy of the Soviet Union and the other centrally planned countries. . . . In developing countries, planning is more feasible and more desirable than in developed market economies. The greater feasibility is a result of the smaller number of variables that must be taken into consideration, and the greater desirability stems from the fact that the automatic mechanisms for co-ordination of individual actions function less satisfactorily in developing than in developed economies. Planning in developing countries is made necessary by, inter alia, the inadequacies of the market as a mechanism to ensure that individual decisions will optimize economic performance in terms of society's preferences and economic goals. . . . The inadequacy of the market mechanism as a means of allocating resources for industrial development sometimes results from government policy itself or because the theoretical assumptions (particularly with respect to the mobility of the factors of production) do not apply to the actual economic situation. Even more importantly, the market mechanism cannot properly allow for the external effects of investment.[17]

Besides the market failure argument, other arguments used to justify economic planning in the developing countries include a resource mobilization and allocation argument that gives to economic planning a better role in the channeling of scarce resources to development; an attitudinal or psychological argument that gives to economic planning a better success in rallying people behind development; and a foreign aid argument that makes economic planning a better base used by donor countries in granting financial and technical assistance.[18]

The planning process is characterized by some common elements that are apparent in all contexts and some specific elements that characterize specific country and contexts. Common elements are apparent in the following characteristics of the planning process:

1. Starting from the political views and goals of the government planning attempts to define policy objectives, especially as they relate to the future development of the economy.
2. A development plan sets out a strategy by means of which it is intended to achieve these objectives, which are normally translated into specific targets.
3. The plan attempts to present a centrally coordinated, internally consistent set of principles and policies, chosen as the optimal means of implementing the strategy and achieving the targets and intended to be used as a framework to guide subsequent day-to-day decisions.
4. It comprehends the whole economy (hence it is "comprehensive," in contrast to "colonial" or "public sector" planning).
5. In order to secure optimality and consistency, the comprehensive plan employs a more-or-less formalized macroeconomic model (which, however, will often remain unpublished), and this is employed to project the intended future performance of the economy.
6. A development plan typically covers a period of, say, 5 years and finds physical expression as a medium-term plan document, which may, however, incorporate a longer-term perspective plan and be supplemented by annual plans.[19]

Economic planning seeks the achievement of full employment of resources and social economic progress through existing and new institutions. Its aims are economic growth and structural change through a conscious effort by a state and its people. Development planning has spread all over the world, acquiring even in the special states in developed countries the form of "industrial policy." In socialized countries it took the form of central planning, with the state controlling, through regulations and directives, the level of savings, the amount and composition of output and investment, and the structure of prices. In mixed economies it is distinguished by three approaches: a project-by-project approach focusing on selected public investment projects; integrated public investment planning, focusing on a well-prepared investment plan rather than the piecemeal basis of the project-by-project approach; and comprehensive planning, focusing on an overall planning of the economy of a nation, including both an integrated public investment plan and a plan for the private sector.[20]

The desirability of comprehensive planning is stated as follows: "In the long run, comprehensive planning based on growth models may give better results than partial planning. Comprehensive planning's view of an economy as a whole and its emphasis on internal consistency allow economic comparisons and judgments to be made which are not generally possible with partial planning.''[21] Comprehensive planning or development planning rely on a development plan or public investment plan that has the force of law, at least in administrative units accountable to the central government. Development plans are short-term, medium-term, and long-term, linked by a degree of flexibility and continuity. A short-term plan can be renewed and ''rolled'' forward in time.

The plan includes the basic development objectives of a given country to be carried out through a variety of economic and social policies. The size of a plan is a fraction of a country's willingness to accept current sacrifices for future benefits. Three approaches may be used for the determination of the size of a plan: ''One is to have the country's requirements determine it; another is to have the country's resources fix it; the third is to set it somewhere between the two points where the requirements and resource approaches would have left it.''[22] The requirements approach is the most useful for a developing country.

Planning Model

Planning models are generally divided into two basic categories: aggregate growth models and multisector input-output models.[23]

Aggregate Growth Models

These, generally based on the Harrod-Domar model, are to predict output and employment growth by examining relationships between important macroeconomic variables, such as savings, investment, capital stocks, exports, imports, foreign assistance, and so on. A generally used modified Harrod-Domar growth equation is as follows:[24]

$$k\,(g + \delta) = (s_\pi - s_w)\,(\pi/Y) + s_w \tag{3.1}$$

where

k = the average (equal to marginal) capital-output ratio

g = targeted growth rate of output

δ = the fraction of the capital shock depreciated in each period

s = share of output Y that is saved

π = profit income

W = wage income

s = propensity to save out of profit income

sw = propensity to save out of wage income

The formula can be used for the evaluation of the adequacy of current saving out of profit and wage income. Taylor gives the following example:

> For example, if a 4 percent growth rate is desired, while the following parameters values hold: $\delta = 0.033$, $K = 3.0$ $(\pi/y.) = 0.5$, then [the growth equation] reduces to $0.42 = s_\pi + s_w$. If the savings rate out of capital income is 30 percent, then labor income recipients must save at a 12 percent rate to maintain the postulated rate of growth. This would be considered a considerable saving rate for low-income people.[25]

Using the same example as Taylor, Todaro reaches the following conclusions: "If savings out of capital income amount to 25%, then wage earners must save at a 17% rate to achieve the targeted rate of growth. In the absence of such a savings rate out of labor income, the government could pursue a variety of policies to raise domestic saving and/or seek foreign assistance."[26]

The Two-Gap Model

Rather than the strict Harrod-Domar models, the two-gap model is needed in these cases where the lack of foreign exchange reserves acts as a constraint over growth. The two-gap model is generally formulated as follows:

1. A *saving-constraint or gap.* It states that the savings generated by capital inflows (i.e., the difference between imports and exports) and the savings generated domestically for the national output is less than or equal to the investment needed. In other words

$$I \leqslant F + sY \tag{3.2}$$

where

F = difference between imports and exports
Y = national output
s = share of output Y that is always saved

2. *A foreign exchange constraint or gap.* It is stated as follows:

$$m_1 I + m_2 Y - E \leqslant F \tag{3.3}$$

where

m_1 = marginal import share from the investment
m_2 = marginal propensity to import out of a unit of GNP
E = Exogenous level of exports

The term F enters both of the inequality constraints of the two-gap model and is critical in the analysis. If in addition to *F,* both output and exports are assigned an exogenous current value, then only one of the two inequalities will be binding—that is, investment (and therefore the output growth rate) will be restricted to a lower level by one of the inequalities. This dichotomy creates a basis of classification of countries in the sense that countries can be classified according to whether the savings or foreign exchange constraint is binding. It also provides a crude means for the assignment of foreign aid since the impact of increased capital inflow on investment is greater when the trade on the foreign exchange gap rather than the savings gap is binding. Todaro suggests accordingly that "two gap models simply provide a crude methodology for determining the relative need and ability of different LDCs to use foreign aid effectively."[27] Taylor gives a more positive assessment:

> As with other models of the Harrod-Domar type, note the mechanistic nature of the forecasts. Imports are strictly linked with output and investment levels, as are savings, while exports and net capital inflows are exogenous. Trying to alter many of these "fixed" parameters is at the heart of planning in a developing economy experiencing structural change. However, for forecasting, this is a less serious objection, and the two-gap specification is widely used. Although extremely simple, two-gap models generalize Harrod-Domar in a relevant way and are consistent with the categories in which national accounts data are usually arranged.[28]

Input-output Models

These present the interrelations between the major sectors of the industrial economy by means of a set of simultaneous algebraic equations expressing the production processes of each industry. Each industry is viewed as a producer of output and a user of input. Two basic sets of equations characterize the mathematical input-output model.

The first set of equations states for each sector that the entire product produced is either consumed by other industries or by final demanders as follows:

$$\sum_{j=1}^{n} x_{ij} + Y_i = X_i \qquad (3.4)$$

where

X_i = annual rate of total output of industry *i*

x_{ij} = Amount of the product of industry *i* consumed annually by industry *j* as an intermediate product

Y_i = Amount of product *i* consumed by a final demand

The second set of equations derives the technical coefficients of production a_{ij} for each industry as follows:

$$X_{ij} = A_{ij} X_j \qquad (3.5)$$

Therefore the symbolic representation of the input-output model of the economy may be as follows:

$$a_{ij} X_j - X_i = Y_i \qquad (3.6)$$

or

$$\begin{aligned} X_1 - A_{11} X_1 - A_{12} X_2 - A_{13} X_3 &= Y_1 \\ X_2 - A_{21} X_1 - A_{22} X_2 - A_{23} X_3 &= Y_2 \\ X_3 - A_{31} X_1 - A_{32} X_2 - A_{33} X_3 &= Y_3 \end{aligned}$$

or

$$\bar{X} - \{A\} \, . \, \bar{X} = \bar{Y} \qquad (3.7)$$

where

X represents a *column vector* of total outputs consisting of n elements [in the above example $n = 3$], each of which numerically represents the total output of one of n industries; $[A]$ is a $n \times n$ square matrix of technical coefficients and Y is a column vector of total final demands.

Equation (1.7) can be solved to yield the following expression:

$$X = [I - A]^{-1} Y \qquad (3.8)$$

where

I = identity matrix

$[I - A]^{-1}$ = Inverted Leontief matrix generally designed by the block letter R

or

$$\bar{X} = R \, \bar{Y} \qquad (3.9)$$

Equation (1.9) can be used to derive the level of output $Xi_{\, i = 1,2,\ldots n}$ of commodity i for a planned final demand $Yj_{\, j = 1,\ldots n}$

Obviously, the reliability of the matrix of technical coefficients is vital to the use of the input-output model in development planning. The reliability is hampered by critical assumption of the model.[29] Linear or nonlinear programming or activity analysis models could be used to alleviate the above problem. However, they are considered not very feasible in most developing countries because of the lack of adequate information.[30]

SOCIAL INDICATORS OF DEVELOPMENT

Social Indicators

Effective data and information are needed for the formulation, implementation, and monitoring of a development plan. Data are needed about natural and human resources. An integrated system of national accounts is a priority in development planning. Planning with inadequate data is a recipe for disaster. There is even the question of whether any planning should start before the creation of data bases. Witness the following comment:

> A county which seeks to improve its statistics for planning must set priorities. It must decide, for example, whether to build up its basic data first or whether it is more desirable to prepare aggregative national accounts estimates, even though the data on which they are based are inadequate. Some experts advocate the first course; others the second. There is also the question whether the available data, although inadequate, should be used to start planning immediately or whether planning should be postponed until improved information is obtained. Some planners prefer to postpone planning for a year or two until they accumulate more reliable information. But this causes great delays in meeting a country's problems through planning and most planners feel that it is preferable to start planning as soon as possible even if there is need to use statistics that are second-best.[31]

What is needed for effective development planning is the creation of development indicators or social indicators.

Social indicators constitute one of the routes chosen in macrosocial accounting toward the evaluation, measurement, and disclosure of national social performance. The approach consists of focusing on a number of social issues to which "measures" are assigned to depict the extent of improvement in these issues. The approach has generated a rich literature on an international scale aimed at producing, testing, and refining an array of "social indicators" on all possible issues of interest to a particular society, nation, or government.

Social indicators have been described as mere statistics that reflect the human condition and that may be helpful to plan for social change. They go beyond economic indicators with their greater orientation toward the needs and goals within the full range of human social activities and a greater emphasis on all the social concerns, processes, and systems deemed essential for an adequate living standard and quality of life. They are essential to an assessment of the state and changing conditions of society, a discovery of the potential and actual social problems, and an evaluation of the effects of social policies and programs.

As such they are a basic component of a macrosocial accounting aimed at measurement, evaluation, and monitoring of social performance of macroeconomic units, from cities to entire governments. In what follows, the origins of the social indicator movement, the nature of social indicators, the construction of social indicators, the actors involved in the production of social indicators, the research approaches and functions of social indicators, and examples of social indicators are examined.

Origins of the Social Indicator Movement

For good reason, the origins of the movement for the production and use of social indicators are generally traced back to biblical times. Concern with social justice and the application of new statistical techniques spurred the social indicators movement. The movement truly emerged, however, in 1966, when the National Aeronautics and Space Administration became concerned with the social effects of its space exploration program and R. A. Bauer and his colleagues examined the need to anticipate the consequences of rapid technological change through a comprehensive system of what they called social indicators.[32] This was followed by the publication of *Toward a Social Report* and Senator Walter Mondale's Full Opportunity and Social Accounting Act of 1967.[33] From there the social indicator movement found followers in many nations and international organizations and established itself as a legitimate research field of relative independence in the social sciences. This effort is evident in the surge of assessments and bibliographical publications,[34] a special newsletter (*Social Indicators Newsletter*), and a specialized journal (*Social Indicators Research*).

The Nature of Social Indicators

There is no agreed definition of social indicators. Various definitions are provided in the literature. Social indicators are:

Quantitative data that serve as indices to socially important conditions of society.[35]

Statistics, statistical services, and all other forms of evidence that enable us to assess where we stand and are going with respect to our values and goals, and to evaluate specific programs and determine their impact.[36]

Statistics which measure social conditions and changes there-in over time for various segments of the population. By social conditions, we mean both the external (social and physical) and the internal (subjective and perceptional) context of human existence in a given society.[37]

Social indicators and social statistics are facts about society in a quantitative form. But social indicators involve not only quantitative measurement of an aspect of the social but also its interpretation in relation to some norm against which statistic represents advance or retrogression.[38]

The first common characteristic of these definitions is their reference to the functions of the social indicators, which are essentially to measure social changes and conditions. The second common characteristic of these definitions is their reference to the nature of the social indicator as a kind of statistic. From these two characteristics we may summarize the nature of social indicators as generally quantitative constructs designed to monitor, measure, and/or report social conditions and changes.

Following a social indicator model introduced and elaborated by Kenneth Land, these constructs may be categorized in one of several types of social indicators:[39]

1. Policy instruments descriptive indicators: These are exogenous descriptive variables that are manipulable by social policy. By exogenous it is meant that they are outside the social system model, a system of relationships connecting all variables and containing analytical indicators.
2. Nonmanipulable descriptive indicators: These are exogenous descriptive variables that are not manipulable by social policy.
3. Output or end product descriptive indicators: These are endogenous descriptive variables that define the social conditions being measured and are the consequences of the social processes embodied within the model.
4. Side-effect descriptive indicators: These are endogenous descriptive variables that influence or are influenced by, but do not define, the social conditions and social processes under consideration.

Land emphasizes also that relationship between these indicators is more of an ideal rather than an actual description of the state of social indicators research.[40]

Social indicators as quantitative constructs generally meet some qualitative characteristics as well:

1. Social indicators are generally normative, in the sense that any move in a particular direction may be interpreted as either good or bad.
2. Social indicators generally relate to outputs rather than inputs of social programs.
3. Social indicators are generally comprehensive and aggregate measures.
4. Social indicators should be genuinely ''indicative'' of something in the sense that they should relate to economic theories and fit into models, whether explanatory or predictive.[41]
5. Social indicators relate to subjects for which problems of measurement are not impossible to handle.
6. Social indicators should tap questions of importance to the general public and related to shared goals. Good health, better education, lower crime rates, improved streets and lighting, and less traffic congestion are goals over which there would be reasonably limited disagreement, even though questions of relative priority inevitably persist.[42]
7. Social indicators are best showing the direct and indirect effects of alternative policies

when they are integrated into a model. This last characteristic argues for analytical as opposed to descriptive indicators. This view is also supported as follows:

In summary, development of a social indicator science requires that concentration be on explanatory, not descriptive, models of social subsystems and attendant indicators. These models should leave operationalized concepts and causal relationships expressed in proportions which will be empirically tested to establish whether linkages exist between indicators and other unobservable variables.[43]

The Construction of Social Indicators

The construction of social indicators ought to rely on a theoretical or formal approach to be able to provide power and precision in its measurement. This approach ought to be deductive, going from the abstract and general to the simple and particular. Such a model has been proposed by Michael Carley[44] and includes the following steps:

development and statement of a theoretical proposition; formulation of an explicit causal model in words and/or some type of diagram, for example, a path diagram; operationalization, that is, the statement in measurable terms of the postulated relationships between social indicators and empirically defined variables, for example, in a system of equations; testing, and perhaps retesting, of the model.[45]

This model allows, for one thing, for the continued development and improvement of social indicators and social theory. Each of the steps requires clear and rigorous thinking, including a precise statement of the theoretical proposition, a carefully defined causal model of the various social relationships underlying the concept being measured, a translation of the relationships into operational and empirically testable forms, and a continuous testing of the model. The ''operationalization'' step rests on making various computational or procedural choices as follows:

1. The construction and interpretation of social indicators generally follows accepted statistical standards.
2. The fact that most indicators may behave in linear or curvilinear forms does not preclude that some indicators may not always fit a well-behaved trend.
3. Ordinal measurement generally used for social indicators requires setting standards of adequacy and around that grade of inadequacy and abundance.
4. When percentage and index numbers are used to screen social indicators, the choice of the base period is important given the way it may affect the interpretation of the social indicators.
5. Indicators may be either open-ended in growth, such as population, or related to a maximum, such as mortality.
6. Indicators may be either ''objective'' indicators based on numerical counts of people, money, and things, or ''subjective'' indicators based on the appraisal of interviewed persons.

7. Indicators may be constructed for all types of goods: free goods, public goods, consumer goods, and/or capital goods.
8. The difficulties with finding indicator units and valuation of intangibles applies also to social indicators.
9. International comparison of indicators may be hampered by the calculation of purchasing power parities that may justify the use of nonmonetary indicators of production and consumption.
10. Social indicators are the result of aggregation of a mass of information into a single or several series.
11. Social indicators should be empirically correlated into the constituent variables of a social concern they are supposed to measure.
12. Social indicators may be based on a common scale, such as money, value, or people, or on different units.
13. Social indicators may be based on either implicit weighing through selection and scaling or explicit weighing.[46]

Actors in the Production of Social Indicators

Various actors are involved in the production of social indicators, including supranational and national agencies, scientific institutions, and individuals.

Of the supranational agencies, the United Nations, the Organization for Economic Cooperation and Development, the European Community, and the Council for Mutual Economic Assistance are very much involved in the production of social indicators. For example, the UN interest started with attempts to define and measure standards and levels of living,[47] before moving to developing a socioeconomic system including a data base and procedures for determining indicators and finally extending the system into a system of demographic and social statistics (SDSS).[48] The SDSS system used principles of economic bookkeeping to suppress the socioeconomic state of the population and its change over time as a set of demographic accounts in the form of an input-output matrix. The data pertain mainly to demographic structure, housing, public order, use of time, and social mobility. The most interesting development in the construction of social indicators is achieved by the OECD.

National agencies in various countries are continuously developing national compendia of social indicators and social reports. A list of national compendia of social indicators and social reports is shown in Exhibit 3.1.

Similarly, various scientific institutions and individual researchers are involved in social indicator research. In Sweden, two theoretical approaches have been used, one characterized by a conception of welfare based on command over resources,[49] and one based on a consideration of needs.[50] This is translated on a practical level in welfare or level-of-living surveys in Sweden,[51] as well as in England,[52] Norway,[53] Austria, and West Germany.

Research Approaches and Functions of Indicators

The term "social indicator" is not associated with a single specific research proposal. The number of approaches for systems of social indicators is on the rise. Most of them attempt to operationalize and measure the components of a multidimensional conception of welfare. Examples include the development of a net national welfare index by the Economic Council of Japan, which measures the annual value of the total economic production available for final consumption,[54] the development of a level-of-living index, or index of measurable welfare, in natural units of goods and services by Jan Drewnovsky,[55] the development of a social indicators battery by J. Q. Wilson for the purpose of ascertaining differences in the quality of life in the United States,[56] the attempt by Nestor E. Terleckyj to calculate the improvements in the quality of life with 31 selected programs in relation to 21 national goals and relying on a large-scale input-output matrix,[57] the development at the United Nations of a system of social and demographic statistics to encourage the national statistical bodies to systematize their entire social statistics in the direction of an integrated system of "stocks" and "flows,"[58] and the development by Erik Allardt of a welfare model of national development based on the theories of social systems, social structure, and needs.[59] These are only examples and are far from exhaustive of all the approaches to social indicator research. It is generally accepted to classify this research into three distinct approaches: those concerned with measuring the quality of life and welfare; those concerned with monitoring social change and socioeconomic development; and those concerned with forecasting social events and evaluation research.[60]

In fact, these three areas follow the main aspects of social reporting—namely, welfare measurement, observation of a social change, prognosis of a social change without intervention, social policy planning to steer society in desired direction, and monitoring of planning performance.[61] V. H. Horn used this sequence to specify the most exhaustive list of the different functions of social indicators as follows:[62]

SOCIAL PROCESS	FUNCTIONS OF SOCIAL INDICATORS
Assessment of welfare elements	Cognition
Observation of welfare trends	Analysis
Clarification of societal interaction	Conceptualization
Prognosis of trend without intervention	Projections
Formulation of social policy alternatives, including priority-rating and trade-offs	Operationalization, direction
Social policy decision	Classification and targeting
Audit of planning progress	Monitoring
Review of plan performance	Retrospective analysis

Exhibit 3.1
List of National Compendia of Social Indicators and Social Reports

Country	Title, Date	Editor
Australia	Social Indicators; 1976, 1978	Australian Bureau of Statistics
Austria	Indikatoren zur gesellschaftlichen Entwicklung; 1976 Soziale Ungleichheit in Österreich; 1979	Österreichisches Statistisches Zentralamt
Brazil	Indicadores sociais para areas urbanas; 1977 Relatorio des indicadores sociais; 1979	Departamento e Indicatores Sociais
Canada	Perspective Canada; 1974, 1977	Statistics Canada
Colombia	Compendio de Indicadores Sociales; 1977	Departemente Administrative National de Estadist tica
Denmark	Levevilkar i Danmark; 1976, 1979	Danmarks Statistik and Socialforskningsinstitutet
Fiji	Social Indicators for Fiji; annually since 1973	Bureau of Statistics
Finland	Levnadsforhallanden: 1950–1975; 1977	Statistikcentralen
France	Données sociales; 1973, annually since	Institut National de la Statistique et des Etudes Economiques (INSEE)
Germany (Fed.Rep.)	Gesellschaftliche Daten; 1973, 1977	Bundesministerium für Arbeit und Sozialordnung
	Basisdaten; 1974	Verlag Neue Gesellschaft GmbH
	Soziologischer Almanach; 1975, 1979 Lebensbedingungen in der Bundesrepublik; 1977	Sozialpolitische Forschergruppe Frankfurt/Mannheim (SPES-Projekt)
India	Social and Economic Indicators; (in preparation)	Central Statistical Organization

Each of these functions constitutes a legitimate avenue in social indicator research.

Examples of Social Indicators of Development

The OECD list of social indicators was intended to measure and report changes in the relative importance of the social demands, aspirations, and problems that are, or could become in the decade ahead, major concerns of the socioeconomic planning process. They are to be viewed as an initial framework subject to any improvements to be brought by member countries. Seven major criteria were used in the final selection of social indicators. The social indicators should:

a. be output-oriented or designed to describe a final outcome, leaving to other statistics the quantification of inputs, through puts or intermediate outputs;

Exhibit 3.1 (*continued*)

Indonesia	Social Indicators; annually since 1971	Central Bureau of Statistics
Israel	Society in Israel; Selected Statistics; 1976	Central Bureau of Statistics
Italy	Statistiche Sociali; 1975	Instituto Centrale die Statistica
Japan	Whitepaper of National Life; 1973 (1975)	Economic Planning Agency
Kenya	Social Perspectives; 1976	Central Bureau of Statistics
Malaysia	Socio-economic indicators and National Policy: Malaysia; 1974	Department of Statistics
Netherlands	Social and Cultural Report; 1974 1976, 1978	Sociaal en Cultureel Planbureau
New Zealand	Social Trends in New Zealand; 1977	Department of Statistics
Norway	Sosialt Utsyn; 1974, 1977	Statistisk Sentralbyra
Panama	Indicadores Economicos y Sociales; 1970	Direción de Estadistica Censo
Philippines	Measuring the Quality of Life: Philippine Social Indicators; 1974	Development Academy of the Philippines
Spain	Espana Panoramica Social; 1974	Instituto National des Estadistica
Sweden	Levnadsföhällanden Arsbok; 1975	Statistiska Centralbyran
Switzerland	Almanach der Schweiz; 1978	Soziologisches Institut der Universität Zürich
Trinidad u. Tobago	Social Indicators; 1975	Central Statistical Office
United Kingdom	Social Trends: annually since 1970	Central Statistical Office
United States	Social Indicators; 1973, 1977	Office of Management and Budget

Source: W. Glatzer, "An Overview of the International Development in Macro-Social Indicators," *Accounting, Organizations and Society* (September 1981): 129. Reprinted with permission.

b. be relevant to policy—i.e., descriptive of prevailing social conditions which are potentially amenable to improvement through collective actions or public policy;

c. be applicable over a long period of time in a substantial number of member countries. Actual values of the indicators may of course differ widely over time and access the whole OECD area;

d. apply to conditions of individual well-being, excluding a number of "indivisible public goods," however desirable these are as an aspect of welfare;

e. be independent of particular institutional arrangements, so as to be reasonably comparable between countries and over time;

f. form part of a comprehensive grid portraying all areas of social concerns;

g. correspond closely to the social concern to which they relate, yet be more than a narrow description of social phenomena;

h. form an integrated framework of definitions, specifications, statistical guidelines, and disaggregations which should be compatible with other important sets of social and demographic statistics.[63]

Based on these criteria a tentative list of eight social concerns and 33 indicators was developed. The indicators present systematically selected statistical measures of individual well-being that can be influenced by social policies and community actions.[64] To give meaningful basic information on the level of individual well-being, some disaggregations are presented as suggestions. The purposes of disaggregation relate to normative considerations, explanatory requirements, and program monitoring and evaluation.[65] Examples of standard disaggregations include age, sex, household type, socioeconomic status, community size, ethnic group, citizenship, region, branch of economic activity, occupation, type of activity, working hours, level of education, tenure status, and/or age of dwelling.

In the developing countries, indicators represent some aspect of development, such as industrialization, equity, health, education, and so on, and play a crucial role in development policy. Examples of indicators, from the study of the contents and measurement of development carried by the UN Research Institute for Social Development (UNRISD) include the following:

1. Expectation of life at birth
2. Percent population in localities of 20,000 and over
3. Consumption of animal protein, per capita, per day
4. Combined primary and secondary enrolment
5. Vocational enrolment ratio
6. Average number of persons per room
7. Newspaper circulation per 1,000 population
8. Percent economically active population in electricity, gas, water, etc.
9. Agricultural production per male agricultural worker
10. Percent adult male labour in agriculture
11. Electricity consumption, kWh per capita
12. Steel consumption, kg. per capita
13. Energy consumption, kg. of coal equivalent per capita
14. Percent G.D.P. derived from manufacturing
15. Foreign trade per capita, in 1960 U.S. dollars
16. Percent salaried and wage earners to total economically active population.[66]

Another study by Adelman and Morris suggests the following social indicators of development:

1. Size of the traditional agricultural sector
2. Extent of dualism
3. Extent of urbanization
4. Character of basic social organization
5. Importance of the indigenous middle class
6. Extent of social mobility
7. Extent of literacy
8. Extent of mass communication
9. Degree of cultural and ethnic homogeneity
10. Degree of social tension
11. Crude fertility rate
12. Degree of modernization of outlook
13. Degree of national integration and sense of national unity
14. Extent of centralization of political power
15. Strength of democratic institutions
16. Degree of freedom of political opposition and press
17. Degree of competitiveness of political parties
18. Predominant basis of the political party system
19. Strength of the labour movement
20. Political strength of the traditional elite
21. Political strength of the military
22. Degree of administrative efficiency
23. Extent of leadership commitment to economic development
24. Extent of political stability
25. Per capita G.N.P. in 1961
26. Rate of growth of real per capita G.N.P.:1950/51–1963/64
27. Abundance of natural resources
28. Gross investment rate
29. Level of modernization of industry
30. Change in degree of industrialization since 1950
31. Character of agricultural organization
32. Level of modernization of techniques in agriculture
33. Degree of improvement in agricultural productivity since 1950
34. Level of adequacy of physical overhead capital
35. Degree of improvement in physical overhead capital since 1950
36. Level of effectiveness of the tax system
37. Degree of improvement in the tax system since 1950

38. Level of effectiveness of financial institutions
39. Degree of improvement in human resources
40. Structure of foreign trade[67]

National Income Accounting

National income accounting constitutes the second route chosen in macrosocial accounting toward the evaluation, measurement, and disclosure of national performance. The first approach taken in national income accounting was to rely on a system of national accounts to measure macroeconomic indicators such as the gross national product. Given the limitations and narrow scope of the GNP, the second approach aims at providing a better measure of social well-being.

National income accounting is the set of rules and techniques for measuring the total flow of output (parts and services) produced and the total flow of inputs (factors of production) used by the economy. It relies on a system of national accounts to measure macroeconomic indicators such as the GNP. Basically, the statement produced is similar to the conventional income statement for a profit-oriented firm. One side of the report shows the total value of the nation's output, classified in terms of its distribution to the four major sectors of the national economy. The other side details the changes against the aggregate national output and includes, therefore, the income accruing to the various factors of production (wages, rent, interest, and profits). The four sectors of the economy considered by the national accounting system are business, consumers (or households), government, and the rest of the world. The aggregate data from each of these sectors are consolidated in order to provide the data for both the national income and product account. The following rules are important to an understanding of the results of national income accounting:

1. The government outputs are valued at the cost of the input needed to produce them.
2. Inventories are treated as if they were "purchased" by the firms producing them.
3. A firm's output is defined to be its value added; that is to say, the value of output minus the value of the inputs it purchased from other firms.
4. Finally, current market prices are used in measuring the value of the economic output.

Conventionally Measured GNP

As stated earlier, the value of the output of the economy can be measured either as the sum of the values of the final products or as the sum of the payments to the various factors of production. In either case the value of the output of the national economy is best exemplified and known as the GNP of the nation. As conventionally known, the GNP is the sum of the values of all final goods and services produced in a specific period of time (usually a year) and valued at current market prices.

Exhibit 3.2
GNP in 1981 as the Sum of Final Demands (billions of dollars)

ITEM	AMOUNT	
Personal consumption expenditures	1,858.1	
Gross private domestic investment	450.6	
Government purchases of goods and services	589.6	
Net exports	23.8	
Exports		366.7
Imports	-------	342.9
GNP	2,922.2	

Two ways have been devised for the measurement of the GNP. The first method measured the GNP as the sum of all final goods and services:

$$GNP = C + I + G + EX - IM \tag{3.10}$$

where

C = sales of goods and services to consumers
I = gross sales of products to business for final use as producers' (capital) goods, including inventory changes
G = sales of goods and services to government
EX = exports
IM = imports

Exhibit 3.2 shows the GNP as the sum of final demands. The second method measures the GNP as the sum of all factor payments—in other words, as the sum of all the incomes in the economy:

$$GNP = W + R + I + P + T + X + D \tag{3.11}$$

where

W = wages
R = rental income of persons
I = net interest paid to households

Exhibit 3.3
GNP in 1981 as the Sum of Incomes (billions of dollars)

ITEM		AMOUNT
Compensation of employees (wages)		1,771.7
Net interest		215.0
Rental income		33.6
Profit		323.4
Corporate profits	189.0	
Proprietors' income	134.4	
National income		2,343.7
Indirect business taxes and miscellaneous items		257.0
Net national product		2,600.0
Depreciation		321.5
GNP		2,922.2

P = profits
T = indirect business taxes
X = business transfer payments
D = depreciation or capital consumption

Exhibit 3.3 shows the GNP as the sum of incomes. Through some recombinations, some other useful macroeconomic measurements may be derived as follows:

Net National Product	$= GNP -$ Depreciation
National Income	$= W + R + I + P$
Personal Income	= National Income − (Corporate Profit Taxes + Retained Earnings + Payroll Taxes) + Transfer Payments
Disposable Personal Income	= Personal Income − Personal Taxes

Both methods of measurement constitute the parts of a dualistic system intended to measure the output of a nation. Both, however, suffer from some limitations as follows. First of all, the GNP includes only market activity and does not include nonmarket activities such as work done by housewives and do-it-yourselfers. It may be inapplicable to some of the Third World countries, where most activities are not conducted in organized markets. Second, the GNP does not include illegal activities; even though some of those activities produce goods and services, few are sold on the market, generating factor incomes. In addition, the GNP does not include factors affecting human welfare. For example, leisure is not included, although it is important for well-being. In brief, the GNP is not a measure of well-being. Third, the GNP includes good as well as bad activities. For example, the outlays necessary to correct the effect of a disaster may cause the GNP to rise. Finally, most of the undesirable effects of economic activities are not deducted from the GNP to give a better measure of the net increase in economic welfare.

Toward a Better Measure of GNP

As stated earlier, the GNP is a measure of the nation's annual production of goods and services. It fails, however, to measure social well-being adequately. Accordingly various attempts have been made to modify conventionally measured GNP to obtain a better measure of social well-being. First, W. Nordhaus and J. Tobin developed a measure of economic welfare as a result of a management of items in the national accounts and addition of items not covered in the GNP computations: household work, leisure, and the services consumers derive from the durable goods such as autos, boats, and appliances.[68] A correction is also made for the "disamenities of urbanization," which include "litter, congestion, noise, insecurity, large buildings, and advertisements offensive to taste."

Second, as stated earlier in the social indicators section, the Economic Council of Japan has developed a net national welfare (NNW) measure to account for the impact on the environment.[69] As in Nordhaus and Tobin, the NNW is a rearrangement of national accounts items, added to imputations for the services of government capital, consumer durables, leisure, and other nonmarket activities, and corrected for "urbanization" and "environmental maintenance costs"—that is, the costs of operating and maintaining pollution control equipment plus the annualized capital costs of purchasing it.

Other attempts were made to provide a framework of modifying the traditional account structure in order to measure the environmental changes. First, M. Olson suggested that the GNP be reduced by an amount equal to the social damage from pollution.[70] Second, O. Herfindahl and A. Kneese suggested that a surrogate for the social damage from pollution is the pollution control expenditures and as such they should be deducted to reduce the GNP.[71] Third, A. Marin also concluded that if we want national income to conform more closely to theoretical concepts of welfare indexes, then we need to include a proxy for the environmental services that would not be completely free goods if it were possible to overcome their inherent nonmarketability.[72] The least unsatisfactory proxy considered for Marin would be spending on environmental protection. Finally, H. M. Peskin, building on an earlier work,[73] suggested a procedure for modifying the conventional income and product accounts so that they can capture certain features of the environment that are at present ignored.[74] It is based on a framework that views the environment as a separate sector subject to both "environmental services" and "environmental damages." As a result, two entries are required to account for these services and damages into a national accounting structure:

> One will describe the productive services the environment provides to business and other consumers of environmental services. This will be entered on the lefthand side of the business accounts and the consolidated national account, along with the other productive inputs. A second entry will describe any loss of environmental services or damage to consumers resulting from the use of the environment by business and other sectors. Since this damage can be viewed as a "bad" produced by the business (as opposed to a "good"), it will be entered negatively on the righthand side of the business accounts and the consolidated national account, along with the other components of output. Since, in general, these two entries will not be equal, a balancing entry will be required if accounting balance is to be maintained.[75]

Peskin has shown that the modified GNP can be defined alternatively as conventional GNP less damages, conventional GNP plus environmental services, and conventional GNP plus net environmental benefits. Efforts to design and implement this modified accounting framework are under way.[76] Finally the per person gross domestic product (GDP) is only an economic measure that does not make any adjustments for quality of life considerations. To compensate for this limitation, the United Nations produces a Human Development Index that combines gross domestic products with other indicators of well-being. This index may be adjusted for life expectancy and literacy; for life expectancy, literacy, and income distribution, and for life expectancy, literacy, and sexual equality. Reliance on either measures of per person GDP or Human Development Index can provide different rankings of countries about their living standards. The developed countries can be used as a good example. The 1990 statistics for the ten best countries in the world are shown in Exhibit 3.4. There are surprising results. Although the United States is number 1 in terms of per person GDP in 1990 using purchasing power parity exchange rates, it is number 7 using market exchange rates. With the 1990 UN Human Development Index adjusted for life expectancy and literacy, Japan comes first although its per capita income is less than two-thirds that of the United States. This is because Japanese citizens tend to live three years longer. The rankings of the United States using the 1990 UN Human Development Index adjusted for life expectancy, literacy,

Exhibit 3.4
The Ten Best Countries in the World: It Depends on the Little Adjustments

	Per person Gross Domestic Product in 1990, using Purchasing Power Parity Exchange Rate	Per person Gross National Product in 1990, using Market Exchange Rate	1990 U.N. Human Development Index Adjusted for Life Expectancy and Literacy	1990 U.N. Human Development Index Adjusted for Life Expectancy and Income Distribution	1990 U.N. Human Development Index Adjusted for Life Expectancy and Sexual Equality
1. United States	$21,449 (1)	21,790 (7)	0.976(7)	0.994(9)	0.809 (10)
2. Switzerland	20,997 (2)	32,680 (1)	0.981(6)	0.961(4)	-
3. Luxembourg	19,340 (3)	-	-	-	-
4. Canada	19,120 (4)	20,470 (8)	0.983(2)	0.948(7)	0.813(9)
5. Germany	18,291 (5)	22,320 (6)	0.971 (10)	-	-
6. Japan	17,634 (6)	25,430 (3)	0.993(1)	0.990(1)	-
7. France	17,431 (7)	19,490 (10)	-	-	0.849(4)
8. Sweden	16,867 (8)	23,660 (4)	0.982(4)	0.963(3)	0.886 (20)
9. Denmark	16,765 (9)	-	-	-	0.878(3)
10. Finland	16,453 (10)	26,040 (2)	-	0.941 (10)	0.902(1)
11. Norway	-	32,120 (5)	0.978(6)	0.956(5)	0.845(5)
12. United Arab Emirates	-	19,860 (9)	-	-	-
13. Iceland	-	-	0.983(3)	-	-
14. Netherlands	-	-	0.976(8)	0.972 (20)	-
15. Australia	-	-	0.973(9)	-	0.843(6)
16. Belgium	-	-	-	0.951 (6)	-
17. Britain	-	-	-	0.948(8)	-
18. Austria	-	-	-	-	0.832(7)
19. Czechoslovakia	-	-	-	-	0.830(8)

and income distribution sinks to the ninth level given the disparities in income distribution. Finally, the 1990 Human Development Index adjusted for life expectancy, literacy, and sexual equality shows Finland in first position and the United States in tenth position, due to the high disparities existing between the men and women in the United States. Czechoslovakia ranks higher than the United States in this dimension.

Other Possible Improvements in National Income Accounting

More and more economists are arguing that the government should keep its books like a business. As a first step the government should adopt a complete balance sheet and income statement that would separate its long-term investment in physical assets from its operating expenses, adjust its assets and debts for inflation, and clarify the way it records nontax revenues and outlays. In addition the government should add a capital account to the government budget that would separate long-term investments from operating squares.

The complete balance sheet would require a detailed inventory of the nation's land and mineral holdings as well as a list of the condition and expected life span of its buildings and a complete record of its finances and investments. These assets and liabilities should be adjusted for inflation to reflect the real net worth of the nation.

ACCOUNTING DEVELOPMENT AND ECONOMIC DEVELOPMENT

Role of Capital Markets

Capital is a scarce but essential commodity for the economic development of developing countries. Capital formation, in the form of domestic capital formation, direct foreign investment, and/or foreign aid are needed for increasing gross national products to the levels set by the development plans. In fact a high rate of capital accumulation is one of the most important goals in economic planning. Institutional arrangements for channeling savings and foreign investments to economic development are, as a result, another important goal of economic planning. These institutional arrangements include commercial and savings banks; investment banks and development financial institutions; insurance, social security, and pension schemes; and securities markets.[77] Their principal operational functions are as follows.

> (a) mobilizing and canalization of savings; (b) granting liquidity; (c) functioning as middlemen in buying and selling of securities, or between interested parties; (d) risk diversification for savers by means of loans and investment in various fields; (e) underwriting of securities; (f) apposing of financial and economic data for investment purposes; (g) supplying various types of auxiliary services to firms and individuals.[78]

In addition to these financial intermediaries, the growth of a capital market in the developing countries is crucial to the task of spurring capital formation. The growth of a capital market allows for the formation of some of the capital needed to sustain local and foreign firms and encourage investment. An efficient capital market, if at all possible, allows risk sharing and risk reduction, and provides through security prices aggregate information about investment opportunity. Unfortunately the capital markets in developing countries are best characterized by thinness and poor management. The following consequences emerge:

1. The individual investor is reduced to financing his or her project out of their proper savings and to acting as the manager of the project.
2. The individual investor may shun risky investments and investments with long-term payoff as a result of hampering the risk sharing fund of a financial market.[79]
3. There is a lack of communication between the management and the shareholders leading the potential investor to be unsure of the price to pay and of the quality of the security.[80]
4. The security's price is decomposed into fundamental value and noise. In the inefficient and thin capital markets of the developing countries, the lack of knowledge about the fundamental value of the security reduces the determination of the security price to "noise." Investing in the capital market now has the equivalence of playing the lottery.

What is evident is that the functioning of capital markets, resource allocation, and the existence of a capital market is not enough if there is no confidence in corporate operation and the working of the capital market. Accounting plays an important role in creating the level of confidence needed for the success of a capital market in a developing country. A sound accounting system that focuses on the reliability and accuracy of the financial statements of corporations creates the right climate of confidence conducive to the functioning of capital markets, resource allocation, and economic growth. Quereshi draws attention to the relationship between financial accounting, capital formation, and economic development as follows:

> The choice is also based on the idea that financial reporting, capital markets, and capital formation interrelate. Capital formation, a strategic factor in economic development, is closely dependent upon financial mechanisms and institution. Studies by such eminent monetarists as Kuznets, Goldsmith, and McKinnon provide a convincing evidence on the parallel between the development of capital markets and economic growth. The development and proper functioning of capital markets in turn is intimately related to the availability of financial information which is provided by the accounting fraction of financial reporting.[81]

The developed countries rely on conventional accounting information for resource allocation decisions. A certain level of market efficiency renders conventional accounting satisfactory in these countries. The developing countries do not have the required market efficiency and other supplementary systems to compensate for the deficiencies of the conventional accounting information system. Some of the reasons follow:

> First, typically, developing countries have economic policies that accompany various forms of government control, which tends to distort the market's ability to make optional resource allocations in the economy. Second, separate information and economic data gathering systems normally do not exist, and even if they do, because of the short history of industrial development, systems are in the fledgling stage and their capacity is invariably limited. Third, apart from the information paucity problem, the flow of information and economic data that exist in the society is generally inhibited owing either to explicit government control or bureaucratic inefficiency. Fourth, the pace of industrial change imposed by internal and external factors is so rapid that the society's fragile information systems are incapable of adjusting themselves organically in the short run. Fifth, and most importantly, the accounting standards and practice in most developing countries are either so archaic or loose in application that information generated from such system is unreliable or limited at best. All these factors of developing countries collectively add up to the condition in which resource allocation for economic development is likely to be distorted, and thus the problem of an information gap between accounting and the planner's needs is serious.[82]

Basically capital formation, as well as the efficiency of capital markets, depends on information production and disclosure. Exhibit 3.5 indicates the relationship among financial information disclosure, capital market efficiency, and economic growth. Gordian Ndubizu explains the relationships depicted (a–g) as follows:

> a. Accounting information disclosure minimizes the capital market uncertainty. This is accomplished through the disclosure of the value and risk of each asset traded on the capital market.
>
> b. The reduced capital market uncertainty encourages more investors to buy and sell securities in the capital market. It has been documented that higher capital market uncertainty induces security buyers to underprice high-quality security. Consequently the seller of such security will withdraw from the market, which reduces the size of the market.
>
> c. The capital market size affects both the market information processing (denoted c) risk sharing (denoted d). Other things being equal, the larger the capital market, the more efficient is the information processing. The capital market information processing generates the security prices. The security prices affect the ability of the capital market to efficiently allocate scarce resources (denoted e).
>
> d. The larger the market portfolio, the smaller the market risk per asset is and the easier

Exhibit 3.5
The Role of Information in Economic Growth

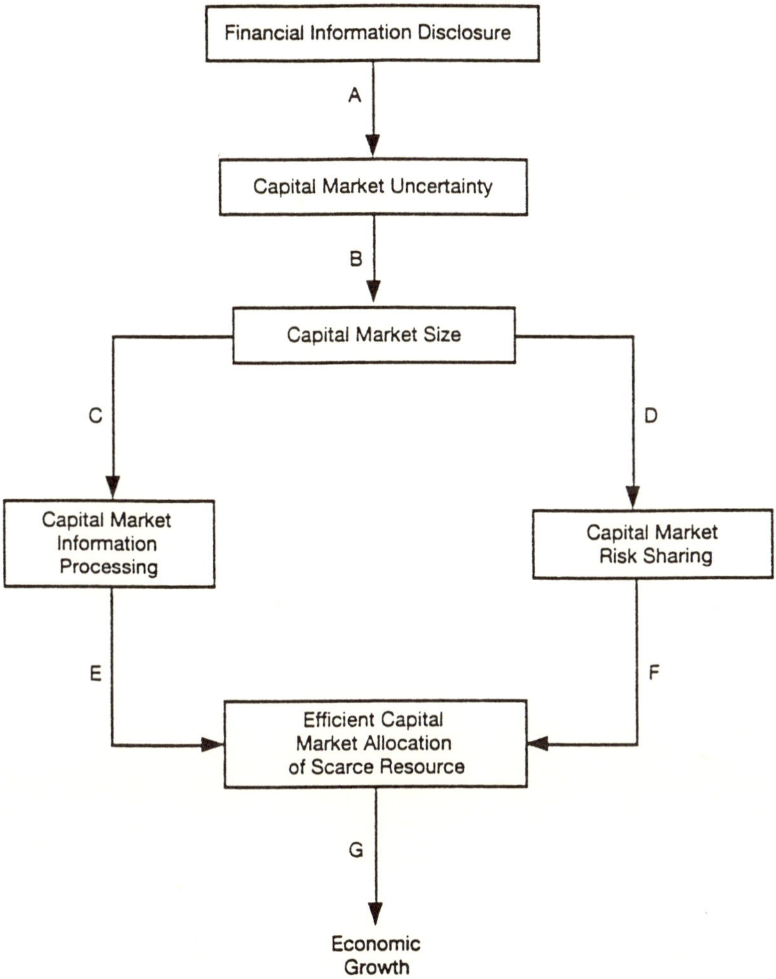

Source: Gordian A. Ndubizu, "Accounting Disclosure Methods and Economic Development: A Criterion for Globalizing Capital Markets," *International Journal of Accounting Education and Research* 27, 2 (1992), p. 153. Reprinted with permission.

it is for investors to hold/purchase an efficient portfolio of securities. The optimal risk sharing leads to an efficient allocation of savings (denoted f).

g. The capital market helps in the development of savings which effect economic growth through investment. The capital market transfers the accumulated savings to the most

Exhibit 3.6
Accounting Environment in Africa

Country	Plan comptable	Standard-setting body		Corporate standards are		None
	By law	Yes	No	By law	Voluntary	
North Africa						
Algeria		x		x		
Egypt			x			x
Morocco		x		x		
Tunisia	x	x		x		
West Africa						
Benin	x	x		x		x
Burkina Faso	x	x		x		
Cameroon	x	x			x	
Chad	x		x			x
Côte d'Ivoire	x		x			x
Gambia			x			x
Ghana		x			x	
Guinea	x	x		x		
Liberia			x			x
Mali			x			x
Mauritania	x	x		x		x
Niger	x	x		x		
Nigeria		x			x	
Senegal	x	x		x		
Sierra Leone		x		x		
Togo	x	x			x	
Zaire	x	x		x		
East Africa						
Burundi	x	x			x	x
Ethiopia			x			x
Kenya		x			x	
Madagascar	x	x		x		x
Mauritius		x		x		
Rwanda	x	x		x		
Uganda			x			x
Southern Africa						
Angola			x			x
Botswana		x			x	
Lesotho		x			x	
Malawi		x		x		
Namibia		x			x	
Swaziland		x		x		
United Republic of Tanzania		x		x		
Zambia		x			x	
Zimbabwe		x			x	

Source: United Nations Center on Transnational Corporations, *International Accounting and Reporting Issues: 1990 Review* (New York: United Nations, 1991), p. 172. Reprinted with permission.

Development standards			Enforcement body		
Own National Standards	Use of international standards: Without modification	Use of international standards: With modification	None	Regulatory agency or standard-setting body	Accounting body
	x			x	
			x		
		x		x	
		x		x	
				x	
	x			x	
	x			x	
			x		
	x			x	
			x		
		x			x
	x			x	
			x		
			x		
				x	
	x			x	
		x			x
	x			x	
	x				x
	x			x	
	x			x	
				x	
			x		
		x			x
			x		
		x		x	
	x			x	
			x		
			x		
		x			x
		x			x
		x			x
		x			x
		x			x
	x				x
	x				x
		x			x

> efficient investment opportunity. This function of the capital market stimulates economic growth.[83]

The accounting infrastructure appears as the cause of capital market thinness. A well-developed accounting infrastructure improves the communication of information to users, allows security holders to better assess the fundamental value of securities, and to monitor management effectively. As stated by C.W.J. Lee,

> good communication makes it possible for the investment of better quality to command a higher price and hence will induce management to seek financing in an organized capital market. When the monitoring cost and signalling cost are zero, information would flow freely among the capital market participants. Consequently, when the accounting infrastructure is well developed, all investment projects would be financed in a centralized and well-organized capital market.[84]

Role of Accounting Infrastructure

The accounting environment of developing countries differs depending on the characteristics used to depict it. See, for example, the accounting environment in Africa as illustrated in Exhibit 3.6. The accounting environment of developing countries has been referred to as either the accounting establishment or the accounting infrastructure. H. P. Holzer and J. S. Chandler defined the accounting establishment as consisting of four components: "the accounting function in indigenous enterprises, the local accounting profession, the accounting function of governmental agencies, and the teaching of accountancy in educational institutions."[85] A systems view of the problems characterizing the accounting establishment in the developing countries is presented in Exhibit 3.7.

As suggested by Lee, the accounting infrastructure is comprised of four elements: (1) the facilities of information production in the nature of the information producer and final user; (2) the framework of information diffusion in the nature of the information intermediaries; (3) the foundation of information monitoring in the nature of the laws and regulations that govern the production, transmission, and usage of information; and (4) the foundation of contract enforcement in the nature of the legal entity that monitors and implements the laws and regulations.[86] The thinness of the capital market in developing countries as well as the failure of security prices to reflect much of the underlying fundamental information can be attributed to deficiencies in the accounting infrastructure. The crucial role of the accounting infrastructure for capital market efficiency is argued as follows:

> The cost of fundamental information depends on the development of the accounting infrastructure. The more advanced the infrastructure, the lower will be the cost of information. In a developing economy where the accounting infrastructure is not well developed, the cost of fundamental information would be high and the percentage of informed investors in the market would be low. As a result, the price of a security can deviate widely from its fundamental value. With a high volume of noise in security price, the

Exhibit 3.7
A Systems View of the Accounting Establishment in Developing Countries

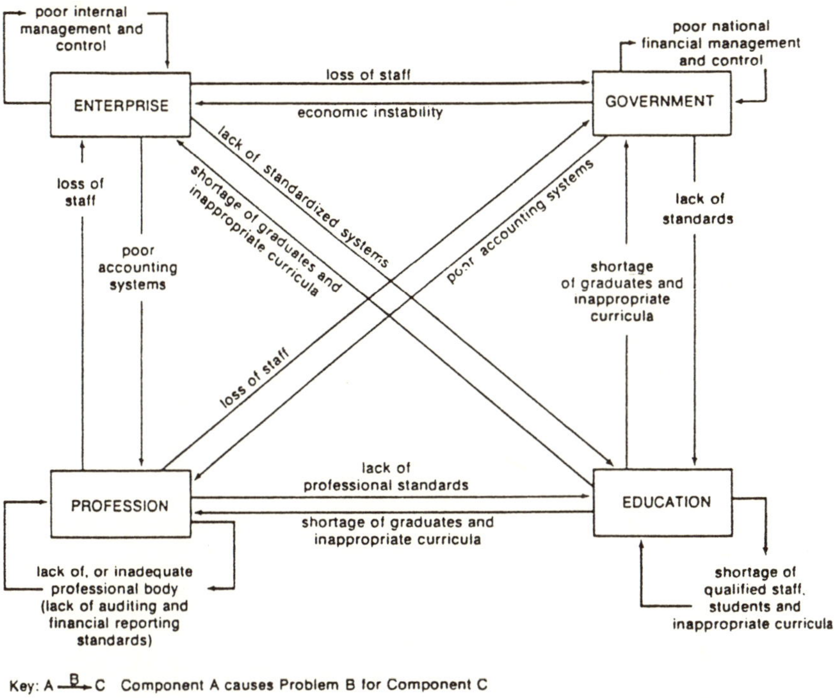

Source: H. P. Holzer and J. S. Chandler, "A Systems Approach to Accounting in Developing Countries," *Management International Review* (Fall 1981), p. 28. Reprinted with permission.

uninformed investors cannot confidently use the security price as a reliable guide to investment decision. Hence, the intertemporal misallocation of resources is a serious issue in developing economies. The development of advanced accounting infrastructure can reduce the information cost and increase the information content of security prices. Because the market price can aggregate relevant fundamental information in the economy, the decision makers can use the market price to enhance their information set and reduce the possible decision bias caused by the bounded rationality. When the capital market is semi-strongly or strongly efficient, then the market price would reflect useful fundamental information and would provide useful guidance to the investment decision.[87]

Another excellent description of accounting infrastructure in the developing countries is provided by R.S.O. Wallace and R. J. Briston and is depicted in

Exhibit 3.8
Elements of Accounting Infrastructure

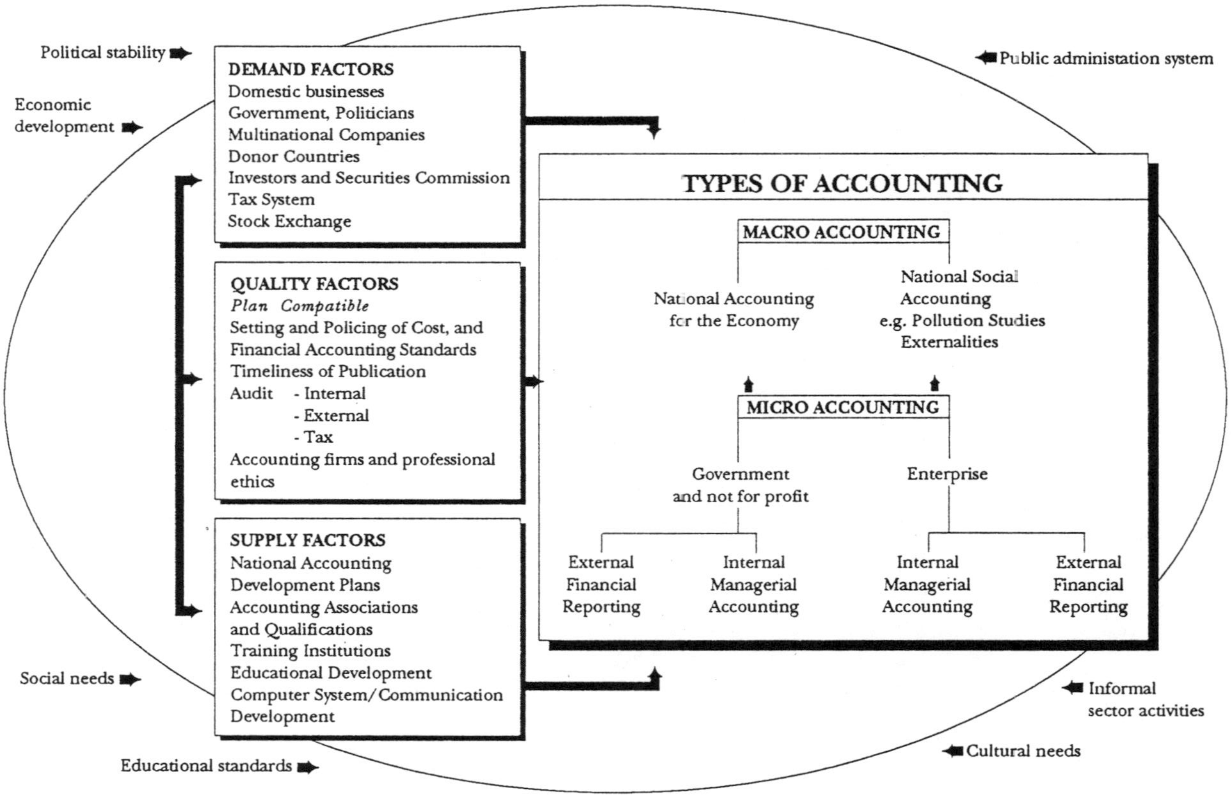

Source: R. S. O. Wallace and R. J. Briston, "Improving the Accounting Infrastructure in Developing Countries," *Research in Third World Accounting* 2 (1992), p. 203. Reprinted with permission.

Exhibit 3.8.[88] The basic elements that make up this information infrastructure include:

> (1) the supply function—the training and education of accountants and auditors (i.e., the information producers) and availability of institutions and equipment in sufficient number and quality to assist the information producer; (2) the demand function—the information user, including information intermediaries, information screening mechanisms such as inter-firm comparison, and stock exchanges and banks; and (3) quality control systems—the laws and regulations that govern the production, transmission and usage of information, the legal entities that monitor and implement the laws and regulations and the personnel that validate the information produced. These basic elements seem to influence, and are influenced by, the types of accounting which exist in a country.[89]

The complexity of this infrastructure points to the problems faced by developing countries in upgrading their accounting environments. Accounting academics have made various suggestions on how best to improve this accounting infrastructure; these approaches are summarized in Exhibit 3.9. Wallace and Briston correctly argue, however, that the national accounting infrastructure development (NAID) program suitable for a country depended on the particular circumstances of a given country.[90] They identified three approaches for developing accounting infrastructure: a dependency approach, a self-reliance (without foreign assistance) approach, and a self-reliance (with foreign assistance) approach.[91] The dependency approach exists generally between a developed country and a developing country that was a colony of the developed country. Basically money, personnel, technology, and administration and accounting systems are transferred from the developed to the developing country to stimulate development. The self-reliance (without foreign assistance) approach exists when the developing country has the appropriate knowledge, skills, and attitude to dictate the evolution of its accounting capability. The self-reliance (with foreign assistance) approach exists when the developing country relies on both its own abilities and external assistance to bring about improvements and upgradings in its accounting infrastructure.

Micro- versus Macroaccounting

Information needs in the developing countries relate to the conduct of both business and government units and of the nation. Micro- and macroaccounting systems, whether or not integrated, are needed. The macro- or national accounting system serves to determine the structure, conduct, and performance of the nation's affairs and implement economic policies. Macroaccounting includes national income accounts, input and output accounts, flow of funds accounts, balance of payments, and national balance sheet. The microaccounting system serves to determine the structure, conduct, and performance of private and public enterprises. Microaccounting includes both enterprise and governmental ac-

Exhibit 3.9
Approaches for Improving Accounting in the Developing Countries

Approaches	*Authors and main thrusts*
(1) The transfer of accounting knowledge from developed to developing countries by designated transfer agents such as transnational accounting firms, multinational enterprises, special projects undertaken by the United Nations and its agencies, or other international or regional agencies (such as European Community) and universities from developed countries.	Engleman (1962), Enthoven (1979), Lowe (1967), Seidler (1969), Needles (1976) and Briston (1978). Transplantation of accounting systems of developed countries into developing countries in accordance with the needs of each country. But needs are determinable by evaluating the gap between what presently exists in a country and what is presumed to be required in that country.
(2) To structure accounting in a developing country so as to provide information which can facilitate the economic evaluation of the activities of an enterprise by management, investors and government. The goal is to base the structuring 'solely on general economic principles of both micro and macro nature rather than on business practice, accounting conventions, tax or other narrowly conceived legislation' (Scott, 1970, p. 149). This model is described by Tipgos (1987) as Economic Evaluation Accounting (EEvA).	Scott (1970) The goal of an accounting development programme should be to serve the end users with its products. The output of an accounting structure should meet users' needs. To ensure that such needs are met, input to accounting structure should be improved—such inputs include education of accountants, legislative control and regulation of accounting and professionals.
(3) The use of existing and potential accounting systems, techniques, procedures and data to enhance economic development within a nation and among nations (AAA 1977, p. 20). This model is described as Economic Development Accounting by Tipgos (1987).	AAA (1977) The vehicle for undertaking the AAA proposal is an economic development educational programme where activities would 'demand a conceptual socio-economic foundation of accounting education and training, a further specialization in various areas (branches) of accounting; a closer linkage between institutional, professional and educational programmes; and a greater focus on forecasting techniques of both, internal and external nature' (AAA, 1977, p. 22).
(4) The development of a two-tier education system (TES) which combines a para professional training for accountants in Third World countries.	Tipgos (1987) and Briston and Wallace (1990). The development of accounting workforce should embrace technical and professional levels. Tipgos (1987) provides an illustration of a two-tier structure in the Philippines while Briston and Wallace (1990) describe the three-tier and three-level structure in Tanzania.

Source: R. S. O. Wallace and R. J. Briston, "Improving the Accounting Infrastructure in Developing Countries," *Research in Third World Accounting* 2 (1992), p. 205. Reprinted with permission.

counting. In the context of an integrated national accounting system, microaccounting is used to serve macroaccounting.[92] Exhibit 3.10 depicts an example of the hierarchy of accounting information measurement systems in a macro-based model. In fact in countries that rely on national economic planning, the two systems are more integrated than in countries relying on market forces. Various authors in international accounting argued for the superiority of an integrated macro-based accounting and advised its adoption by developing countries.[93] Recommendations were also made for its adoption in Kuwait[94] and Syria.[95] The suggestion for linkages between micro- and macroaccounting is made for the sake of success of development planning.[96] The unavailability of reliable information and the unreliability of available information can have adverse effects upon exerted development efforts.[97]

The linkage between micro- and macroaccounting allows for the determination of the type of information outputs for the microaccounting system that is intended to become the information inputs of the macroaccounting system, creating in the process an information feedback loop. The advantages of such a feedback loop are presumed as follows:

1. The preparers of the macroaccounting information would be able to keep track of the changing information needs of the development planning process.
2. The development planners would be able to indicate to the preparers of the macroaccounting information, through negative or positive feedback information, the effectiveness of the information provided in aiding the development planning process. This would, in turn, enable the macroaccounting system to adjust its operations in order to serve the development planning process better.
3. The macroaccounting system would be able to provide negative or positive feedback information to the development planners regarding the progress being made in achieving the objectives of the development plan. This would in turn enable the development planners to revise the development plan, on a timely basis, whenever it is necessary.
4. The developing country would have development planning and macroaccounting systems that are complementary to each other rather than having each system operating in a vacuum. This would save the particular developing country the cost of implementing and later scrubbing development strategies or policies that were ultimately found to have been formulated on the basis of unreliable information.[98]

Mirghani also offers a structure of the macroeconomic system comprised of its method of classification, processing methodologies, and data base, as shown in Exhibit 3.11. The classification system is threefold: the micro units comprising the economy divided into major economic sectors, the macroaccounting system grouped into accounts or subsystems intended to produce specific information output, and the economic transactions of each economic sector worked into the input data for each subsystem of the macroaccounting system. This integration of macroaccounting and microaccounting is prevalent in general in countries expressing some forms of indicative planning and in particular in most

Exhibit 3.10
Hierarchy of Accounting Information Measurement Systems in a Macro-Based Model

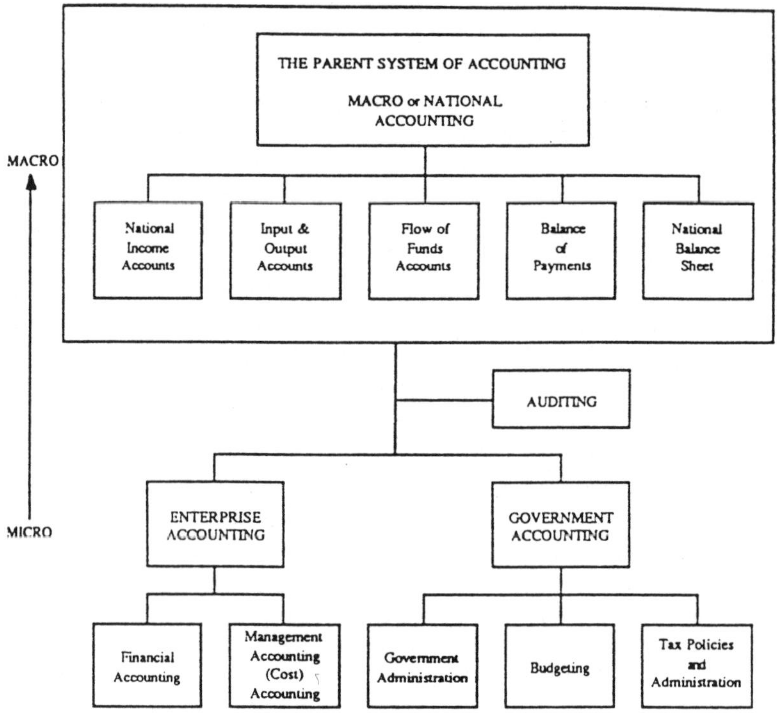

Source: R. S. O. Wallace, "Accounting in Developing Countries: A Review of the Literature," *Research in Third World Accounting* 1 (1990), p. 21. Reprinted with permission.

francophone countries where the French system of uniform accounting for the purpose of assisting national or macroaccounting is adopted. The merge of two systems, while desirable, is not required for an effective macroaccounting system.

Enterprise Accounting

Enterprise accounting, or private-enterprise accounting, contributes to the measurement of the efficiency of the allocation and use of economic resources. It plays a vital role in running firms in developed countries. The low level of enterprise accounting expertise in developing countries and the consequent low reliability of the information provided has the following consequences:

National investors are understandably disinclined to provide the capital necessary to expanding economies, and private-sector capital markets of adequate size fail to materialize. Management reporting is also usually of low caliber and often is almost nonex-

Exhibit 3.11
The Structure of the Macroaccounting System

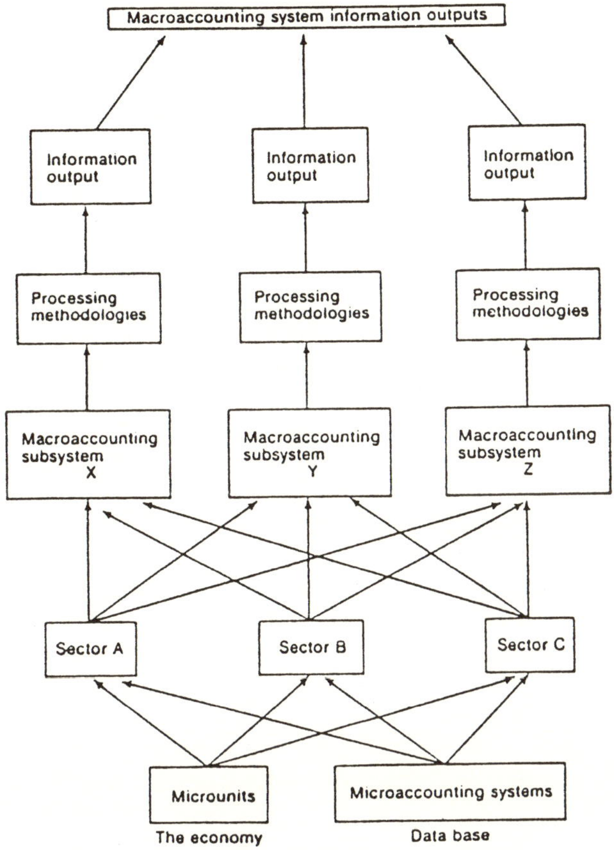

Source: M. A. Mirghani, "A Framework for a Linkage between Microaccounting and Macroaccounting for Purposes of Developing Planning in Developing Countries," *International Journal of Accounting Education and Research* 18 (1982), p. 65.

istent. In developing nations internal reporting may offer management little more than verification of past transactions and management may not realize the potential of accounting as a managerial tool.[99]

This is an unfortunate situation given the importance of enterprise accounting for the integrity and development of capital markets and for economic development in general. Some of the merits of enterprise accounting follow:

1. The skills and techniques that make up enterprise accounting are essential to the development of commerce, industry, and public administration.

2. Economic development rests on successful industrialization and the efficient mobilization of capital. Accounting can help in evaluating the success of both endeavors, as stated by Seidler: "Enterprise accounting is a supplier of information, a device for increasing the efficiency of resource allocations, and a mechanism for controlling productive operations. It seems logical that these skills, normally considered to be tools of private enterprise management, should be equally useful to the management of the development process."[100]
3. Through the production of reliable and timely information, enterprise accounting is essential to the efficient functioning of a capital market necessary to channel funds for development and investment, in the collection of taxes, and in the efficient allocation of scarce resources.
4. Enterprise accounting information is needed by government, capital markets, and business firms in developing nations. First, government needs such information for implementing public policy, controlling and regulating private enterprise, controlling economic cycles, analyzing expenditures for social overhead, measuring national income, constructing input-output and flow of funds systems, disseminating information, and, finally, collecting income taxes.
5. Enterprise accounting information is seen as vital to the emergence of a domestic private capital market, a domestic public capital market, an external private capital market, an external public source of capital, and a capital market consisting of funds from international agencies.
6. Enterprise accounting information is necessary to assist management in its custodial functions, operating decisions, control of subsidiaries and branches, personnel control, real income measurement, budgeting and forecasting, and special management problems.
7. Finally, economic development depends on an efficient use of a country's economic resources. It rests on development planning to guide the efficient use of these resources. To be successful, development planning should be supported by an adequate supply of information, which is one of the prerogatives of accounting.

This last point is eloquently addressed by M. A. Mirghani:

> Since development planning represents a system of decision making under conditions of great uncertainty, it should be supported by an information system capable of generating the types of information necessary for reducing the amount of uncertainty surrounding the economic choices that must be made. The development planning process can be likened to the resource allocation process in a micro-organization. The management of any organization would attempt to select the package of alternative uses that would yield maximum benefits in view of the constraints operating in that organization's specific environment. Such an exercise would not be fruitful without an information system that would enable management to make rational choices among alternative uses.[101]

Enterprise accounting in the developing countries needs, however, to adapt to the specific problems faced by these countries and produce the appropriate report for an understanding of these problems. For example, J. M. Samuels suggested a list of the major problems of developing countries and the types of

Exhibit 3.12
Major Problems of Developing Countries and Types of Accounting Statements That Would Help in Their Solution

	Problems	*Relevant accounting reports and statements*
(1)	Economic growth	(a) Profit and loss account (b) Balance sheet (with notes) based on inflation adjusted figures
(2)	Unemployment	Employment report
(3)	Balance of payments	Statement of transactions in foreign currency
(4)	Income/wealth distribution	(a) Adapted value added statement (b) Analysis of shareholders
(5)	Level of Technology	Education/training report
(6)	Regional imbalances	(a) Regional flow of funds statements (b) Regional distribution of assets
(7)	Safety/security	Empolyment report
(8)	Impact of environment	Special report
(9)	Corruption	Audit report

Source: J. M. Samuels, "Accounting for Development: An Alternative Approach," *Research in Third World Accounting* 1 (1990), p. 80.

accounting statements for an understanding of these problems.[102] These problems and statements are shown in Exhibit 3.12.

Specific economic data and information are required for economic planning. Some of this information includes competitive advantage, effective interest rates, value added, productivity, employment, market structure, export and import dependence, local contents, effective tariff rates, shadow price, linkage relations, input-output ratios, investment coefficients, effect of price-level change, energy requirements, water requirements, environmental pollution, technology and skill level, and R&D capability.[103] Most of these data and information are not provided by the conventional accounting system of either developed or undeveloping countries. The scope of accounting information obviously needs to be expanded to include the production and reporting of these important indicators of development planning. Enthoven advocated that critical information for economic planning—such as value added, profitability, capital coefficient, price level change, human resources, and productivity—should be included in the accounting scope in a manner that integrates enterprise, government, and macroaccounting in the whole process of economic analysis, policy, and planning.[104]

Developing countries rely to a large extent on economic development planning to achieve a certain measure of growth. To avoid misallocation of resources in the planning process, reliable economic data and information are needed and are generally presumed to be provided by the accounting and information system. This is generally not the case. As stated by S. Yu and J. Lee,

> economic data and information required for industrial development planning by developing countries are much more diverse and intense than traditional accounting's income based, one-dimensional approach. Development planning typically requires, apart from profitability at the micro level and fiscal and monetary policy at the macro level, such information as value added, productivity, export dependence, local contents, linkage relations, investment coefficients, energy requirement, technology level, and R&D capability. Most of this information is required not only at the project level, but also at the industry and national levels. Currently, they are obtained not through routine accounting information systems, but through *ad hoc* efforts or separate information and data gathering systems established purposefully or developed indigenously within the economy.[105]

Accounting for Inflation

The differences between price change models rest in the differences in their implicit or explicit specification of a valuation model or a measured attribute for assets and liabilities, and a capital maintenance concept. Various studies provided a taxonomy of price change models based on a useful algebraic approach.[106] Lenny Chasteen's approach will be used here to illustrate the different price change models.[107] He based his analysis on the assumptions and price change data in 12 price change models, based on an attribute measured/capital maintenance concept:

1. Historical cost/nominal dollars (HC/N$) model
2. Historical cost/constant dollars (HC/C$) model
3. Historical cost/constant dollars model a la Ijiri
4. Historical cost/constant dollars model using the one-line adjustment
5. Current cost/nominal dollars (CC/N$) model
6. Current cost/constant dollars (CC/C$) model
7. Current cost/physical capital (CC/PC) model
8. Current cost/physical capital model that incorporates purchasing power gains and losses on monetary items based on specific price changes.
9. Current cost/physical capital model that incorporates both a specific price change adjustment as in the previous model and a "gearing" adjustment.
10. Current exit value/nominal dollars (EV/N$)
11. Current exit value/constant dollars (EV/C$) a la Sterling
12. Current exit value/constant dollars a la Chambers

The algebraic formulations of each model follow.

1. The historical cost/nominal dollars model:

$$M + N = L + \underbrace{R}_{(t\,=\,1\text{ capital})} \tag{3.12}$$

Both inventory and equity security may be reported at $N(1 + s_1)$ or $N(1 + s_2)$ if s_1 and s_2 were negative.

2. The historical cost/constant dollars model:

$$M + N(1 + p) = L + \underbrace{R(1 + p)}_{(t\,=\,1\text{ capital})} \quad \underbrace{-\, p(M - L)}_{(\text{income [loss]})} \tag{3.13}$$

3. The historical cost/constant dollars model based on Ijiri's interpretation[108]:

$$M + N(1 + p) = L + \underbrace{R(1 + p)}_{(t\,=\,1\text{ capital})} + \underbrace{Np - Rp}_{(\text{income [loss]})} \tag{3.14}$$

Where Np is a price level holding gain and Rp a price level capital change

4. The historical cost/constant dollars model based on the one-line adjustment[109]:

$$M + N = L + \underbrace{R(1 + p)}_{(t\,=\,1\text{ capital})} - \underbrace{Rp}_{(\text{loss})} \tag{3.15}$$

5. The current cost/nominal dollars model[110]:

$$M + N(1 + s_1) = L + \underbrace{R}_{(t\,=\,1\text{ capital})} \quad + \quad Ns_1 \tag{3.16}$$

allowing the disaggregation of the firm's replacement or current cost income into two elements: (1) the current operating profit (revenues less the current costs of earning the revenues) and (2) holding gains (Ns_1).

6. The current cost/constant dollars model:

$$M + N(1 + s_1) = L + \underbrace{R(1 + p)}_{(t\,=\,1\text{ capital})} + \underbrace{N(s_1 - p) - p(M - L)}_{(\text{income [loss]})} \tag{3.17}$$

where $N(s_1 - p)$ is the holding gain or loss resulting from the specific price level changes, and $p(M - L)$ is the purchasing power gain or loss resulting from the general price level changes.

7. The current cost/physical capital model:

$$M + N(1 + s_1) = L + \underbrace{R + Ns_1}_{(t\,=\,1\text{ capital})} \tag{3.18}$$

where, unlike the current cost/nominal dollars model, the holding gains are considered a capital maintenance adjustment rather than an element of income.

8. The current cost/physical capital model that incorporates purchasing power gains and losses on monetary items based on specific price changes[111]:

$$M + N(1 + s_1) = L + \underbrace{R + Rs_1}_{(t\,=\,1\text{ capital})} - \underbrace{s_1(M - L)}_{(\text{income [loss]})} \tag{3.19}$$

9. The current cost/physical capital model that incorporates losses, a specific price change adjustment, and a "gearing" adjustment[112]:

$$\begin{aligned} M + N(1 + s_1) = {} & L + \underbrace{R + Ns_1[R/(L + R)] + Ms_1[R/(L + R)]}_{(\text{t}\,=\,1\text{ capital})} \\ & + \underbrace{Ns_1[L/(L + R)] - Ms_1[R/(L + R)]}_{(\text{income})} \end{aligned} \tag{3.20}$$

where the gearing adjustment is calculated by allocating the holding gain (specific price increase) on nonmonetary assets between income and capital as follows: Income portion = $[L/(L + R)]\,Ns_1$; Capital maintenance portion = $[R/(L + R)]\,Ns_1$.

10. The current exit value/nominal dollars model:

$$M + N(1 + s_2) = L + \underbrace{R}_{(\text{t}\,=\,1\text{ capital})} + \underbrace{\text{N}s_2}_{(\text{income})} \tag{3.21}$$

11. The current exit value/constant dollars (EV/C$) a la Sterling[113]:

$$\begin{aligned} M + N(1 + s_2 = {} & L + \underbrace{R(1 + p)}_{(t\,=\,1\text{ capital})} \\ & + \underbrace{N(s_2 - p) - p(M - L)}_{(\text{income})} \end{aligned} \tag{3.22}$$

where the nonmonetary assets are valued at exit prices instead of replacement costs.

12. The current exit value/constant dollars a la Chambers[114]:

$$M + N(1 + s_2) = L + \underbrace{R(1 + p)}_{(t\,=\,1\text{ capital})} + \underbrace{Ns_2 - Rp}_{(\text{income})} \tag{3.23}$$

The 12 models described in this section represent some of the models that can be used or adapted by any country to deal with inflation. The easiest and most practical models that could be adopted by developing countries include the historical cost/constant dollars model (no. 1), the current cost/nominal dollars model (no. 5), and the current cost/constant dollars model (no. 6). They can provide relevant information about the impact of price changes on the financial structure, performance, and conduct of firms in the developing countries.

CONCLUSIONS

Macro- and microaccounting information is needed by governments, capital markets, and business firms to insure a proper conduct of the planning process, generally required for the economic development of the developing countries. This chapter shows the importance of this role of accounting in both the planning process and economic development.

NOTES

1. *New Left Review* (1963), p. 4.
2. H. Liebenstein, "Allocative Efficiency v. X-Efficiency," *American Economic Review* (June 1966), pp. 352–415.
3. W. J. Baumol and A. S. Binder, *Economics: Principles and Policy*, 2nd ed. (New York: Harcourt Brace Jovanovich, 1982), p. 760.
4. Nasir Islam and Georges M. Henault, "From GNP to Basic Needs: A Critical Review of Development and Development Administration," *International Review of Administrative Sciences* 2 (1979), pp. 253–267.
5. Ibid.
6. W. W. Rostow, "The Stages of Economic Growth," *Economic History Review* (August 1959).
7. Talcott Parsons, *The Social System* (Glencoe, Ill.: Free Press, 1951).
8. Islam and Henault, "From GNP to Basic Needs," p. 254.
9. Ibid.
10. Marc Nefron, "Introduction," in Marc Nefron, ed., *Another Development: Approaches and Strategies* (Uppsala: Dag Hammarskjold Foundation, 1977), p. 10.
11. Benjamin J. Cohen, *The Question of Imperialism: The Political Economy of Dominance and Dependence* (New York: Basic Books, 1973).
12. Mahbub Ul Haq, "An International Perspective on Basic Needs," in World Bank, *Poverty and Basic Needs* (September 1980), p. 32.
13. Paul Streeten, "From Growth to Basic Needs," in ibid., p. 6.
14. Frances Stewart, "Country Experience in Providing Basic Needs," in ibid., p. 9.
15. Norman L. Hicks, "Is There a Tradeoff Between Growth and Basic Needs?" in ibid., p. 25.
16. UN Department of Economic Affairs, *Measures of Economic Development of Underdeveloped Countries* (New York: UNDEA, 1951), p. 63.
17. R. Helfgoth and S. Schiano-Campo, "An Introduction to Development Plan-

ning,'' *United Nations Industrial Development Organization (UNIDO), Industrialization and Productivity Bulletin* 16 (1920), p. 11.

18. Michael P. Todaro, *Economic Development in the Third World* (New York: Longman, 1985), pp. 466–468.

19. T. Killick, ''The Possibilities of Development Planning,'' *Oxford Economic Papers* (July 1976).

20. Albert Waterson, *Development Planning: Lessons of Experience* (Baltimore: Johns Hopkins University Press, 1969), pp. 61–65.

21. Ibid., p. 98.

22. Ibid., p. 156.

23. Todaro, *Economic Development in the Third World,* p. 468.

24. Ibid., p. 470.

25. Lance Taylor, ''Theoretical Foundations and Technical Implications,'' in C. R. Blitzer, P. B. Clark, and L. Taylor, eds., *Economy-wide Models and Development Planning* (London: Oxford University Press, 1975), p. 39.

26. Todaro, *Economic Development in the Third World,* p. 470.

27. Ibid., p. 449.

28. Taylor, ''Theoretical Foundations and Technical Implications,'' p. 41

29. Todaro, *Economic Development in the Third World,* p. 473.

30. Ibid., p. 480.

31. Waterson, *Development Planning,* p. 199.

32. R. A. Baucr, cd., *Social Indicators* (Cambridgc, Mass.: MIT Prcss, 1966).

33. U.S. Department of Health, Education and Welfare, *Toward a Social Report* (Washington, D.C., 1965).

34. Leslie D. Wilcox et al., *Social Indicators and Social Monitoring: An Annotated Bibliography* (Amsterdam: Elsevier Scientific, 1972); and Kenneth C. Land, ''Social Indicator Models: An Overview,'' in Kenneth C. Land and Seymor Spilerman, eds., *Social Indicator Models* (New York: Russell Sage Foundation, 1975).

35. A. D. Biderman, ''Social Indicators and Goals,'' in *Social Indicator Models,* p. 69.

36. R. A. Bauer, ''Detection and Anticipation of Impact: The Nature of the Task,'' in *Social Indicators* p. 1.

37. Kenneth C. Land, ''Theories, Models and Indicators of Social Change,'' *International Social Science Journal,* No. 1 (1975).

38. P. M. Hauser, *Social Statistics in Use* (New York: Russell Sage, 1975).

39. Kenneth C. Land, ''On the Definition of Social Indicators,'' *American Sociologist* (November 1971): pp. 322–325; Land, ''Social Indicator Models: An Overview.''

40. Land, ''Theories, Models and Indicators of Social Change,'' p. 35.

41. Sir Claus Moser, ''Social Indicators: Systems, Methods and Problems,'' *Review of Income and Wealth* (June 1973), pp. 135–136.

42. Terry Nichols Clark, ''Community Social Indicators: From Analytical Models to Policy Applications,'' *Urban Affairs Quarterly* (September 1973), p. 6.

43. Michael J. Carley, ''Social Theory and Models in Social Indicator Research,'' *International Journal of Social Economics* 6, 1 (1979), p. 42.

44. Ibid., pp. 33–44.

45. Ibid., p. 42.

46. R. V. Horn, ''Social Indicators: Meaning, Method and Applications,'' *International Journal of Social Economics* 7, 8 (1980), pp. 440–441.

47. United Nations, *International Definition and Measurement of Standards and Lev-*

els of Living 1V, 5 (New York, 1954); United Nations, *International Definition and Measurement of Levels of Living, An Interim Guide* 1V, 7 (New York, 1961).

48. United Nations, *Social and Demographic Statistics: Draft Guidelines on Social Indicators* (New York: United Nations, 1976); United Nations, *Toward A System of Social and Demographic Statistics,* prepared by Richard Stone, ST/STAT. 68 (New York: United Nations, 1973).

49. Sten Johansson, "The Level of Living Survey: A Presentation," *Acta Sociologica* (1973); *Toward a Theory of Social Reporting* (Stockholm: Swedish Institute for Social Research, 1976).

50. Erik Allardt and Hannu Uusitalo, "Dimensions of Welfare in a Comparative Study of the Scandinavian Societies," *Scandinavian Political Studies* (1972).

51. Johansson, "The Level Living Survey."

52. J. P. Roos, "The Way of Life in Social Change: A Comparative Study," *Acta Sociologica* (1978).

53. Stein Ringen, *An Introduction to the Level of Living Study,* Memorandum no. 23 (Bergen, Norway, 1973).

54. Economic Council of Japan, *Measuring Net National Welfare of Japan* (Tokyo: Economic Research Institute, 1973).

55. Jan Drewnovsky, *Studies in the Measurement of Levels of Living and Welfare,* UNRISD Report, no. 703 (Geneva: United Nations, 1970).

56. John Q. Wilson, *Quality of Life in the United States* (Kansas City, Mo.: Mid-West Research Institute, 1969).

57. Nestor Terleckyj, *Elements of Possibilities for Improvements in the Quality of Life in the USA, 1971–1981* (Washington, D.C.: National Planning Association, 1978).

58. United Nations, *Toward a System of Social and Demographic Statistics.*

59. Erik Allardt, "A Welfare Model for Selecting Indicators of National Developments," *Policy Sciences* 4 (1973), pp. 63–74; Erik Allardt, "Individual Needs, Social Structures and Indicators of National Development," in S. N. Eisenstadt and S. Rokkan, eds., *Building States and Nations,* vol. 1 (Beverly Hills, Calif.: Sage, 1973), pp. 259–273.

60. Wolfgang Glatzer, "An Overview of the International Development in Macro Social Indicators," *Accounting, Organizations and Society* 6, 3 (1981), p. 224.

61. W. Zapf, "Soziale Indikatoren: Eine Zwischenbilanz," *Allgemeines Statistisches Archiv* 1 (1976), p. 432.

62. Horn, "Social Indicators," p. 432.

63. Organization for Economic Cooperation and Development, *The OECD List of Social Indicators* (Paris: OECD, 1982), p. 10.

64. Ibid., p. 12.

65. Organization for Economic Cooperation and Development, *Measuring Social Well-Being: A Progress Report on the Development of Social Indicators* (Paris: OECD, 1976), pp. 31–33.

66. United Nations Research Institute for Social Development, *Contents and Measurement of Socio-Economic Development* (Geneva: UNRISD, 1970), p. 63.

67. I. Adelman, and C. T. Morris, *Society, Politics and Economic Development* (Baltimore: John Hopkins University Press, 1967), pp. 16–17.

68. W. Nordhaus and J. Tobin, "Is Growth Obsolete?" in F. Thomas Juster, ed., *Economic Growth* (Ann Arbor: University of Michigan, Institute of Social Research, 1972).

69. Economic Council of Japan, NNW Measurement Committee, "Measuring Na-

tional Welfare of Japan'' (Report prepared for the Japanese Ministry of Finance, Tokyo, April 30, 1974).

70. M. Olson, ''The Treatment of Externalities in National Income Statistics,'' in L. Wings and A. Evans, eds., *Public Economics and the Quality of Life* (Baltimore: Johns Hopkins University Press, 1977).

71. O. Herfindahl and A. Kneese, ''Measuring Social and Economic Change: Benefits and Costs of Environmental Pollution,'' in M. Moss, ed., *Measurement of Economic and Social Performance* (New York: Columbia University Press, 1973).

72. Ibid.

73. H. M. Peskin and J. Peskin, ''The Valuation of Nonmarket Activities in Income Accounting,'' *Review of Income and Wealth* 71 (March 1978); and H. M. Peskin, ''A National Accounting Framework for Environmental Assets,'' *Environmental Economics and Management* 255 (1976).

74. H. M. Peskin, ''National Income Accounts and the Environment,'' in H. M. Peskin, P. R. Portney, and A. V. Kneese, eds., *Environmental Regulation and the U.S. Economy* (Baltimore: John Hopkins University Press, 1981).

75. Ibid.

76. Ibid., p. 84.

77. Adolf J. H. Enthoven, *Accountancy and Economic Development Policy* (Amsterdam: North-Holland, 1973), p. 196.

78. Ibid.

79. C. W. J. Lee, ''Accounting Infrastructure and Economic Development,'' *Journal of Accounting and Public Policy* (Summer 1987), p. 77.

80. Ibid., p. 82.

81. Mahmood Quereshi, ''Economic Development, Social Justice and Financial Reporting: Pakistan's Experience with Private Enterprise,'' *Management International Review* 6 (1975), p. 71.

82. Sengjae Yu, and Jungho Lee, ''Functions of Accounting in Developing Countries for Economic Planning,'' in Kyojiro Someya, ed., *Accounting Education and Research to Promote International Understanding* (Westport, Conn.: Greenwood Press, 1988).

83. Gordian A. Ndubizu, ''Accounting Disclosure Methods and Economic Development: A Criterion for Globalizing Capital Markets,'' *International Journal of Accounting Education and Research* 27, 2 (1992), p. 153.

84. Lee, ''Accounting Infrastructure and Economic Development,'' p. 82.

85. H. P. Holzer and J. S. Chandler, ''A Systems Approach to Accounting in Developing Countries,'' *Management International Review* (Fall 1981), pp. 23–32.

86. Lee, ''Accounting Infrastructure and Economic Development,'' p. 79.

87. Ibid., p. 83.

88. R. S. O. Wallace and R. J. Briston, ''Improving the Accounting Infrastructure in Developing Countries,'' *Research in Third World Accounting* 2 (1992), pp. 201–224.

89. Ibid., p. 202.

90. Ibid., p. 206.

91. Ibid., pp. 206–210.

92. R. S. O. Wallace, ''Accounting in the Developing Countries: A Review of the Literature,'' *Research in Third World Accounting* 1 (1990), p. 20.

93. B. E. Needles, ''Implementing a Framework for the International Transfer of Accounting Technology, *International Journal of Accounting Education and Research* 12 (1976), pp. 45–62.

94. S. A. Shuaib, ''Accounting Information and the Development Planning Process in Kuwait,'' *International Journal of Accounting Education and Research* 15 (1980), pp. 129–141.

95. A. Abdeen, ''The Role of Accounting in Project Evaluation and Control: The Syrian Experience,'' *International Journal of Accounting Education and Research* 15 (1980), pp. 143–58.

96. M. A. Mirghani, ''A Framework for a Linkage between Microaccounting and Macroaccounting for Purposes of Developing Planning in Developing Countries,'' *International Journal of Accounting Education and Research* 18 (1982), pp. 57–68.

97. Ibid.

98. Ibid., p. 63.

99. George M. Scott, ''Private Sector Enterprise Accounting in Developing Nations,'' *International Journal of Accounting Education and Research* 14 (1986), p. 52.

100. Lee J. Seidler, *The Function of Accounting in Economic Development: Turkey as a Case Study* (New York: Praeger, 1967), p. 7.

101. Mirghani, ''A Framework for a Linkage,'' p. 593.

102. J. M. Samuels, ''Accounting for Development: An Alternative Approach,'' in R. S. O. Wallace, J. M. Samuels, and R. J. Briston, eds., *Research in Third World Accounting* 1 (1990), p. 80.

103. Yu and Lee, ''Functions of Accounting in Developing Countries for Economic Planning,'' p. 474.

104. Adolf H. Enthoven, *Mega Accountancy Trends: Extended Accountancy Dimensions in Challenging Social Patterns* (Richardson, Tex.: Center for International Accounting Development, University of Texas at Dallas, 1985).

105. Yu and Lee, ''Functions of Accounting in Developing Countries for Economic Planning,'' p. 472.

106. R. J. Chambers, ''The Use and Misuse of a Notation: The History of an Idea,'' *Abacus* (December 1978), pp. 122–144; A. Barton, *An Analysis of Business Income Concepts,* ICRA Occasional Paper No. 7, International Center for Research in Accounting (University of Lancaster, 1975); Lenny Chasteen, ''A Taxonomy of Price Change Models,'' *The Accounting Review* (July 1984), pp. 515–523.

107. Chasteen, ''A Taxonomy of Price Change Models.''

108. Y. Ijiri, ''The Price-level Restatement and Its Dual Interpretation,'' *The Accounting Review* (April 1976), pp. 227–243.

109. Chambers, ''The Use and Misuse of a Notation;'' P. Grady, ''Purchasing Power Accounting,'' *Price Waterhouse Review* (1975), pp. 3–5; S. Agrawal, and K. Roseinzweig, ''One-Line Adjustment Methods of Accounting for the Effects of Inflation,'' *Collected Abstracts of the AAA Annual Meeting* (AAA, 1982), p. 29.

110. E. Edwards and P. Bell, *The Theory and Measurement of Business Income* (Berkeley: University of California Press, 1961); R. A. Samuelson, ''Should Replacement-Cost Changes Be Included in Income?'' *The Accounting Review* (April 1980), pp. 254–268.

111. R. Gynther, *Accounting for Price Level Changes* (New York: Pergamon Press, 1966).

112. ''Statement of Standard Accounting Practice No. 16: Current Cost Accounting,'' *Accountancy* (April 1980), pp. 99–100.

113. R. R. Sterling, *Theory of the Measurement of Enterprise Income* (University of

Kansas, 1970); R. R. Sterling, "Relevant Financial Reporting in an Age of Price Changes," *Journal of Accountancy* (February 1975), pp. 42–51.

114. R. J. Chambers, "NOD, COG and PuPu: See How Inflation Teases," *Journal of Accountancy* (September 1975), pp. 56–62.

REFERENCES

Abdeen, A. (1980). "The Role of Accounting in Project Evaluation and Control: The Syrian Experience." *International Journal of Accounting Education and Research* 15: 143–158.

Abdelsalam, M. (1990). "The Use of Corporate Financial Reports by Investors in Saudi Arabia." In K. S. Most (ed)., *Advances in International Accounting* 3, pp. 25–39. Greenwich, Conn.: JAI Press.

Abdelsalam, M. and D. Satin (1988). "The Impact of Published Annual Financial Reports on Share Prices in Saudi Arabia." *International Journal of Accounting Education and Research* 23: 113–124.

Agami, A. M. and Y. A. Alkafaji (1987). "Accounting Education in Selected Middle Eastern Countries." *International Journal of Accounting Education and Research* 23: 145–168.

Aitken, M. J. and M. A. Islam (1984). "Dispelling Arguments against International Accounting Standards." *International Journal of Accounting Education and Research* 19: 35–46.

Alhashim, D. D. (1977). "Social Accounting in Egypt." *International Journal of Accounting Education and Research* 12: 127–142.

Amer, M. B. (1969). "Impact of Public Ownership on the U.A.R. Accounting Profession." *International Journal of Accounting Education and Research* 4: 49–62.

American Accounting Association (1977). "Report of the 1975–76 Committee on International Accounting Operations and Education." *The Accounting Review* 52 (Supplement): 65–132.

———. (1980). *Accounting Education and the Third World.* Sarasota, Fl.: AAA Report of the Committee on International Accounting Operations and Education 1976–1978.

American Institute of Certified Public Accountants (AICPA). (1964). *Professional Accounting in 25 Countries.* New York: AICPA.

———. (1975). *Professional Accounting in 30 Countries.* New York: AICPA.

Ariyo, A. (1988). "Economic Considerations in the Choice of Depreciation Methods: Some Additional Evidence from Nigeria." In K. S. Most (ed.), *Advances in International Accounting* 2, pp. 89–97. Greenwich, Conn.: JAI Press.

Ba-Eissa, M. O. (1984). *The Professionalisation of Accounting: A Study of the Development of Accounting Profession with Special Reference to Great Britain, The United States and Saudi Arabia.* Doctoral Thesis, University of Kent at Canterbury.

Bai, Z. L. (1988). "Accounting in the People's Republic of China—Contemporary Situations and Issues." In V. K. Zimmerman (ed.), *Recent Accounting and Economic Developments in the Far East.* Center for International Education and Research in Accounting, University of Illinois at Urbana-Champaign, pp. 27–50.

Bait-et Mal, M. M., C. H. Smith, and M. E. Taylor (1973). "The Development of Accounting in Libya.'' *International Journal of Accounting Education and Research* 8: 83–102.

Benjamin, B. Y. Tei et al. (1990). ''Non-Compliance with Disclosure Requirements in Financial Statements; the Case of Hong Kong Companies.'' *International Journal of Accounting Education and Research,* 25, 2: 99–112.

Bernstein, M. H. (1955). *Regulating Business by Independent Commission.* Princeton, N.J.: Princeton University Press.

Berry, M. (1988). ''The Cultural Development of Accounting in the People's Republic of China.'' In V. K. Zimmerman (ed.), *Recent Accounting and Economic Developments in the Far East.* Center for International Education and Research in Accounting, University of Illinois at Urbana-Champaign, pp. 1–25.

Bond, R. R. (1970). ''Emerging Nations and Emerging Institutions.'' *International Journal of Accounting Education and Research* 6: 83–90.

Bose, A. (1988). ''The Indian Accounting Profession: Its Origins and Current Status.'' In V. K. Zimmerman (ed.), *Recent Accounting and Economic Developments in the Far East.* Center for International Education and Research in Accounting, University of Illinois at Urbana-Champaign, pp. 149–162.

Bose, M. (1977). ''The Growth of Accountancy in India.'' *Accountancy* 88: 36–38.

Briston, R. J. (1974). ''The Accountancy Profession in a Developing Country: an Indonesia Case Study.'' *The Accountant's Magazine* August: 314–315.

———. (1978). ''The Evolution of Accounting in Developing Countries,'' *International Journal of Accounting Education and Research* 14: 105–120.

———. (1979). ''The Changing Role of Government Audits in Developing Countries: Its Implications for UK Accounting Firms.'' *Accountant's Magazine* August: 25–27.

———. (1984). ''Accounting Standards and Host Country Control of Multinationals.'' *British Accounting Review* 16: 12–26.

Briston, R. J. and A. A. El-Ashker (1984). ''The Egyptian Accounting System: A Case Study in Western Influence.'' *International Journal of Accounting Education and Research* 19: 129–155.

Briston, R. J. and F. S. Liang (1990). ''The Evolution of Corporate Reporting in Singapore.'' In R.S.O. Wallace, J. M. Samuels, and R. J. Briston (eds.), *Research in Third World Accounting* 1, pp. 281–299. London: JAI Press.

Briston, R. J., F. S. Liang, and H. Yunus (1990). ''Accounting Education and Work Force Requirements in Indonesia.'' In B. E. Needles, Jr. and V. K. Zimmerman (eds.), *Comparative International Accounting Education Standards.* Center for International Education and Research in Accounting, University of Illinois at Urbana-Champaign, pp. 147–173.

Briston, R. J. and R.S.O. Wallace (1990). ''Accounting Education and Corporate Financial Reporting In Tanzania.'' In R.S.O. Wallace, J. M. Samuels, and R. J. Briston (eds.), *Research in Third World Accounting* 1, pp. 288–301. London: JAI Press.

Briston, R. J. and R.S.O. Wallace (1990). ''Accounting Education and Corporate Disclosure Regulations in Tanzania.'' In R.S.O. Wallace, J. M. Samuels, and R. J. Briston (eds), *Research in Third World Accounting* 1, pp. 281–299.

Brookner, L. and E. Heilman (1960). ''Technical Assistance in Accounting in Turkey.'' *Accounting Review* 25: 33–36.

Campbell, L. (1985). ''Financial Reporting in Japan.'' In C. W. Nobes and R. H. Parker (eds.), *Comparative International Accounting,* 2nd ed. Deddington, U.K.: Philip Allan.

Cassell, M. E. (1979). "Economic Development Accountancy." *Management Accounting* (UK) May: 23–24.

Chaderton, R. (1990). "The Education of Professional Accountants in the Barbados." In B. E. Needles and V. K. Zimmerman (eds.), *Comparative International Accounting Education Standards.* Center for International Education and Research in Accounting, University of Illinois at Urbana-Champaign, pp. 273–243.

Chan, A. M. (1988). "The Speculative Accounting System in Hong Kong; Understanding Hong Kong's Accounting Reality." In V. K. Zimmerman (ed.), *Recent Accounting and Economic Developments in the Far East.* Center for International Education and Research in Accounting, University of Illinois at Urbana-Champaign, pp. 197–218.

Chandler, J. S. and H. P. Holzer (1985). "Preconditions for the Introduction of Computer-Aided Accounting Systems in Less Developed Countries." *Management International Review* 25: 53–66.

Cheng, C. (1980). "Political Accounting in China: What the West Should Know." *Journal of Accountancy,* January: 76–82, 85.

Cheng, P. C. and T. N. Jain (1973). "Economic Perspective and Accounting Practices in South Korea." *International Journal of Accounting Education and Research* 8: 123–142.

Chiu, J. S. and D. L. Chang (1979). "Management Accounting in Taiwan." *Management Accounting* (U.S.) 60: 50–55.

Choi, F.D.S. (1979). "ASEAN Federation of Accountants: A New International Accounting Force." *International Journal of Accounting Education and Research* 15: 53–75.

Choi, F.D.S. and G. L. Mueller (1984). *International Accounting.* Engelwood Cliffs, N.J.: Prentice-Hall.

Chow, C. W. and A. Wong-Boren (1986). "Audit Firm Size and Audit Quality: Some Evidence from Mexico." *International Journal of Accounting Education and Research* 21: 1–25.

———. (1987). "Voluntary Financial Disclosure by Mexican Corporations." *Accounting Review* 62: 533–541.

Chu, J. M. (1973). "Accounting Principles and Practices in Panama." *International Journal of Accounting Education and Research* 9: 43–52.

Clapp, C. L. (1967). "National Variation in Accounting Principles and Practices." *International Journal of Accounting Education and Research* 3: 29–42.

Cooke, T. E. and R.S.O. Wallace (1990). "Financial Disclosure Regulation and its Environment: A Review and Further Analysis." *Journal of Accounting and Public Policy* 9: 79–110.

Costouros, G. J. (1975). "Accounting Education and Practices in Greece." *International Journal of Accounting Education and Research* 11: 95–106.

da Costa, R. C., J. C. Bourgeois, and W. M. Lawson (1978). "A Classification of International Financial Accounting Practices." *International Journal of Accounting Education and Research* 13: 73–85.

Dahmash, N. H. (1982). "Public Auditing Developments in the Arab States: A Comparative Study." *International Journal of Accounting Education and Research* 18: 89–114.

Dev, S. and E. L. Inanga (1979). "Educating Accountants in Nigeria." *Accountancy* 90: 127–129.

Elliot, E. L. (1968). *The Nature and Stages of Accounting Development in Latin America.*

Center for International Education and Research in Accounting, University of Illinois at Urbana-Champaign.

———. (1972). "Accounting and Economic Development in Latin America." *International Journal of Accounting Education and Research* 8: 89–98.

Elliot, E. L., J. Larrea, and J. M. Rivera (1968). "Accounting Aid to Developing Countries: Some Additional Considerations." *Accounting Review* 43: 763–768.

Engleman, K. (1962). "Accountancy Problems in Developing Countries." *Journal of Accountancy,* January: 53–56.

Enthoven, A.J.H. (1965). "Economic Development and Accountancy." *Journal of Accountancy,* August: 29–35.

———. (1967). "Accounting and Development Programming." *International Journal of Accounting Education and Research* 3: 107–120.

———. (1969). "Accountancy for Economic Development." *Finance and Development,* September: 24–29.

———. (1973). *Accounting and Economic Development Policy.* Amsterdam: North Holland.

———. (1976). "Scope of Accountancy Planning in Developing Countries." *Accounting and Business Research,* No. 22: 135–139.

———. (1979). *Accountancy Systems in Third World Economies.* Amsterdam: North Holland.

———. (1981a). "Accounting in Developing Countries." In C. W. Nobes and R. H. Parker (eds.), *Comparative International Accounting,* 1st ed. pp. 217–237. Deddington, U.K: Philip Allan.

———. (1981b). *Accounting Education in Economic Development Management.* Amsterdam: North-Holland.

———. (1983). "Price-Level Accounting in a Developing Economy (The Case of Zaire)." *The Government Accountants Journal,* Summer: 33–40.

Falk, H., S. Frumer, and J. A. Heintz (1974). "Accounting for Stock Reacquisitions: Israel and the United States Compared." *The International Journal of Accounting Education and Research* 9: 118–124.

Fantl, I. (1971). "The Case Against International Uniformity." *Management Accounting* (UK) May: 13–25.

Fleming, R. (1979). "New Concepts in Brazilian Accounting for Inflation." *The Accountant's Magazine,* April: 162–165.

Foroughi, T. K. (1981). "Accounting in Developing Countries before and after Social Crises: The Case of Iran." *Journal of International Accounting Education and Research* 17: 181–223.

Forrester, D. (1983). "Comment va-t-il in Africa?: A Study of the Influence of French Accounting." *AUTA Review* 15: 230–240.

Frank, W. G. (1979). "An Empirical Analysis of International Accounting Principles." *Journal of Accounting Research* 17: 593–605.

Frankel, H. S. (1949). "Psychic and Accounting Concepts of Income and Welfare." *Econometrica* 17 (Supplement), July.

Fu, P. Y. (1968). *A Study of Governmental Accounting in China: With Special Reference to the Sung Dynasty (960–1279).* Doctoral Dissertation, University of Illinois at Urbana-Champaign.

Gbenedio, P. O. (1977). *The Challenge to the Accounting Profession in a Developing Country: The Nigerian Case.* Doctoral dissertation, University of Cincinnati.

Ghandhi, N. W. (1976). "The Emergence of the Post Industrial Society and the Future of the Accounting Function.'' *International Journal of Accounting Education and Research* 11: 33–50.

Ghartey, A. (1978). ''A New Perspective for Accounting Education in Ghana.'' *International Journal of Accounting Education and Research* 14: 121–132.

Ghartey, J. B. (1985). ''Accountability, the Threshold of Political Instability, Underdevelopment and Misery: The Case of Africa.'' *International Journal of Accounting Education and Research* 21: 143–158.

Ghosh, S. N. (1990). ''A Comparative International Study of the Education of Professional Accountants: A Case Study of Bangladesh.'' In B. E. Needles, Jr. and V. K. Zimmerman (eds.), *Comparative International Accounting Education Standards.* Center for International Education and Research in Accounting, University of Illinois at Urbana-Champaign, pp. 97–108.

Goodrich, P. S. (1980). ''Grouping National Accounting Policies: A Q-Factor Analysis.'' School of Economic Studies, University of Leeds, Discussion Paper No. 96.

———. (1982). ''Accounting and Political Systems.'' School of Economic Studies, University of Leeds, Discussion Paper No. 109.

Graves, O. F. and M. Berry (1989). ''Accounting's Role in Successful Economic Development: Some Normative Evidence from the German Democratic Republic.'' *International Journal of Accounting* 24: 189–220.

Gul, F. A. and T. H. Yap (1984). ''The Effect of Combined Audit and Management Services on Public Perception of Auditor Independence in Developing Countries: The Malaysian Case.'' *Journal of International Accounting Education and Research* 20: 95–107.

Hardman, D. J. (1984). ''Accounting Development in the Solomon Islands.'' *International Journal of Accounting Education and Research* 20: 141–152.

Heintz, J. A. and J. Han (1985). ''A Study of Audit Judgement of Korean CPAs.'' *The International Journal of Accounting Education and Research* 21: 21–38.

Holzer, H. P. and J. S. Chandler (1981). ''A Systems Approach to Accounting in Developing Countries.'' *Management International Review,* Fall: 23–32.

Holzer, H. P. and D. Tremblay (1973). ''Accounting and Economic Development: The Cases of Thailand and Tunisia.'' *The International Journal of Accounting Education and Research* 9: 67–80.

Hove, M. R. (1986). ''Accounting Practices in Developing Countries: Colonialism's Legacy of Inappropriate Technologies.'' *International Journal of Accounting Education and Research* 22: 81–100.

Hove, M. R. (1989). ''The Inappropriate Uses of International Accounting Standards in Less Developed Countries: The Case of International Accounting Standard Number 24–Related Party Disclosures–Concerning Transfer Prices.'' *International Journal of Accounting* 24: 165–79.

IASC (1988). *Survey of the Use and Application of International Accounting Standards.* London: IASC.

Iino, T. and R. Inouye (1984). ''Financial Accounting and Reporting in Japan.'' In H. Peter Holzer et al. (eds.), *International Accounting.* New York: Harper & Row.

Inanga, E. L. (1976). ''The Information Content of Published Accounts of Nigerian Public Limited Companies.'' *Nigerian Journal of Economic and Social Studies* 18: 237–259.

Jagetia, L. C. and E. C. Nwadik (1983). ''Accounting Systems in Developing Nations: The Nigerian Experience.'' *International Journal of Accounting Education and Research,* 18: 69–81.

Jaggi, B. L. (1970). "A Review of the Accounting Profession in India." *International Journal of Accounting Education and Research* 6: 35–51.

———. (1973). "Accounting Systems in Developing Countries: An Assessment." *International Journal of Accounting Education and Research* 9: 159–170.

———. (1975). "The Impact of the Cultural Environment of Financial Disclosures." *International Journal of Accounting Education and Research* 10: 75–84.

Jaruga, A. A. (1980). "The Accounting Profession in a Centrally Planned Economy: The Polish Case." *Calcutta Management Association Newsletter,* May. (Reprinted in *Accountants Digest,* September 1980, pp. 20–23.)

Johnson, T. L. and M. Caygill (1971). "The Development of Accounting Links in the Commonwealth." *Accounting and Business Research,* Spring: 155–173.

Jones, G. M. and J. Kinfu (1971). "The Birth of an Accounting Profession: The Ethiopian Experience." *International Journal of Accounting Education and Research* 7: 89–98.

Juchau, R. H. (1978). "Accounting Practice Problems in Papua New Guinea and Fiji." *The Australian Accountant,* March: 110–113.

Juchau, R. H., M. White, and R. Hopkins (1986). "Tertiary Education Strategies for Accounting in Developing Societies—The South West Pacific as a Case Study." *International Journal of Accounting Education and Research* 21: 145–160.

Kapadia, G. P. (1973). *History of the Accounting Profession in India.* New Delhi: Institute of Chartered Accountants of India.

Kohlmeies, L. M. (1969). *The Regulators.* New York: Harper & Row.

Kraayenhof, J. (1963). "International Challenges in Accounting." *Journal of Accountancy.* January: 36.

Kwang, C. (1966). "The Economic Accounting System of State Enterprises in Mainland China." *International Journal of Accounting Education and Research* 1: 61–99.

Lee, S.A.A. (1965). "Korean Accounting Revaluation Laws." *Accounting Review* 40: 622–625.

Lev, B. (1976). "The Formulation of Accounting Standards and Rules: A Comparison of Efforts in Israel and the United States." *International Journal of Accounting Education and Research* 11: 121–132.

Lev, B. and B. Yahalomi (1972), "The Effect of Corporate Financial Statements on the Israeli Stock Exchange." *Management International Review* 12: 145–150.

Lowe, H. D. (1967). "Accounting Aid for Developing Countries." *The Accounting Review* 42: 356–360.

Mahon, J. J. (1965). "Some Observations on World Accounting." *Journal of Accountancy,* January: 15–23.

Markell, W. (1968). "Accounting Education—Its Importance in Developing Countries: Israel—A Case Study." *International Journal of Accounting Education and Research* 3: 125–133.

Marston, C. (1986). *Financial Reporting in India.* London: Croom Helm.

Mason, A. K. (1978). "The Development of International Financial Reporting Standards." ICRA Occasional Paper No. 17, International Center for Research in Accounting, University of Lancaster.

Mensah, Y. W. (1979). *A Database Approach to the Design of Macro-Oriented Enterprise Accounting Systems in Developing Countries.* University of Illinois at Urbana-Champaign.

———. (1981). "Financial Reporting Model for Dependent Market Economies." *Abacus* 17: 161–173.

Mepham, M. J. (1977). "The Accountancy Profession in Jamaica." *The Accountant's Magazine,* November: 468–470.

Mirghani, M. A. (1979). *The Role of Accounting in the Economic Development of Developing Countries: The Case of the Sudan.* Graduate School of Business, Indiana University.

———. (1982). "A Framework for a Linkage between Microaccounting and Macroaccounting for Purposes of Developing Planning in Developing Countries." *International Journal of Accounting Education and Research* 18: 57–68.

Mora, R. E. (1972). "The Accounting Profession in Mexico and Why." *International Journal of Accounting Education and Research* 8: 17–24.

Nair, R. D. and W. G. Frank (1980). "The Impact of Disclosure and Measurement Practices on International Accounting Classifications." *Accounting Review* 55: 426–450.

Ndubizu, G. A. (1984). "Accounting Standards and Economic Development: The Third World in Perspective." *Journal of International Accounting Education and Research* 19: 181–196.

Needles, B. E. (1976a). "Implementing a Framework for the International Transfer of Accounting Technology." *International Journal of Accounting Education and Research* 12: 45–62.

———. (1988). "Auditing Standards in the Far East: An Overview." In V. K. Zimmerman (ed.), *Recent Accounting and Economic Developments in the Far East.* Center for International Education and Research in Accounting, University of Illinois at Urbana-Champaign, pp. 65–95.

Niarchos, N. and M. Georgkopulus (1986), "The Effect of Annual Corporate Profit Reports on the Athens Stock Exchange: An Empirical Investigation." *Management International Review* 26, 1: 64–72.

Ninsuvannakul, P. (1966). "Education for Accountancy in Thailand." *International Journal of Accounting Education and Research* 2: 77–114.

———. (1988). "The Development of the Accounting Profession of the ASEAN Countries: Past, Present, and Future." In V. K. Zimmerman (ed.), *Recent Accounting and Economic Developments in the Far East.* Center for International Education and Research in Accounting, University of Illinois at Urbana-Champaign, pp. 115–148.

Nobes, C. W. (1981). "An Empirical Analysis of International Accounting Principles: A Comment." *Journal of Accounting Research* 19: 268–270.

———. (1983). "A Judgemental International Classification of Financial Reporting Practices." *Journal of Business Finance and Accounting* 10: 1–19.

Nobes, C. W. and J. Matatko (1980). "Classification of National Systems of Financial Accounting." *AUTA Review* 12: 57–78.

Nobes, C. W. and R. H. Parker (1985). *Comparative International Accounting,* 2nd ed., pp. 174–184. Deddington, U.K.: Philip Allan.

Ogundele, B. (1969). "The Accounting Profession in Nigeria: An International Perspective." *International Journal of Accounting Education and Research* 5: 101–106.

———. (1970). *Accounting and Economic Development: The Case of Nigeria.* Doctoral Dissertation, University of Illinois at Urbana-Champaign.

Park, S. and I. S. Cho (1988). "The Korean CPA Profession: Its Role in the Economic Development of Korea." In V. K. Zimmerman (ed.), *Recent Accounting and Economic Developments in the Far East.* Center for International Education and Research in Accounting, University of Illinois at Urbana-Champaign, pp. 97–113.

Parker, R. H. (1987). "Importing and Exporting Accounting: The British Experience." In *International Pressures for Accounting Change.* Englewood Cliffs, N.J.: Prentice-Hall/ICAEW.

Pena, P. A. (1976). "Special Report: A Comparison of the Accounting Professions of Colombia and the United States." *International Journal of Accounting Education and Research* 11: 143–177.

Perera, M.H.B. (1975). "Accounting and Its Environment in Sri Lanka." *Abacus* 11: 85–96.

———. (1989). "Accounting in Developing Countries: A Case for Localised Uniformity." *British Accounting Review* 21: 141–157.

Price Waterhouse International (1973). *Accounting Principles and Reporting Practices: A Survey in 38 Countries.* London: ICAEW.

———. (1975). *Accounting Principles and Reporting Practices: A Survey of 46 Countries.* London: ICAEW.

———. (1979). *International Survey of Accounting Principles and Reporting Practices in 64 Countries,* R. D. Fitzgerald, A. D. Stickler, and T. R. Watts (eds.). Scarborough, Ont.: Butterworths.

Quereshi, M. A. (1974). "Private Enterprise Accounting and Economic Development in Pakistan." *International Journal of Accounting Education and Research* 9: 125–142.

———. (1975). "Economic Development, Social Justice and Financial Reporting: Pakistan's Experience with Private Enterprise." *Management International Review* 2: 52–75.

Radebaugh, L. H. (1975). "Environmental Factors Influencing the Development of Accounting Objectives, Standards and Practices in Peru." *International Journal of Accounting Education and Research* 11: 39–56.

Rahman, M. Z. (1987). "Accounting Reports and Performance Measurement of Multinational Enterprises in Less Developed Countries." *Management International Review* 27, 2: 35–46.

Rivera, J. M. (1990). "The Accounting Profession and Accounting Education in Panama: A Survey." In B. E. Needles, Jr. and V. K. Zimmerman (eds.), *Comparative International Accounting Educational Standards.* Center for International Education and Research in Accounting, University of Illinois at Urbana-Champaign, pp. 175–192.

Rogness, E. C. (1977). "For Export: Accounting Expertise." *Management Accounting* (U.S.) 58: 19–20.

Rostow, W. W. (1956). "The Take-off into Self Sustainable Growth." *Economic Journal* 66: 25–48.

———. (1960). *The Stages of Economic Growth, A Non-Communist Manifesto.* London: Cambridge University Press.

Rydell, F. (1963). "The Accounting Profession in Pakistan, India, Burma and Thailand: A Comparative Study." Institute of Business Administration, University of Karachi, pp. 155–176.

Salas, C. A. (1976). "Accounting Education and Practice in Spanish Latin America." *International Journal of Accounting Education and Research* 3: 67–86.

Samuels, J. M. (1990). "Accounting for Development: An Alternative Approach." In R.S.O. Wallace, J. M. Samuels, and R. J. Briston (eds.), *Research in Third World Accounting* 1, pp. 67–86. London: JAI Press.

Samuels, J. M. and J. C. Oliga (1982). "Accounting Standards in Developing Countries." *International Journal of Accounting Education and Research* 18: 69–88.

Samuels, J. M. and A. G. Piper (1985). *International Accounting: A Survey.* London: Croom Helm.

Scott, G. M. (1986). "Private Sector Enterprise Accounting in Developing Nations." *International Journal of Accounting Education and Research* 14: 51–66.

———. (1970). *Accounting and Developing Nations.* University of Washington Graduate School of Business Administration, Seattle.

Seidler, L. J. (1967a). "International Accounting—The Ultimate Theory Course." *Accounting Review* 4: 775–781.

———. (1967b). *The Function of Accounting in Economic Development: Turkey as a Case Study.* New York: Praeger.

———. (1968). "Teaching Business Administration Overseas: The Case of the Ugly American." *International Journal of Accounting Education and Research* 4: 145–53.

———. (1969). "Nationalism and the International Transfer of Accounting Skills," *International Journal of Accounting Education and Research,* Fall: 35–46.

Seidler, R. E. (1966). "Accounting Information Systems and Underdeveloped Countries." *Accounting Review* 25: 652–656.

Shinawi, A.A.K. and W. F. Crum (1971). "The Emergence of Professional Accounting in Saudi Arabia." *International Journal of Accounting Education and Research* 6: 103–110.

Shuaib, S. A. (1980) "Accounting Information and the Development Planning Process in Kuwait." *International Journal of Accounting Education and Research* 15: 129–141.

Singh, D. R. and B. N. Gupta (1977). "Corporate Financial Disclosure in Indian Companies." *Indian Journal of Accounting,* June and December: 21–37.

Singhvi, S. S. (1967). *Corporate Disclosure through Annual Reports in the USA and India.* Doctoral Dissertation, Graduate School of Business, Columbia University.

———. (1968). "Characteristics and Implications of Inadequate Disclosure: A Case Study of India." *International Journal of Accounting Education and Research* 3: 29–44.

Sishtla, V. S. (1990). "Economic Change under Five-Year Plans and Accounting Education in India." In B. E. Needles, Jr. and V. K. Zimmerman (eds.), *Comparative International Accounting Education Standards.* Center for International Education and Research in Accounting, University of Illinois at Urbana-Champaign, pp. 213–236.

Solomons, D. (1980) "Foreword to AAA Report." In *Accounting Education and the Third World.* Sarasota, Fl.: AAA.

Sombart, W. (1902). *Der moderne Kapitalismus,* 6th ed. Munich and Leipzig (1924).

SyCip, W. (1967). "Professional Practice in Developing Economies." *Journal of Accountancy,* January: 41–45.

———. (1981). "Establishing and Applying Standards in Diverse Economic and Social Environments." In J. C. Burton (ed.), *The International World of Accounting: Challenges and Opportunities* (1980 Proceedings of the Arthur Young Professors' Roundtable), pp. 85–96. Reston, Va.: The Council of Arthur Young Professors' Roundtable.

Tai, B. Y. (1988). "The Accounting Profession in Hong Kong: Problems and Challenges." In V. K. Zimmerman (ed.), *Recent Accounting and Economic Developments in the Far East.* Center for International Education and Research in Accounting, University of Illinois at Urbana-Champaign, pp. 219–228.

Talaga, J. A. and B. Ndubizu (1986). "Accounting and Economics Development: Relationships Among the Paradigms." *International Journal of Accounting Education and Research* 21: 55–68.

Tipgos, M. A. (1987). "A Comprehensive Model for Improving Accounting Education in Developing Countries," in K. Most (ed.), *Advances in International Accounting* 1, 383–404. Greenwich, CT: JAI Press.

United Nations Centre on Transnational Corporations (1985a). *International Accounting and Reporting Issues: 1984 Review.* New York: United Nations.

———. (1985b). *International Accounting and Reporting Issues: 1985 Review.* New York: United Nations.

Vanderdries, R. (1970). "Social Accounting and Its Applications in Peru." *International Journal of Accounting Education and Research* 6: 91–100.

Wallace, R.S.O. (1987). *Disclosure of Accounting Information in Developing Countries: A Case Study of Nigeria.* Doctoral Thesis, University of Exeter.

———. (1988a). "Corporate Financial Reporting in Nigeria." *Accounting and Business Research* 18: 352–362.

———. (1988b). "Intranational and International Consensus on the Importance of Disclosure Items in Financial Reports: A Nigerian Case Study." *British Accounting Review* 20, 223–265.

Walton, P. (1986). "The Export of British Accounting Legislation to Commonwealth Countries." *Accounting and Business Research* 16: 353–357.

Whiteley, J. (1976). "Third World Aid: How and Why Are We Going Wrong?" *Accountancy* 87: 42–44.

Whittle, J. D. (1980). "The Accountancy Profession in Thailand." *Accountant's Magazine,* March: 112–113.

Wilkinson, T. L. (1965). "United States Accounting as Viewed by Accountants of Other Countries." *International Journal of Accounting Education and Research* 1: 3–14.

Winjum, J. O. (1971). "Accounting and the Rise of Capitalism: An Accountants View." *Journal of Accounting Research* 9: 333–350.

———. (1972). *The Role of Accounting in the Economic Development of England 1500–1750.* Center for International Education and Research in Accounting, University of Illinois at Urbana-Champaign.

World Bank (1985). *World Development Report 1985.* New York: Oxford University Press.

Wu, F. H. and D. W. Hackett (1977). "The Internationalization of US Public Accounting Firms: An Empirical Study." *International Journal of Accounting Education and Research* 12: 81–92.

Xu-Ying, Y. (1988). "The General Character of Chinese and U.S. Management Accounting and Analysis of the New Chinese Management Accounting Style." In V. K. Zimmerman (ed.), *Recent Accounting and Economic Developments in the Far East.* Center for International Education and Research in Accounting, University of Illinois at Urbana-Champaign, pp. 51–64.

Yamey, B. S. (1964). "Accounting and the Rise of Capitalism: Further Notes on a Theme by Sombart." *Journal of Accounting Research* 2: 117–136.

Zeff, S. A. (1972). *Forging Accounting Principles in Five Countries.* Champaign, Ill.: Stripes Publishing.

Zhou, Z. H. (1988). "Chinese Accounting Systems and Practices." *Accounting, Organizations and Society* 13: 207–224.

4

Project Appraisal in the Developing Countries

Economic development in the developing countries rests on the quantity and quality of economic, social, and/or political projects that are implemented in the development process. The success of these projects rests also on a proper appraisal and evaluation. Accordingly, this chapter covers the techniques used in both appraisal and evaluation of projects in the developing countries.

COST-BENEFIT ANALYSIS

Nature of Cost-Benefit Analysis

Project appraisal in development planning rests to a large extent on the use of cost-benefit analysis. It is a method used to assess the desirability of projects when it is necessary to take both long and wide views of the impact of a proposed project in the general welfare of a society.[1] A good definition of cost-benefit analysis follows:

> Cost-benefit analysis is a quantitative technique to help guide investment decisions in a systematic fashion. Based on a comparison of the costs and benefits of a particular project or program, it tries to answer the practical questions of whether, on balance, an investment is worthwhile; whether its worth could be increased by altering design parameters such as location, timing, scale, composition, technology, or method of implementation; and whether the policy environment bearing on the project or program is, or could be made, conductive to its successful implementation and operation. Thus, cost-benefit analysis seeks to determine not only if a project can be expected to provide a satisfactory return to the economy, but also if there is an alternative way of achieving the project's objectives that would offer a higher return.[2]

Cost-benefit analysis calls for enumeration and evaluation of all the relevant costs and benefits the project may generate and, above all, for choosing the alternative that maximizes the present value of all benefits less costs, subject to specified constraints and specified objectives. Cost-benefit analysis is useful when all economic impacts of a project, side effects as well as direct effects, have to be considered. It is a favorite method of analysis by governmental agencies for assessing the desirability of particular program expenditures or policy changes. In fact, it has been formally adopted into U.S. federal government budgetary procedures under the Planning-Programming-Budgeting System (PPBS). It acts as a structure of a general theory of government resource allocation. There are five major principles of cost-benefit analysis: (1) What are the objectives and constraints to be considered? (2) Which costs and benefits are to be included? (3) How are the costs and benefits to be valued? (4) What are the investment criteria to be used? (5) Which discount rate should be used?

Objectives and Relevant Constraints of Cost-Benefit Analysis

The main objective of cost-benefit analysis is to determine whether a particular expenditure is economically and socially justifiable. The basic criterion used is an efficiency criterion, such as Pareto optimality. A program is said to be Pareto-efficient if at least one person is made better off and no one is made worse off. The criterion is too impractical for cost-benefit analysis given that few programs are likely to leave some individuals better off and no one worse off. A weaker notion of efficiency, known as the Kaldor-Hides criterion, is generally used for cost-benefit analysis. Under this criterion, also known as the ''potential'' Pareto improvement criterion, a program is acceptable if it is Pareto-optimal or if it could redistribute the net benefits to everyone in the community so that everyone is at least as well off as he or she was before initiation of the program.[3] Basically, a program is efficient and should be undertaken if its total discounted societal benefits exceed the total discounted costs.

Besides the objectives of cost-benefit analysis that are basically to maximize society's wealth, it is important to recognize some of the constraints. Otto Eckstein provided a helpful classification of constraints:[4]

1. *Physical constraints:* The program alternatives considered may be constrained by the state of technology and more generally by the production function, which relates the physical inputs and outputs of a project.
2. *Legal constraints:* The program alternatives considered must be done within the framework of the law. Examples of legal constraints include property rights, time needed for public inquiries, regulated pricing, the right of eminent domain, limits to the activities of public agencies, and so on.
3. *Administrative constraints:* Each of the alternative programs requires the availability and hiring of individuals with the right administrative skills.
4. *Distributational constraints:* Any program is bound to generate gainers and losers.

The unfavorable effects on income distribution may be alleviated by expressing the objective of cost-benefit analysis as either maximizing the excess of total benefits less costs of particular groups, or maximizing the net gain (or minimizing the net loss) to a particular group subject to a constraint relating to total benefits and costs.

5. *Political constraints:* Political considerations may act as constraints, shifting the decision from what is *best* to what is *possible.* Regional differences and presence of various competing interest groups are examples of actors bound to create political constraints on the choice of the best program.
6. *Budgetary constraints:* Capital rationing and evaluating may act as constraints, shifting the objective function from maximizing to suboptimizing of net benefit given a target budget.
7. *Social and religious constraints:* Social and religious taboos are bound to act as constraints, shifting the decision from what is *best* to what is *acceptable.*

Enumeration of Costs and Benefits

Enumeration of costs and benefits is important because it deals with the question of determining which of the costs and benefits of a particular project should be included in a cost-benefit analysis. Benefits and costs may be real or pecuniary. Real benefits are those resulting from changes in total production possibilities and consumption opportunities. For example, if a dam causes a reduction of flooding and a more pleasant scenery, these benefits are real benefits. Pecuniary benefits are those that alter the distribution of total income without changing its volume. They generally take the form of lower input costs, increased volumes of business, or changes in the economy values. Pecuniary benefits and costs result from changes in relative prices occurring as the earning adjusts itself to the production of the public service and the changes in resource demands. Only real benefits and costs should be included in the analysis; pecuniary benefits and costs of a project should be excluded from the enumeration of benefits and costs of a project, because they do not reflect net gains or costs to society as a whole. The point is emphasized as follows:

> As labor is hired and a road is constructed, the wage rates for construction workers may rise because the relative scarcity of their skills is increased. At the same time, increased taxes needed to pay for the road may result in reduced amounts for other services, and a loss of income elsewhere in the system. Such pecuniary changes do not reflect net gains or losses to society because they are matched by offsetting losses or gains. They must be distinguished from real costs and benefits which do. The latter must be allowed for and pecuniary changes should not enter into the evaluation. Such at least is the case unless distributional weights are to be attached to the particular gains or losses which accrue to various individuals, or unless such changes occur outside the jurisdiction within which the project is evaluated.[5]

Briefly, in enumerating the costs and benefits of a project, the analyst must be careful to distinguish their allocative effect from their pecuniary or distributional effects. In fact, the confusion of pecuniary and allocative effects constitutes a primary defect in many analyses of the efficiency of public projects. The only effects that should be taken into account in enumerating the costs and benefits of a public project are the real or technological externalities—that is, those that affect total opportunities for production and consumption, as opposed to pecuniary externalities, which do not affect production or consumption.

Various types of real benefits and costs can be determined. The classifications can be in terms of direct versus indirect, tangible versus intangible, and intermediate versus final benefits and costs.

Benefits and costs can be either direct or indirect. Direct (primary) benefits of a project are those that accrue directly to the users of the service provided by the project. They consist of "the value of goods or services that result from conditions with the project as compared to conditions without the project."[6] Indirect (secondary) benefits are those accruing to entities other than the users of the service provided by the project. Similarly, direct costs are those that are incurred directly by the users of the service provided by the project. They include capital costs, operating and maintenance costs, and personnel expense required by the project.

Benefits and costs can be either tangible or intangible. The tangible benefits and costs are those that can be valued by the market. Although difficult to specify, both intangible benefits and costs should be considered in the analysis.

Benefits and costs can be either intermediate or final. If they provide benefits and income costs directly to the final users, they are final. If they enter in the production of other goods, they are intermediate.

Valuation of Cost and Benefits

In general, benefits should measure the value of the additional goods or services produced or the value of cost savings in the production of goods or services, while costs should measure the value of real resources displaced from other users.

Assuming a competitive economy, the benefits and costs are valued on the basis of the observable market prices of the outputs and inputs of the program. More precisely, the benefits are valued by either the market price of the output of the program or by the amounts the users are willing to pay if they were charged (that is, the consumers' surplus), which is the difference between the aggregate willingness to pay and the costs of the projects. The costs are measured by the monetary expenditures required by the project.

Where market prices do not reflect the value of market transactions to society as a result of externalities, shadow prices, as adjusted input prices, may be used. The general principle for estimating shadow prices for the output of public projects is to stimulate what users would be willing to pay if they were charged as if the goods were sold in perfectly competitive markets. Shadow prices are needed in case of unperfect markets, taxes included in market prices, and unemployed resources.

In valuing costs and benefits of public projects, the following rules must be followed:

- Only real costs and benefits should be included and pecuniary costs and benefits should be excluded.
- Both direct and indirect costs and benefits should be included.
- Valuation of intangible benefits and costs is more difficult than and poses problems similar to those caused by the valuation of social goods.
- Intermediate-type benefits can be valued more readily than benefits of the final type.
- Even if intangible benefits can not be valued readily, cost-effectiveness analysis may be helpful.
- Shadow pricing corrects for distributions introduced by monopoly, taxes, and unemployed resources.[7]

Investment Criteria

Cost-benefit analysis is a method used to evaluate long-term projects. As such, the benefits and costs of each project have to discounted to be comparable at time 0 when evaluation and decisions on the projects have to be made. There is a need to rely on some form of discounting in the choice of investment criteria. There are three possible investment or decision criteria.

The first is the net present value method. Under this method the present value of a project is obtained by discounting the net excess of benefits (B_t) over costs (C_t) for each year during the life of the project back to the present time using a social discount rate. More explicitly,

$$V = \sum_{t=1}^{\alpha} \frac{B_t - C_t}{(1 + r)^t} \tag{4.1}$$

where

B = Value of the project

B_t = Benefit in year t

C_t = Cost in year t

r = Social discount rate

α = Life of the project

Basically, a project is found acceptable if the present value *V* is positive. If there are binding constraints on a project (for example, budget appropriation, foreign exchange, private investment opportunity foregone), then the following model proposed by George Steiner[8] would be more appropriate:

$$V = \sum_{t=1}^{\alpha} \frac{B_t - C_t}{(1 + +r)^t} - \sum_{j=1}^{n} p_j k_j \tag{4.2}$$

where

P_j = Shadow price of a binding constraint
K_j = Number of units of a constrained resource

Second is the benefit/cost ratio. Under this method the decision criterion is expressed in terms of the ratio of the present value of benefits to the present value of costs (both discounted at the social discount). More explicitly, the benefit/cost ratio is:

$$\frac{\sum_{t=1}^{\alpha} \frac{b_t}{(1 + r)^t 1'}}{\sum_{t=1}^{\alpha} \frac{c_t}{(1 + r)^t}} = 0. \tag{4.3}$$

Basically, all projects that are not mutually exclusive with a benefit/cost ratio in excess of 1 are acceptable.

Last is the internal rate of return. Under this method the decision criterion is expressed in terms of the internal rate of return; that is, the discount rate will equate the net benefits over the life of the project with the original cost. In other words, 2 is the rate of interest for which

$$\sum_{t=1}^{\alpha} \frac{b_t}{(1 + r)^t} - \sum_{t=1}^{\alpha} \frac{C_t}{(1 + r)^t} = 0 \tag{4.4}$$

Basically, all projects with an internal rate of return that exceeds the closer social discount rate are deemed acceptable.

Choice of a Discount Rate

The choice of a discount rate is important for at least two reasons. A high rate will mitigate against the firm or the government undertaking the project, while a low rate may make the project more acceptable from a return point of view. Furthermore, a low discount rate tends to favor projects yielding net benefits further into the future relative to projects yielding more current net benefits. Choosing the appropriate interest rate therefore becomes an important policy question. There are several possible alternative rates.

The first is the marginal productivity of capital in private investment. Given that the discount rate allows the allocation of resources between the public and private sectors, it should be chosen so that it indicates when resources should be transferred from one sector to another. This means that the discount rate should represent the opportunity cost of funds withdrawn from the private sector to be used in the public sector. As William Baumol states, "the correct discount rate for the evaluation of a government project is the percentage rate of return that the resources utilized would otherwise provide in the private sector."[9]

The following considerations enter into the choice of the marginal productivity of capital as a discount rate: an effort to minimize governmental activity, a concern for efficiency, and a belief that the source of funds for government investment in the private sector will displace private investment that would otherwise be made.[10]

Second is the social rate of time preference, which expresses a concern for future generations in the sense that the welfare of future generations will be increased if investments are made now. It follows that the discount rate should be the social rate of time preference—that is, the compensation required to induce consumers to refrain from consumption and to save. One study committee argued that the federal government should use the "administration's social rate of time discount" to be established by the president in consultation with advisors such as the Council of Economic Advisers.[11] The strongest argument for the social rate of time preference was made by A. C. Pigou, when he suggested that individuals were short-sighted about the future ("defective telescopic faculty") and the welfare of future generations would require governmental intervention.[12]

Advantages and Limitations of Cost-Benefit Analysis

There are thousands of cost-benefit analyses of government projects. The popularity of the method is a witness to some of its advantages; there are also some limitations well recognized in the literature. Among the advantages are: (1) It has been pointed out that cost-benefit analysis is most effective in dealing with cases of intermediate social goods.[13] (2) It established a framework for a reasonably consistent evaluation of alternative projects, especially where the choice set is narrow in the sense that the projects are not only similar but generate the same volume of externalities. (3) It allows decisions to be made that are most advantageous in terms of the objectives accepted. Among the limitations are: (1) There are limits within which social objectives can be measured in money terms. An example of nonefficiency objectives that are not measurable in dollar terms is an equitable distribution of income. (2) Cost-benefit analysis falls under what is known as partial equilibrium analysis. It is useful in evaluating only those projects that have negligible impact outside the immediately affected areas of the economy. (3) There are obvious problems of enumeration and evaluation of the costs and benefits of particular projects.[14] A committee of the U.S. House of Representatives, pointing to the difficulty inherent in estimating the direct effects of a policy and assigning dollar terms to them, argued that such estimates are seldom accurate.[15] Similarly, Michael Baram cites an inappropriate treatment of factors that transcend economies.[16]

Other Issues in Cost-Benefit Analysis

These issues include the following:

1. Because projects may be incurred to meet a number of objectives, different types of benefits and costs are generated. In evaluating these projects, relative weight should be attributed to the benefits and costs to reflect the different importance of the objectives. The use of distributional weights in cost-benefit analysis is used as a means of distributional connection. They are specified and entered into the objective function defining the social welfare to be maximized. Such an objective function can be specified as follows:

$$W_s = \alpha \sum_{i=1}^{m} (G_i - L_i) + \beta \sum_{j=n}^{z} (G_j - L_j) \qquad (4.5)$$

where gains G and losses L of individuals a to n are given weight α, while those of individuals n to z are given weight β.[17] The weights may be assigned as follows:

> In specifying the weights to be assigned to consumption gains accruing to different income levels, a distinction between only a few levels may suffice. The weights may be made consistently progressive—the lower the income level, the greater the weight, with a weight of unity being given to the national per capita level. Alternatively, equal weights may be assigned to all income groups except the lowest. The traditional practice of assigning equal weights to all income levels is clearly a special case.[18]

2. Projects can be divisible projects in the sense that they may be increased and decreased by small amounts, or lumpy projects. Efficient use of scarce resources dictates a different approach to both projects. The following rules are suggested:

- Where projects are freely divisible the best solution is reached by equating the marginal benefits from the last dollar in each project (where the budget is fixed) and in public and private projects (where the budget total is open).

- Lumpy projects in a fixed budget should be chosen so as to maximize the sum of net benefits. In an open budget such projects should be adopted as long as total benefits exceed costs.[19]
- The outcomes of public projects are not always of certain value. Make allowance for risky outcomes, the benefits may be weighted by probabilities that sum to zero. The expected value of the benefits E(B) are then expended as follows:

$$E(B) = p_1B_1 + p_2B_2 + \ldots p_nB_n \text{ where } p_1 + p_2 \ldots + p_n = 1 \qquad (4.6)$$

In cases where the probabilities are not known, R. Dorfman suggests the use of various techniques derived from game theory.[20]

Particular Issues for the Developing Countries

Institutional analysis is as important as technical economic and financial analyses. Institutions are vital to the implementation of projects and the efficient safeguarding of the resources devoted to the project. Problems facing project institutions include scale management, poor financial control, and lack of training to name only a few. Obstacles facing project institutions include a counterproductive policy environment, complex objectives fixed for projects, and overemphasis on the short-term implementations of new investments.[21] Strong project institutions are needed to obscure these problems. As described by Baum and Tolbert,

> new institutions have to take root in their societies and adapt their plans for change and modernization to their cultural milieu. Technical and managerial competence must be improved gradually, to bring about effective policy planning, work programming, financial and personnel management, and all the other essential functions of modern organization.[22]

In addition to technical, economic, and financial analyses, a social analysis of the project is generally required to ensure the suitability of the project. The following constitute social analysis:

- The sociocultural and demographic characteristics of a project population—its size and social structure, including ethnic, tribal and class composition
- The way in which the project population has organized itself to carry out productive activities, including the structure of households and family, availability of labor, ownership of land, and access to and control of resources
- The project's cultural acceptability; that is, its capacity both for adapting to and for bringing about desirable changes in people's behavior and in how they perceive their needs
- The strategy necessary to elicit commitment from the project population and to ensure

their sustained anticipation from design through to successful implementation, operation, and maintenance.[23]

The recovery of costs of a project is important for the sake of equity among citizens. As stated by Baum and Tolbert, "failure to recoup these costs from the users—through some form of price, tax, or other charge—creates a privileged class of beneficiaries, who in effect receive a subsidy or income transfer from the rest of society, while it deprives the project entity of resources that could be used to extend the product or service to additional users."[24] Basically, the users and beneficiaries of the project need to pay back the costs.[25]

The role of prices is important to any macroeconomic policy agenda, by efficiently allocating and mobilizing resources. The developing countries' experiences with pricing policies reveal serious distortion of prices as a result of a multiplicity of government actions or policies, many of them ill-considered.[26] These distortions result from:

- Overvalued exchange rate, especially when the governments are reluctant to devalue their currencies appropriately in order to ease the trade and payments problems.
- Overpricing of industrial products above world market levels, especially as a result of import restrictions.
- Underpricing of agricultural products that also slows agricultural growth.
- Underpricing of capital resulting from low and controlled interest rates as well as credit rationing.
- Overpricing of labor resulting from the encouragement of trade union activities and the promotion of minimum wage legislation to provide an "adequate" income for workers.
- Underpricing of infrastructural services such as power and transport determined by a public authority rather than the market.
- High and accelerating inflation affecting the efficiency of resource allocation.[27]

PROJECT RESULT ASSESSMENT: PROJECT EVALUATION

One way to assess the results of projects is to make an evaluation judgment about the worth of the project. This evaluation judgment is explicated as follows:

This judgement often is arrived at by grading or by ranking something according to how well the object fulfills a set of standards or criteria. Evaluation is essentially comparative, and usually explicitly so. This means there must be a set of standards and a class to which the object is compared. If the object is graded as "good" or "bad," the class of comparison is the entire class of objects or the average object of the class. If the object is ranked as "best" or "worst," it is compared directly to a particular subset of similar objects, e.g., a car compared to four other cars in its price range.[28]

Evaluation of projects requires setting standards and a final comparison of actual results against these standards. There are various approaches to evaluation.[29] Exhibit 4.1 presents a taxonomy of major evaluation models. Each model can be applied to the evaluation of projects in the developing countries. Each model favored by different groups proposes a different way of defining the criteria and/or standards of output, and of comparing the end results to the standards.

PROJECT RESULT ASSESSMENT: VALUE-FOR-MONEY AUDITING

Nature of Value-for-Money Auditing

Value for money is associated in Canada with the comprehensive auditing concept. The Canadian Comprehensive Auditing Foundation's *Comprehensive Auditing: Concepts, Components and Characteristics* provides the following definition:

A comprehensive audit is an examination that provides an objective and constructive assessment of the extent to which:

- Financial, human and physical resources are managed with due regard to economy, efficiency and effectiveness; and
- accountability relationships are reasonably reserved. The comprehensive audit examines both financial and management controls, including information systems and reporting practices, and recommends improvements where appropriate.[30]

The concept rests on two principles:

1. Principle I: Public business should be conducted in a way that makes the best possible use of public funds.
2. Principle II: Those who conduct public business should be accountable for the prudent and effective management of the resources entrusted to them.[31]

Comprehensive auditing invokes financial statement auditing, compliance auditing, and value-for-money auditing. Financial statement auditing is aimed at assuring that management assertions in the financial statements of the public projects are complete and accurate. Compliance auditing is aimed at providing assurance of the authority and legality attending the management of public projects. Finally, value-for-money auditing is aimed at providing assurance that the projects have been managed economically and efficiently and the results have been effective. Value-for-money auditing focuses on

- economy in the sense of obtaining the appropriate quality and quantity of goods and services from the project at the appropriate time and at the best prices.

Exhibit 4.1

A Taxonomy of Major Evaluation Approaches

Model	*Major Audiences or Reference Groups*	*Assumes Consensus On*	*Methodology*	*Outcome*	*Typical Questions*
Systems analysis	Economists, managers	Goals, known cause and effect, quantified variables	PPBS, linear programming, planned variation, cost-benefit analysis	Efficency	Are the expected effects achieved? Can the effects be achieved more economically? What are the *most* efficient programs?
Behavioral objectives	Managers, psychologists	Prespecified objectives, quantified outcome variables	Behavioral objectives, achievement tests	Productivity, accountability	Is the program achieving the objectives? Is the program producing?
Decision-making	Decision-makers, especially administrators	General goals, criteria	Surveys, questionnaires, interviews, natural variation	Effectiveness, quality control	Is the program effective? What parts are effective?
Goal-free	Consumers	Consequences, criteria	Bias control, logical analysis, modus operandi	Consumer choice, social utility	What are *all* the effects?
Art criticism	Connoisseurs, consumers	Critics, standards	Critical review	Improved standards, heightened awareness	Would a critic approve this program? Is the audience's appreciation increased?
Professional review	Professionals, public	Criteria, panel, procedures	Review by panel, self study	Professional acceptance	How would professionals rate this program?
Quasi-legal	Jury	Procedures and judges	Quasi-legal procedures	Resolution	What are the arguments for and against the program?
Case study	Client, practitioners	Negotiations, activities	Case studies, interviews, observations	Understanding diversity	What does the program look like to different people?

Source: Ernest R. House, *Evaluating with Validity* © 1980 by Sage Publications (Beverly Hills, Calif.) p. 23. Reprinted by permission of Sage Publications, Inc.

- efficiency in the sense of achieving the best possible productive use of goods, people, and money, and its assessment leads to an examination of performance measures and similar productivity indicators.
- effectiveness in the sense of insuring that the projects deliver what they were intended to do.[32]

Value-for-money auditing consists of economy efficiency and effectiveness. There is a distinction between auditing in the financial field on the basis of rigorous auditing technique and auditing in the area of effectiveness on the basis of subjective techniques. Pomeranz et al. made the same distinction: ''Efficiency and economy audits can be undertaken by highly specified detailed and structured examinations, while program effectiveness involves subjective judgements, although an efficiency and economy audit may shed some light on program effectiveness, additional measures are needed to determine if a program or activity objective are being met.''[33]

The distinction between economy and efficiency audit and effectiveness audit is also emphasized by the U.S. General Accounting Office (GAO), which views an audit as comprising the following three elements: financial and compliance, economy and efficiency, and program results.

Level I (Financial and compliance)

An examination of financial transactions, accounts and reports, including an evaluation of compliance with applicable laws and regulations. (Purpose: to evaluate whether operations and resources are properly accounted for and presented in reports and whether legal requirements are being met.)

Level II (Economy and efficiency)

A review of efficiency and economy in the use of resources. (Purpose: to evaluate whether the management operates with due regard to conserving its monetary, property and human resources.)

Level III (Program results)

A review to determine whether desired results are effectively achieved. (Purpose: to evaluate the extent to which statutory or other goals are being achieved and whether alternative methods of operation should be considered.)[34]

In fact, the GAO refers to performance audits as a similar concept to the value-for-money audit referred to in Canada. Similarly to value-for-money audits, performance audits include economy, efficiency, and program audits, defined as follows:

a. Economy and efficiency audits include determining (1) whether the entity is acquiring, protecting, and using its resources (such as personnel, property, and space) economically and efficiently, (2) the causes of inefficiencies or uneconomical practices, and

(3) whether the entity has complied with laws and regulations concerning matters of economy and efficiency.

b. Program audits include determining (1) the extent to which the desired results or benefits established by the legislature of another authorizing body are being achieved, (2) the effectiveness of organizations, programs, activities, or functions, and (3) whether the entity has complied with laws and regulations applicable to the program.[35]

The office of the Auditor General of Canada has developed the acronym FRAME, which identifies and explains the components of a value-for-money audit (or, in their terms, "Comprehensive Audit"):

F *Financial Controls*—an evaluation of the controls over revenues, expenditures, assets and liabilities, including the organization of the financial function and its place in the general management structure; the qualifications and suitability of financial personnel to the needs of the organization; the appropriateness of the accounting systems and procedures, and the appropriateness and adequacy of budgeting and financial reporting systems.

R *Reporting to Parliament*—an evaluation of the nature, content, adequacy, reliability and timeliness of financial and related nonfinancial information presented in reports to Parliament. The principal formal reports to Parliament include the Estimates, the Public Accounts and the Auditor General's Annual Report.

A *Attest and Authority*—the expression of an opinion on financial statements and the verification of parliamentary and governmental authority for expenditures.

M *Management Control*—an evaluation of the system of management information and controls, including the internal audit/evaluation/review functions, so as to ensure there is due regard to economy and efficiency and that appropriate procedures to evaluate and report on programme effectiveness, where such are feasible, are in place and operating satisfactorily—in short, value for money auditing.

E *EDP Controls*—an evaluation of controls over financial and other information processed by computers and for management controls over the use of computer related sources.[36]

The acronym is exhaustive in the sense that it brings together all the characteristics required by value for money auditing. Value for money auditing needs to be coordinated, cyclical, and constructive.[37]

Economy and Efficiency Auditing

Economy and efficiency are the first two objectives of value-for-money auditing. Economy is a concern with the acquisition of resources of the right quality at a minimum cost. Efficiency is a concern with reaching the maximum output for a minimum input. It is different from productivity. The *Audit Guide* on efficiency produced by the office of the Auditor General of Canada draws the following important distinction between efficiency and productivity:

- productivity is the arithmetical ratio between the amount of goods or services produced and the amount of resources used in the course of production—the ratio between output and input.
- Efficiency is the relationship of actual output/input (productivity) to a performance standard. This relationship is usually expressed as a percentage.[38]

Efficiency is best measured by a rate of return on production. It is a unit cost of a finished good or service. It is measured at standard and compared to actual performance.

Effectiveness Auditing

Effectiveness judgments involve value judgments that can change depending on the time, the environment, the ideology, and the temperaments of individuals, to cite only a few factors. Forming effectiveness judgments calls for a reliance on various attributes, generally thought to be important to the understanding of effectiveness. The following list of attributes has been provided for effectiveness:

- *management direction:* the extent to which the objectives of an organization, its component programs or lines of business, and its employees are clear, well-integrated and understood, and appropriately reflected in the organization's plans, structure, delegations of authority and decision-making processes
- *relevance:* the extent to which a program or line of business continues to make sense in regard to the problems or conditions to which it is intended to respond
- *appropriateness:* the extent to which the design of a program or its major components, and the level of effort being made, are logical in light of the specific objectives to be achieved
- *achievement of intended results:* the extent to which goals and objectives have been realized
- *acceptance:* the extent to which the constituencies or customers for whom a program or line of business is designed judge it to be satisfactory
- *secondary impacts:* the extent to which other significant consequences, either intended or unintended and either positive or negative, have occurred
- *costs and productivity:* the relationships among costs, inputs and outputs
- *responsiveness:* an organization's ability to adapt to changes in such factors as markets, competition, available funding or technology
- *financial results:* the matching of, and the accounting for, revenues and costs and the accounting for and valuation of assets, liabilities and equity

Exhibit 4.2
Categories of Service Efforts and Accomplishments Indicators

A. Indicators of Service Efforts

1. Inputs—Dollar costs of the service during the period.
   a. In "current" dollars.
   b. In "constant" dollars, that is, adjusted for price level changes.
   c. Per household or per capita, and in either current or constant dollars.
2. Inputs—Amounts of *non*monetary resources expended, especially the amount of work time expended during the period (for the service). These might be expressed in such units as full-time-equivalent years or employee-hours.

B. Indicators of Service Accomplishments

1. Outputs—Amount of workload accomplished.
2. Outcomes—A numeric indicator of program results. This category includes indicators of service quality (such as timeliness), effectiveness, and amount or proportion of "need" that is (or is not) being served.

C. Indicators That Relate Service Efforts to Service Accomplishments
(These can also be labeled efficiency indicators,[a] which for the purposes of this report include both input/output and input/outcome indicators.)

1. Amount of input related to (divided by) amount of *output.* "Input" can be any of the variations included under Section A, and "output" refers to B.1, not B.2.
2. Amount of input related to (divided by) amount of *outcomes or results.* Again, "input" can be any of the variations noted in Section A. "Outcome" refers only to B.2, not B.1.

- *working environment:* the extent to which the organization provides an appropriate work atmosphere for its employees, provides appropriate opportunities for development and achievement, and promotes commitment, initiative and safety
- *protection of assets:* the extent to which important assets—such as sources of supply, valuable property, key personnel, agreements, and important records or information—are safeguarded so that the organization is protected from the danger of losses that could threaten its success, credibility, continuity and, perhaps, its very existence
- *monitoring and reporting:* the extent to which key matters pertaining to performance and organizational strength are identified, reported and carefully monitored.[39]

Information about all these attributes can allow one to form a good judgment about the effectiveness of an organization.

Exhibit 4.2 *(continued)*

3. Productivity (or efficiency) *indexes.* These traditionally have been used in reporting national productivity trends. Indexes are calculated by relating the ratio of productivity in the current year to that of a preselected base year. These indexes have the advantage that the productivity ratios for different activities for a service, or across services, can be combined by weighting each ratio by the amount of input for each activity.

D. Explanatory Information

This is a term used to cover a variety of information relevant to a service that helps users understand the performance on the SEA indicators and factors affecting an organization's performance. The explanatory information should be grouped into two categories:

1. Elements substantially outside the control of the public agency, such as demographic characteristics.
2. Elements over which the agency has significant control, such as staffing patterns.

Source: Governmental Accounting Standards Board, *Service Efforts and Accomplishments Reporting: Its Time Has Come, An Overview* (Norwalk, Conn.: GASB, 1990), pp. 12–13. Reprinted with permission.

Management Representations in Effectiveness

The public in the developing counties relied on better information about the effectiveness, efficiency, and economy of public projects. The managers of these public projects provided information in the form of representation that can help the public form judgments about the economy, efficiency, and effectiveness of public projects. These management representations are a key to the value-for-money auditing.[40] By providing representations, managers provide information about effectiveness that can be audited by auditors who can offer opinions about the fairness of these representations.[41]

These management representations on the effectiveness of public projects will be useful to the auditors, to the government bodies and to the general public. These representations are audited for their fairness, resulting in an audit assurance. The audit assurance becomes the ultimate and final test on the effectiveness of the public project, assuring the auditors have abided by a strong test of independence. Because an audit follows the management representations, the following guidelines have been offered for making representations:

Exhibit 4.3

Recommended SEA Indicators for Colleges and Universities

Indicator	Rationale for Selecting Indicator
Input:	
Instructional Expenditures: Current dollars Constant dollars	To provide a measure of the resources used to provide instruction
Number of Faculty: Full-time Total FTE	To provide a measure of the number of faculty available to provide instruction
Output:	
Number of Degrees and Certificates Awarded	To provide a measure of students satisfactorily completing educational requirements
Number of Student Credit Hours (SCH) Generated: Unweighted Weighted	To provide a measure of work load and productivity (Weighting can be used to equate differences among disciplines and course levels.)
Number of FTE Students (fall semester)	To provide a measure of work load and productivity; FTE students are derived from student credit hours
Outcomes:	
Academic Test Scores: General education National exams Average percentile score Percentage scoring above 50th percentile Local exams Average score Percentage scoring 70% or above	To provide direct measures of student learning across the general education field, and comparisons with selected standards

Indicator	Purpose
Major field National exams Average percentile score Percentage scoring above 50th percentile Local exams Average score Percentage scoring 70% or above	To provide direct measures of students' learning in their chosen fields of study, and comparisons with selected standards
Student Ratings of Select Aspects of College,† e.g.: Help in reaching select goals Increasing knowledge in major field Learning life-enriching skills Improving self-image Improving leadership skills Adequacy of general education program in developing: Effective writing and speaking skills/habits Independent work skills/habits Understanding of different philosophies and cultures Ability to define, analyze, and solve problems Adequacy of academic major program in areas such as: Gaining knowledge of issues and trends pertinent to specialty Applying knowledge in defining and solving problems Identifying values and responding ethically Integrating career and personal goals	To provide student perceptions of the quality of instruction and guidance received; both cognitive and noncognitive dimensions are addressed

The recommended indicators presented in this exhibit are illustrative. They are intended to serve as a starting point for use in the development of a comprehensive set of SEA indicators for external reporting of an entity's results of operation.

This exhibit does not provide illustrations of indicator disaggregation or of comparison data such as trends, targets, or other comparable entities. Both disaggregation and comparison data are important aspects of SEA reporting. They are discussed in the chapter and in the Overview.

†These sample criteria were taken or adapted from survey instruments used at Northeast Missouri State University.

Exhibit 4.3 *(continued)*

Indicator	Rationale for Selecting Indicator
Outcomes: (continued)	
Alumni Ratings of Select Aspects of Their Instruction Program,† such as: Overall impression of general education courses Overall impression of courses in major field Overall quality of instruction in major Overall quality of faculty academic advising Help in achieving occupational goals	To provide alumni perceptions of the quality of instruction received (*Note:* Some institutions may also wish to obtain responses to some or all the questions asked of students per the above measure, providing a "second look" perspective.)
Licensure and Certification Exam Results Number Taking Exams Percentage Passing Exams	To provide a measure of student success in meeting criteria established by professional groups; also, can suggest currentness and relevance of curricula
Retention/Graduation Rates, such as: Percentage of entering first-time, full-time freshmen still enrolled/graduated after 4 years 5 years 6 years	To provide a measure of success in retaining students until they complete their degree objective (*Note:* Similar measures can be developed for two-year and certificate programs.)
Employment and Graduate Study Rates, such as: After one year, percentage of graduates' indicating: They were currently employed full-time They were currently enrolled in a program of study	To provide measures of student success in obtaining employment and student interest in further study as evidenced by enrollment in programs of study

Employers' Satisfaction[†] with Graduates': Knowledge/skills specific to the job Reading and writing skills Work attitudes General academic preparation Overall rating of the graduate	To provide a measure of employer satisfaction with graduates
Efficiency Measures:	
Instructional Expenditures/Student Credit Hour (SCH): Unweighted Weighted	To provide a measure of the cost of generating a unit of output; measures one dimension of efficiency
FTE Students/FTE Faculty (fall semester): Unweighted Weighted	To provide a measure of work load and productivity; measures one dimension of efficiency
Explanatory Data:	
Role and Mission Statement State Appropriations: Total Per FTE student Average Class Size Other: Faculty data Enrollment data Entering-student test scores Listing of degree programs Other explanatory data and notes as needed	To provide information on factors that affect student learning and development, and the efficiency and effectiveness with which instructional services are delivered

Source: Governmental Accounting Standards Board, *Service Efforts and Accomplishments Reporting: Its Time Has Come, An Overview* (Norwalk, Conn.: GASB, 1990). Reprinted with permission.

Exhibit 4.4

Recommended SEA Indicators for Economic Development: Business Attraction/Marketing Programs

Indicator	Rationale for Selecting Indicator
Inputs:	
Dollars spent on the program's activities (current and constant dollars)	Provide information on the resources available to the program
Number of staff-hours expended by the program	
Outputs:	
Number and percentage of business prospects identified that may be interested in locating	Measure of the program's outreach function
Number of businesses from target industries identified that are interested in locating	Identifies success with targeted industries
Number of contacts made with firms interested in locating	Measure of program follow-up
Number of firms that received assistance from the program (by type of assistance)	Provides indication of the number of actual program clients
Percentage of leverage (nongovernmental) funds used to finance project	Estimate of amount of other funds leveraged by a project

Outcomes:	
Intermediate outcomes:	
Number of visits by interested businesses that received assistance	Measures important intermediate response by clients
Number and percentage of responses to advertising or direct mail solicitations	Provides information on number of potentially interested businesses
Longer-term outcomes:	
Number and percentage of firms that received assistance and located elsewhere	Indication of program failures
Number and percentage of firms receiving assistance that located in jurisdiction and that felt that assistance contributed to their location decision	Major performance indicator for the program; measures the contribution of services to the observed outcomes
Number of actual jobs created by assistance 12 months/24 months after their initial contact with the program (and comparison with projected number of jobs to be created)	Major stated goal of business attraction programs
Average wage of jobs created by locating firms that receive assistance	Partial measure of job "quality"
Dollars of capital investment made by locating firms receiving assistance 12 months/ 24 months after the announcement of their location decision	Provides an indication of the local economic impact of the firm location

The recommended indicators presented in this exhibit are illustrative. They are intended to serve as a starting point for use in the development of a comprehensive set of SEA indicators for external reporting of an entity's results of operation.

This exhibit does not provide illustrations of indicator disaggregation or of comparison data such as trends, targets, or other comparable entities. Both disaggregation and comparison data are important aspects of SEA reporting. They are discussed in the Economic Development Programs chapter and in the Overview.

Exhibit 4.4 *(continued)*

Indicator	Rationale for Selecting Indicator
Outcomes (continued):	
Amount of added tax revenues relating to assisted firms that located in the jurisdiction	Government return on investment in the program
Percentage of clients rating the *timeliness* of each service they received as excellent, good, fair, or poor	Service quality indicator
Percentage of clients rating the *helpfulness* of each service they received as excellent, good, fair, or poor	Service quality indicator
Percentage of clients locating elsewhere for reasons over which agency had some influence	Indicates potential problems within the program or agency
Estimated number of workers displaced by assisted firms that located	Measures a negative impact of business attraction programs
Efficiency:	
Program expenditures per actual job created at 12 months/24 months after receiving assistance	Measures program costs for each job created
Program expenditures per estimated tax dollar generated by client firms	Compares program expenditures with direct return through taxes

Source: Governmental Accounting Standards Board, *Service Efforts and Accomplishments Reporting: Its Time Has Come, An Overview* (Norwalk, Conn.: GASB, 1990). Reprinted with permission.

Guideline 1: All applicable attributes of effectiveness should be considered in making management representations, and an explanation should be given where any attribute otherwise expected is not used.

Guideline 2: Representations should reflect the full range of information generated in their preparation and contain whatever explanations or qualifications about the information and analysis that may be necessary to allow users to make informed judgments.

Guideline 3: Representations should be prepared in such a way as to take into account the interests of governing bodies.

Guideline 4: Representations should be made at the highest meaningful level, and to accomplish this, top management must be involved in preparing them.

Guideline 5: Each organization should establish a comprehensive strategy for reporting management representations on effectiveness over an agreed period of time.[42]

The management representations should include the service efforts and accomplishments (SEA) of the project. The categories of SEA indicators are expected to include input indicators, output indicators, outcome indicators, efficiency (and cost-effectiveness) indicators, and explanatory information. A suggested definition of these categories follows:

1. *Input indicators.* These are designed to report the amount of the resources, either financial or other (especially personnel), that have been used for a specific service or program. Input indicators are ordinarily presented in budget submissions and sometimes external management reports.
2. *Output indicators.* These report units produced or services provided by a service or program.
3. *Outcome indicators.* These are designed to report the results (including quality) of the service. Examples of outcome indicators are the change in students' test scores, the percentage of hypertensives treated who now have controlled blood pressure, and the value of property lost due to crime.
4. *Efficiency (and cost-effectiveness) indicators.* These are defined as indicators that measure the cost (whether in dollars or employee-hours) per unit of output or outcome. Examples are cost per million gallons of drinking water delivered to consumers, or cost per thousand gallons of effluent treated to a certain level of quality.
5. *Explanatory information.* This includes a variety of information about the environment and other factors that might affect an organization's performance on SEA indicators. Examples would be weather conditions for road maintenance, percentage of students with English as a second language for education, or quality of source water for water service.[43]

Examples of categories of service efforts and accomplishment indicators are shown in Exhibit 4.2. Recommended SEA indicators for colleges and universities and economic development programs are shown in Exhibits 4.3 and 4.4.

CONCLUSION

Project appraisal and evaluation are essential to the success of projects in particular and economic development in general in the developing countries. This chapter elaborated on cost-benefit analysis as used in project appraisal, and on project evaluation and value-for-money auditing as used in project assessment.

NOTES

1. A. R. Prest, and R. Turvey, "Cost-Benefit Analysis: A Survey," *The Economic Journal* (December 1965), pp. 683–735.
2. Warren C. Baum, and Stokes M. Tolbert, *Investing in Development: Lessons of World Bank Experience* (Oxford: Oxford University Press, 1985).
3. Another test for potential Pareto improvements is that everyone in society could be made better off by means of a costless redistribution of the net benefits.
4. Otto Eckstein, "A Survey of the Theory of Public Expenditure Criteria," in James M. Buchanan, ed., *Public Finances: Needs, Sources and Utilization* (Princeton, N.J.: Princeton University Press, 1961).
5. Richard A. Musgrave, and Peggy B. Musgave, *Public Finance in Theory and Practice,* 5th ed. (New York: McGraw-Hill, 1989), p. 138.
6. Jesse Burkhead and Jerry Miner, *Public Expenditure* (Chicago: Aldine-Atherton, 1971), p. 255.
7. Musgrave and Musgrave, *Public Finance in Theory and Practice,* pp. 161–162.
8. George A. Steiner, "Problems in Implementing Program Budgeting," in David Novic, ed. *Program Budgeting* (Cambridge, Mass.: Harvard University Press, 1965), pp. 87–88.
9. William J. Baumol, "On the Discount Rate for Public Projects," in Robert and Julius Margolis, eds., *Public Expenditures and Policy Analysis* (Chicago: Markham, 1970), p. 274.
10. Burkhead and Miner, *Public Expenditure,* p. 232.
11. Report of Panel of Consultants, Bureau of the Budget, *Standards and Criteria for Formulating and Evaluating Federal Water Resources Development* (Washington, D.C., 1961), p. 67.
12. A. C. Pigou, *The Economics of Welfare,* 4th ed. (London: Macmillan, 1932).
13. R. A. Musgrave, *Fiscal Systems* (New Haven, Conn.: Yale University Press, 1969), pp. 797–806.
14. Prest and Turvey, "Cost-Benefit Analysis," pp. 729–731.
15. U.S. House of Representatives, Committee on Interstate and Foreign Commerce, Subcommittee on Oversight and Investigations, *Federal and Regulation and Regulatory Reform (1976),* Chap. 15, 94th Cong., 2nd sess., (Subcommittee print).
16. Michael S. Baram, "Cost Benefit Analysis: An Inadequate Basis for Health, Safety, and Environmental Regulatory Decision-Making," *Ecology Law Quarterly* 8 (1980), pp. 473–531.
17. Musgrave and Musgrave, *Public Finance in Theory and Practice,* p. 149.

18. Anandarup Ray, *Cost-Benefit Analysis: Issues and Methodologies* (Baltimore: John Hopkins University Press, 1984), p. 17.

19. Musgrave and Musgrave, *Public Finance in Theory and Practice,* p. 161.

20. R. Dorfman, "Decision Rules under Uncertainty," in R. Layand, ed., *Cost-Benefit Analysis: Selected Readings* (Baltimore: Penguin, 1972), Ch. 15.

21. Baum, and Tolbert, *Investing in Development,* p. 501.

22. Ibid.

23. Ibid., p. 474.

24. Ibid.

25. Ibid., p. 452.

26. Ibid., p. 33.

27. Ibid., pp. 34–42.

28. Ernest R. House, *Evaluating with Validity* (Beverly Hills, Calif.: Sage, 1980), p. 18.

29. Ibid., p. 27.

30. Canadian Comprehensive Auditing Foundation, *Comprehensive Auditing: Concepts, Components and Characteristics* (Ottawa, 1981), p. 8.

31. Canadian Comprehensive Auditing Foundation, *Value for Money in Municipalities* (Ottawa, 1984), p. 8.

32. Ibid., p. 13.

33. F. Pomeranz, A. Cancellieri, J. Stevens, and J. Savage, *Auditing in the Public Sector* (New York: Warren, Gorham and Lamont, 1976).

34. Martin Grimmood, and Cyril Tomkins, "Value for Money Auditing—Towards Incorporating a Naturalistic Approach," *Financial Accountability and Management* (Winter 1986), p. 253.

35. U.S. General Accounting Office, *Government Accounting Standards* (July 1988), pp. 2–3 and 2–4.

36. John J. Glynn, *Value for Money Auditing in the Public Sector* (Englewood Cliffs, N.J., Prentice-Hall, 1985), pp. 22–23.

37. Ibid., p. 81.

38. Office of the Auditor General of Canada, *Audit Guide: Auditing the Efficiency* (Ottawa, 1981), p. 2.

39. Canadian Comprehensive Auditing Foundation, *Effectiveness: Reporting and Auditing in the Public Sector* (Ottawa, 1987), pp. 22–23.

40. Ibid., p. 11.

41. Ibid., p. 69.

42. Ibid.

43. Government Accounting Standard Board, *Research Report: Service Efforts and Accomplishment Reporting: Its Time Has Come* (Norwalk, Conn.: GASB, 1990), p. 10.

SELECTED READINGS

Baram, Michael S. "Cost-Benefit Analysis: An Inadequate Basis for Health, Safety, and Environmental Regulatory Decision Making." *Ecology Law Quarterly* 8 (1980), pp. 473–531.

Baum, Warren C. and Stokes M. Tolbert. *Investing in Development: Lessons of World Bank Experience.* Oxford: Oxford University Press, 1985.

Buchanan, James M. ed. *Public Finances: Needs, Sources and Utilization.* Princeton, N.J.: Princeton University Press, 1961.

Canadian Comprehensive Auditing Foundation. *Comprehensive Auditing: Concepts, Components and Characteristics.* Ottawa, 1981.

Glynn, John J. *Value for Money Auditing in the Public Sector.* Englewood Cliffs, N.J.: Prentice-Hall, 1985.

Grimmood, Martin and Cyril Tomkins. ''Value for Money Auditing—Towards Incorporating a Naturalistic Approach.'' *Financial Accountability and Management* (Winter 1986), pp. 251–272.

House, Ernest R. *Evaluating with Validity.* Beverly Hills, Calif.: Sage, 1980.

Layand, R. ed. *Cost-Benefit Analysis: Selected Readings.* Baltimore: Penguin, 1972.

Musgrave, Richard A. and Peggy B. Musgrave. *Public Finance in Theory and Practice,* 5th ed. New York: McGraw-Hill, 1989.

Pomeranz, F., A. Cancellieri, J. Stevens, and J. Savage. *Auditing in the Public Sector* New York: Warren, Gorham and Lamon, 1976.

Prest, A. R. and R. Turvey. ''Cost-Benefit Analysis: A Survey.'' *The Economic Journal* (December 1965), pp. 683–735.

5

Public Enterprises and Privatization in the Developing Countries

Most of the developing countries have a mixed economy comprising both public and private sectors. The public sector includes the central government; local, provincial, and other levels of government; and public enterprises or state-owned enterprises (SOEs). The private sector is characterized by the private ownership of firms, and it functions in the framework of markets and the so-called price mechanism. The mixed economy is a hybrid of pure socialism and pure capitalism. While both sectors are expected to coexist and contribute to the economic development of the country, they are generally the subject of a debate about the role of state-owned enterprises versus private enterprises. The debate centers basically on whether SOEs should be privatized to better improve the economic development of the developing countries. Accordingly this chapter examines the role of both SOEs and privatization in the development context of the developing countries.

VIEWS OF GENERAL WELFARE

The societal optimal choices about SOEs depend on the views of society about general welfare in the face of market failures, and the nature of the SOEs themselves. General welfare is secured by an efficient production of all the goods necessary for society to maintain an adequate quality of life. It depends on the working of the economy and particularly the public and private sectors. In what follows, both systems are examined in terms of their contribution to the public interest.

THE PUBLIC AND PRIVATE SECTORS

The economy of most nations is very complex. The production of goods and services is shared by both public and private sectors. The output of the public sector includes products such as education, national defense, and police and fire protection. The output of the private sector includes commodities such as food, medical care, housing, and investment goods such as residences, business structures, and producers' equipment and inventories. This type of economy, which combines outputs produced by both public and private sectors, is referred to as a mixed economy. The nature of the mixed economy in terms of the public and private sectors' contribution to the GNP has been changing over the years. While the trend seems toward a steady increase of the public sector's contribution, there is a lack of public consensus on which sector should be dominating.

One school of thought argues forcefully for a major role of the private sector, while another argues for a more important role for the public sector and for government intervention. The private-sector argument is well represented by the following quote from Milton Friedman, an ardent advocate of private-sector dominance:

> Every act of government intervention limits the area of individual freedom directly and threatens the preservation of freedom indirectly. . . . The widespread use of the market reduces the strain on the social fabric by rendering conformity unnecessary with respect to any activities it encompasses. The wider the range of activities covered by the market, the fewer are the issues on which explicitly political decisions are required and hence on which it is necessary to achieve agreement. In turn, the fewer the issues on which agreement is necessary, the greater is the likelihood of getting agreement while maintaining a free society. . . . A government which maintained law and order, defined property rights, served as a means whereby we could modify property rights and other rules of the economic game, adjudicated disputes about the interpretation of the rules, enforced contracts, promoted competition, provided a monetary framework, engaged in activities to counter technical monopolies and to overcome neighborhood effects widely regarded as sufficiently important to justify government intervention, and which supplemented private charity and the private family in protecting the irresponsible, whether madman or child—such a government would clearly have important functions to perform. The consistent liberal is not an anarchist.[1]

The public sector is also well represented by John Galbraith, an ardent advocate of public-sector dominance:

> This disparity between our flow of private and public goods and services is no matter of subjective judgment. On the contrary, it is the source of the most extensive comment which only stops short of the direct contrast being made here. In the years following World War II, the papers of any major city—those of New York were an excellent example—told daily of the shortages and shortcomings in the elementary municipal and metropolitan services. The schools were old and overcrowded. The police force was under

strength and underpaid. The parks and playgrounds were insufficient. Streets and empty lots were filthy, and the sanitation staff was under-equipped and in need of men. Access to the city by those who work there was uncertain and painful and becoming more so. Internal transportation was overcrowded, unhealthful, and dirty. So was the air. Parking on the streets had to be prohibited, and there was no space elsewhere. These deficiencies were not in new and novel services but in the old and established ones. Cities have long swept their streets, helped their people move around, educated them, kept order, and provided horse rails for vehicles which sought to pause. That their residents should have a nontoxic supply of air suggests no revolutionary dalliance with socialism.[2]

The debate centers on the merits and/or deficiencies of the market system. An examination of the structure and the performance of the market system followed by a discussion of the economic effectiveness of public sector decisions will clarify the arguments in the debate.

The Working of the Market System

The private market economy consists of two primary actors, households and businesses, and two markets, the product market and the factor market. Households buy and businesses sell products in the product market, while households sell and businesses buy factor services in the factor market. The prices of either products or factors of production are set in the two markets in an automatic process referred to as the law of supply and demand. For these two markets to function efficiently, the following conditions must be met:

1. *Perfect competition in all markets:* Enough buyers and sellers exist in the market that no one has control over the price of goods or services exchanged.
2. *Increasing costs in all industries:* Each industry experiences increasing costs, to where the costs are either constant or decreasing corresponds to a natural monopoly.
3. *Exclusion principle:* Each good, service, or factor of production is exclusive in the sense that they provide satisfaction only to the buyer of the good, service, or factor. Goods, services, or factors of production that are not consistent with the exclusion principle possess *spillover effects.*
4. *Absence of Public Goods:* This assumption eliminates all goods that possess spillover effects.
5. *Complete Knowledge:* All buyers and sellers have full knowledge of all the options in the market.
6. *Complete Mobility.* All resources are mobile in response to changes in prices.

If all these assumptions are met, the private market system will work efficiently and in the public interest: it will produce what is desired by people, it will produce it most efficiently, and it will distribute it according to the individual's contribution to the total social output.

Market Failure and the Need for Collective Action

Markets are in general not perfectly competitive because of failure to meet one or several of the above assumptions. Market failure requires that some economic goals be attained with collective action. As a first example, some firms are experiencing decreasing costs, leading to a situation of natural monopoly. A situation where only a few firms can function efficiently leads to natural oligopolies. In both cases competition is decreased, requiring correction of various forms of regulation—antitrust legislation, public regulation, public ownership. As a second example, the complicity of society leads to the creation of spillover cost or benefit in violation of the exclusion principle. These arise whenever one individual's action benefits or harms someone else with or without his or her consent. These spillovers create inefficiencies in the market because they are not internalized in the decision making of the individual creating them or consuming them. In the case of spillover benefits, as in the case of education, the free market produces a smaller output than the socially optimum output. In the case of spillover costs, as in the case of pollution, the free market produces a greater output than the socially optimum output, taking into account social costs and benefits. In both cases, collective action is required to correct the economic inefficiency and misallocation of resources.

Collective action may take the form of government production of the good as a public good, levying a special tax and granting inducements to correct for a spillover cost or to reward for a spillover benefit, use of administrative regulation, or use of persuasive power. This collective action is generally initiated and implemented by the public sector to compensate for the failure of the market system to produce the optimal social output. Robert Haveman states the problem as follows: "Because the private economy sometimes fails to operate in the public interest, sometimes fails to achieve an efficient allocation of society's resources, and sometimes generates an income distribution which violates ethical sensibilities, collective action through a public sector is required."[3] Accordingly, in what follows, the working of the public sector is examined.

The Working of the Public Sector

Public and nonprofit organizations go beyond the efficiency objective sought by profit-oriented firms to include various goals such as achieving an "equitable" distribution of income, maintaining economic stability and full employment, and controlling the balance of payments. The range of problems addressed by the public sector includes those relating to the provision of public and private education; transportation services; health care services for the poor, the military, and the aged; recreational facilities; and national defense. In addition, the public sector is heavily involved in managing hospitals, natural resources, income maintenance and income transfer programs, research support programs, the production of energy, and the provision of public and fire protection.

Various alternative ways are used by the public sector to engage in these activities. The commonly used alternative is direct action, whereby the government (local or federal) takes an active role in providing such goods as national defense, highways, low-income housing, recreational facilities, postal services, police and fire services, and sewage treatment facilities. Direct action may take the form of either explicit expenditures to provide these services or cash and/or tax subsidies to encourage private initiative to deal with these problems. In addition, the government is involved in various income transfer and maintenance programs, such as social security, welfare and unemployment compensation, and transfer in-kind programs in the form of food, health care, education, and housing redistribution.

It is generally accepted to divide the economic activities of the government into three branches: allocative, distributional, and stabilization, each pursuing a single objective and producing one type of public good.[4] The allocative branch pursues the efficiency objective, which is the efficient allocation of resources. The stabilization branch is concerned with the formulation and execution of macroeconomic policies to effect full employment. The distribution branch is concerned with the equity objective, which is to promote a desirable distribution of income. Since this chapter is not concerned with macroeconomic policy, only allocative and distributional branches are examined.

Income Distribution

The market system rewards people for their output performance and not for their efforts. Consequently, people who are not endowed with the necessary skills required by the market system—such as education, training, or capital endowment—may earn little. These skills may also change in response to changes in consumer preferences and demands, leading to changes in the rewards received by people. Finally, social problems and particularly racial tension and discrimination may create inequitable and "inefficient" income distribution. For these and other reasons, the government is justified in undertaking some forms of income redistribution.

Burton Weisbrod suggested a number of alternative approaches to be used by a government that desires to alter the distribution of income, which involve programs to transfer money, to transfer income in kind, or to enhance earning power for the group to be aided.[5] He also suggested six standards for judging the desirability of any alternative means for redistribution income, namely, the administrative cost, the target efficiency, the allocative efficiency, the nondemeaning benefits, consumer versus taxpayer sovereignty, and flexibility over time.[6]

First, the administrative cost is judged relevant to program selection. Target efficiency is the second standard for ensuring that the "deserving" and only the deserving are aided. The degree to which a program benefits only the "target" group is termed the program's *vertical target efficiency.* The degree to which the program benefits all members of the "target" group is termed its *horizontal target efficiency.* Third, allocative efficiency refers to the need to minimize the negative effects of the redistributional scheme on the incentives of those who benefit from the redistribution and of those who are made worse off by it. Fourth, nondemeaning benefits refers to the need to ensure that the benefits are not provided in a manner that tends to stigmatize or destroy self-respect. Fifth, consumer versus taxpayer sovereignty reflects a choice regarding who ought to determine the pattern of consumption by beneficiaries of a public program. The conflict between the two criteria reflects two distinct views of society.[7] Sixth and last, flexibility over time refers to the need to evaluate the desirability of the program over time and to verify whether it will remain satisfactory as conditions change.[8]

Allocative Function

The allocative function of government is concerned with an efficient allocation of resources for the benefit of the public interest. The definition of the public interest involves making a distinction between collective action and individual action and between public action and private action. Collective action or public action arises any time a group desires provision of goods or services that it cannot have through individual or private action. These goods or services are produced for the public interest and are known as pure public goods and quasipublic goods.

Pure private goods and services are divisible and excludable—divisible in the sense that they may be divided into finite units of consumption and excludable in the sense that nonbuyers may be excluded from the benefits of consumption. In addition, to the goods efficiently produced by the private market system, private goods must be produced under nonmonopoly conditions, be unassociated with significant production or consumption externalities, and assorted with low cost information concerning the quality of competing products.

At the extreme opposite pole to pure private goods are pure public goods. Unlike pure private goods, pure public goods are indivisible and imperfectly excludable, may be associated with significant production or consumption externalities, are often produced under conditions of decreasing costs of production, and may not be assorted with accurate and inexpensive market information.

A general definition of a public good is that of the perfect collective consumption good:

> There are certain goods that have the peculiarity that once they are available no one can be precluded from enjoying them whether he contributed to their provision or not. These are the public goods. Law and order is an example, and there are many others too familiar to make further exemplification worthwhile. Their essential characteristic is that they are enjoyed but not consumed [and that their benefits are derived] without any act of appropriation.[9]

This definition is restricted, however, to a collective consumption good that does not embrace much of what public expenditure policy concerns. As a result, Peter Steiner defined a public good as any publicly induced or provided collective good.[10] He also distinguished between three types of public goods: public goods arising from nonmarketable services of particular goods, public goods arising from market imperfections, and public goods arising because of concern with the quality of the environment.[11]

The first type of public good arises when collective concern and public action are needed to allocate resources in accord with "true valuations." They are particularly needed when the production of a good or service creates side effects whose value is not reflected in the prices of the outputs sold or the resources used, which is the case when external economies or diseconomies are produced. Familiar examples are discharges of noxious wastes into water or air, downstream navigational or flood control consequences of a private power dam, and civic beautification or uglification incident upon the building of private golf courses, factories, or slaughterhouses.[12]

The second type of public good arises when public collective action is needed to correct market failure caused by market imperfections. Imperfections that may hinder the efficiency of the market include inadequate information, monopoly power, time lags, and high transaction costs.

The third type of public good arises when, even with existing perfectly functioning markets, people choose collective action rather than market solutions to allocative problems with respect to the distribution of income, the nature or quality of goods produced, or the patterns of consumption that markets produce.

A pure public good is characterized by indivisibilities in production or jointness in supply and the impossibility or inefficiency of excluding a person from the enjoyment of a particular commodity once it has been made available to other individuals in society. For these goods a collective voice process or nonmarket decision making is necessary to reveal individual preferences and achieve Pareto efficiency.[13] For the private goods the preferences are expressed by the purchases (entry or exit) of buyers. There are, however, some goods, labeled either quasipublic goods or mixed goods, that fall between the two extremes of public and private goods and that may require a mixture of exit and voice processes.

Dennis C. Mueller, in a seminal article later expanded into a book, identified four strategies for deciding the quantities of quasipublic goods, namely: voting with the feet, the theory of clubs, voting with the feet in the presence of jointness of supply, and the theory of revolution.[14]

If joint supply property is relaxed and a limited degree of exclusion is assumed, people can reveal their preference by moving into the community providing the most desirable fraction of the public good. This strategy, voting with the feet, allows people to group themselves into groups of like tastes.[15]

If exclusion is possible and economies of scale exist (joint supply property), people can reveal their preference by forming clubs where members have identical taste for the public good.[16] Any effort to discriminate against an individual will induce him or her to exit and join another club or create a new one. This is the theory of clubs.

When public goods are produced with economies of scale, people can reveal their preference with a combination of voting with the feet and the ballot. People moving from one community to another may be offered a subsidy or asked to pay a tax depending upon whether they impose an external economy or diseconomy on the new community. A central authority may be asked to levy the taxes and offer subsidies. The solution based on a central authority "vests the entire population with a property right in both communities and achieves allocational efficiency by taking all members of the favored community to subsidize the disfavored community."[17] This is Mueller's "voting with the feet in the presence of jointness of supply."

The theory of revolution strategy is eloquently stated by Mueller as follows: "When neither the ballot, nor the feet constitute adequate models of expression, there is still Chairman Mao's barrel of the gun."[18] The strategy calls for the creation of a new polity by revolution. Gordon Tullock proposed a model to explain a revolutionary's behavior as follows:

$$R = BP + D - C \tag{5.1}$$

where

R = potential revolutionary's action
B = new government's public good benefits
P = probability that the individual's participation brings about success
D = private gains from participation in the revolution
C = private costs

A positive R induces the individual to participate in a revolution while a negative R creates the opposite attitude.[19]

The Public Interest

The creation of public goods for the public interest identified earlier requires a conceptualization of the notion of the public interest. Steiner has identified three points of view of the public interest: individual utility, willingness to pay, and an aggregate social welfare function.[20]

The point of view of individual utility considers the public interest of a society as simply an aggregate of the private interests of the individuals comprising that society. The individuals are assumed to desire both private and public goods, which legitimizes the dual role of private markets and the government. This point of view assumes that unanimity prevails and that individual utilities can be measured and compared. This point of view is not, however, without its criticisms. Consider the following:

> The major objection to a utility consensus view of social welfare functions is that it is nonoperational and does not seem to provide guidance to the decisions of real societies. Certainly we do take decisions with less than unanimous consent. Certainly, too, many public goods provide benefits in excess of their contributions only to very small minorities of the society, but with the evident acquiescence of sizeable majorities. One can argue that, ex post, individuals are thus revealed to value the benefits which accrue primarily to others. But this rationalization leads us back to a de facto definition: whatever the government does is revealed to be desired by people.[21]

The point of view of willingness to pay asks not how much an individual values a given public good but how much he or she is willing to be taxed to provide it. Placed in the context of the pure theory of public expenditure,[22] this view implies that a good is worth producing if the aggregate sum of the willingness to pay of different individuals exceeds the cost.

One limitation of this point of view is the distributional question. More explicitly, some of the taxpayers may end up receiving more than they are willing to pay for and being coerced to provide what others want. Consider the following:

> Citizens have social values about appropriate tax policies, too. Suppose we are building a public playground to be used by underprivileged children. If A is a rich misanthrope and B a poor Samaritan, there is no compelling reason why B should carry more of the tax burden, even though he may be willing to do so.[23]

The point of view of an aggregate social welfare function assumes that individuals voluntarily yield certain coercive powers to a government that determines social priorities by an aggregation process. In this view the political process articulates the public interest by determining the aggregate social values. In doing so, competing objectives are reconciled by a process of implicit or explicit "weighting." J. C. Harsanyi proved that individuals and social preferences satisfy the von Neumann and Morgenstern-Marschak postulates and if each individual is indifferent between two states of the world implies social indifference between the states, then social welfare is a weighted sum of individual utilities:[24]

$$W = \sum_{i=1}^{n} a_i U_i \qquad (5.2)$$

An example is the Bergson-Samuelson social welfare function:[25]

$$W = W(Z_1, Z_2, \dots) \qquad (5.3)$$

where W is a real value function of all variables (Z_i's) that might affect social welfare; the Z_i's and W are assumed to represent the ethical values of a society or of individuals in it. Needless to say, this social welfare function is difficult to determine and may require the introduction of value judgments or ethical postulates.

Kenneth Arrow introduced five axioms that he argued every social welfare function should meet because they may be considered as the basic value judgments of the community contained in the social contract or constitution.[26] These five axioms may be stated briefly as follows:

1. *Unlimited domain:* All possible orderings of individual preferences are possible.
2. *The Pareto postulate.*
3. *Transitivity:* The social welfare function gives a consistent ordering of all feasible alternatives.
4. *Nondictatorship:* No individual can impose his or her preferences.
5. *Independence of irrelevant alternatives:* The social choice between any two alternatives is independent of preferences over any other alternatives.

Arrow showed that no social welfare function satisfies these five postulates. To get rid of the paradox, researchers relied on a relaxation of each of the assumptions and found that such a procedure raises more difficult questions of choices.[27] Consider the following statement:

> From a public choice perspective, relaxation of either the independence or unrestricted domain axioms appears to be the most appealing way out of the paradox. Each in turn raises questions as to what issues are to be decided, who is to decide, and of those who decide, which preferences shall be weighted. Such choices directly or indirectly involve interpersonal utility comparisons and must rest on some additional value postulates, which if explicitly introduced would imply specific interpersonal utility comparisons. The latter cannot be avoided.[28]

Given a choice of any view of the public interest, it is left to the political process to implement it. Two views of the nature of the political process may be identified: majority principle and pluralism.

Majority principle derives from a theory of leadership motivation put down by Anthony Downs.[29] In *An Economic Theory of Democracy* he hypothesized that "parties in democratic politics are analogous to entrepreneurs in a profit-seeking company. So as to attain their private ends, they formulate whatever policies they believe will gain the most votes, just as entrepreneurs produce whatever products will gain the most profits."[30] In brief, they will attempt to maximize political support. To do so they will rely on the majority principle in their policy decisions, which basically correspond to the level of support at which the marginal gains of those supporting the policy equal the marginal losses of those rejecting the policy.

The pluralistic nature of the political process assumes that decisions are the result of the interaction of various important special interest groups. The general view is that pluralism generates a socially desirable outcome, given that it represents an equilibrium and consensus among competing groups. This view has, however, been challenged by various authors. The most effective objection was advanced by M. Olson, who argued that there is a systematic bias in a pluralistic society that causes only special interest groups to exercise political power.[31] An expression of the special interest groups is evident in their lobbying effort.

STATE-OWNED ENTERPRISES

Nature of State-Owned Enterprises

Government policies are generally aimed at the user of GNP. However, in most countries government is also involved in the production of GNP, making the public sector an owner, producer, and manager of certain state-owned enterprises whose outputs are sold or distributed. This public endeavor is made in the name of the public interest, and the resulting state-owned enterprises are assumed to work for the public interest. SOEs are created as separate entities from the government, sometimes incorporated under a general corporation act, sometimes under a specific act for government operations, sometimes according to a special act for each corporation, with the government as the legal owner of the shares of these enterprises. The legal forms are justified as follows:

> The purpose of these legal forms is to free the enterprise from rules and regulations of the government that may prevent flexibility and reduce operating efficiency, and to achieve some sort of separation of the activities of the government as both a ruler of the country and as owner of economic units engaged in production, exchange and distribution. It is hoped that these legal forms would permit public accountability combined with maximum management freedom and flexibility.[32]

State-owned enterprises are assumed to meet the following three criteria:

1. That the government is the principal stockholder in the enterprise, or otherwise has the ability or the potential to exercise control over the broad policies followed by the enterprise, and to appoint and remove enterprise management.
2. That the enterprise is engaged in the production of goods and/or services for sale to the public, or to other private or public enterprises.
3. That, as a matter of policy, the revenues of the enterprise are supposed to bear some relation to its costs.[33]

They are basically hybrid organizations where, as in the private sector, they are generally expected to generate a profit, pay taxes, and manage their own budgets; and as in the public sector, they are expected to conform to a host of formal and informal state controls in exchange for special privileges or subsidies.

Various distinctions can be made among different types of SOEs. W. G. Shepherd made the useful distinction between negative and positive types of SOEs.[34] Negative types include:

1. Public sponsorship of activities used mainly by the wealthy, such as the tax support of university education for children from upper economic levels.
2. The ''sick industry'' public firm that often uses large volumes of capital and sells primarily to private firms and unneedy customers.
3. The capital-intensive ''utility'' monopoly that breeds internal inefficiency.[35]

Positive types include:

1. A public-firm competitor that has some mixture of private-public ownership and motivation.
2. A public entity exerting monopsony power against private market power, which appears to be beyond other public constraints.
3. Activities with high, progressive benefits spread widely throughout society such as in the case of public universities.
4. Units whose outputs go mainly to upper-wealth groups, which maximize profits such as state universities, performing arts programs, and high quality medical care.[36]

Shepherd distinguished between the following three different types of SOEs: the conventional public corporation, the financial public enterprises, and the social enterprise.[37] They are defined as follows:

1. *The conventional public corporation* is commonly in a ''utility'' or heavy industry, with high capital intensity. Its degrees of public ownership and monopoly are total, or nearly so. Its capital is usually supplied directly by the Treasury, and—despite a degree of formal autonomy—the government does influence (or even control) some policies. When these outside interventions are large, and when the market is shrinking, the public firm often has financial deficits.
2. *Financial public enterprises* are public banks that range from standard deposit and clearing banks to special lending units and insurance systems; they can also be public investment banks. . . . The investment banks are distinctive in several ways. They have partial holdings and can often shift these holdings flexibly. They are usually independent and unsubsidized. They are a newer type, with several subcategories, and their experience is growing. Some are directed to specific aims: to assist mergers, foster small business, or protect national sovereignty, for example. Others are simply general-purpose investment banks, free to follow commercial opportunities. Such public investment banking has recently grown, but it is still experimental.
3. *Social enterprises* come in a wide array of purposes and conditions, often with a degree of subsidy and direct governmental control, but also ranging into independent

and self-sustaining social enterprises. These too are evolving in many ways, and they are an important part of all governmental activity. They can usefully be evaluated and predicted as public enterprises, rather than just as units of public finance, as they traditionally have been. Indeed, their defects often arise from neglect of the fact that they are enterprises, with (1) inputs, (2) a production process which needs to be managed, costed, and evolved, (3) outputs (physical units or services), (4) demand characteristics, much like those of standard enterprises, and (5) market positions and monopoly characteristics.[38]

SOEs derive their funds from annual appropriations of a government budget, and as such may act as a tool of government strategies, a vehicle for political patronage, yet still a revenue-producing and self-supporting enterprise, aimed at selling the goods or services they either purchased or produced. National interest remains the ultimate goal of SOEs. They are expected to adopt managerial policies that ensure the "national interest."

SOEs differ from one country to another, espousing from each country administrative, organizational, and managerial traits more in line with the culture of each country. Witness the following characterization of SOEs:

Local business norms and administrative culture shape the way state-owned enterprises are set up in the first place, and determine how they are run thereafter. At the danger of caricature we can say that emerging Asian economies with a tradition of family-owned private enterprise set up public firms along similar lines. These countries follow the market model and establish state-owned enterprises with a distinct identity separate from government. They must jostle with other firms in the capital market, compete against imports within reasonable bounds set for an infant industry, and follow the commercial principles of a family-owned firm. Public enterprises in South Korea and Taiwan conform closely to this ideal type. They broadly rely on market forces to shape the destiny of the state-owned sector, although governments in both countries lean on state and private companies alike if they want to nudge the economy in a particular direction. Ironically, occupation of these countries by Japan until the second war left a colonial legacy which now reverberates in tough, state-sponsored competition threatening Japanese firms forty years on.[39]

There is also a great organizational variety in SOEs, including organizations producing a single product or multiple products in a given sector, organizations operating in more than one sector, organizations operating in more than one location, and organizations operating through different segments.[40] An illustrative description of this variety follows:

a. An organisation with a more-or-less single product and in a single location: e.g. (the former) Heavy Electricals Ltd. in Bhopal (India), and Mumias Sugar Company Ltd. (in Kenya).

b. An organisation with dispersed plants but operating in a more-or-less single sector: e.g., British Steel Corporation, Bharat Heavy Electricals Ltd. (in India), and Steel Authority of India Ltd. (in India).

c. An organisation with diversified plants and operating in different sectors: e.g., Hindustan Machine Tools (in India), and Ghana Industrial Holding Company (in Ghana).

d. An organisation with legally separate parts engaged

i. either in a more-or-less single sector—e.g., National Textile Corporation Ltd. (in India), Mineral Development Corporation (in Zambia) and Kenya Tourist Development Corporation;

ii. or in different sectors, of which the most well-known example is IRI of Italy. Other examples are National Development Corporation (Tanzania), Pernas (Malaysia), Temasek (Singapore), National Enterprise Board (UK), Industrial and Commercial Development Corporation (Kenya), and Guystac (Guyana).

e. An organisation with almost all public enterprises in its fold. There are not many examples of this structure. ZIMCO in Zambia is a conspicuous one, having under it such large holding companies as INDECO (for industry), MINDECO (for mining), FINDECO (for finance) and so on. A nearly similar organisation was set up in Argentina, Corporacion de Empresas Nacionales, which covered all public enterprises with the exception of banks, provincial and municipal, and armed forces enterprises. GUYSTAC is another near example (in Guyana), though the big DEMBA (Bauxite) enterprise stands outside it.[41]

Motives for SOEs

State-owned enterprises have grown steadily not only as a response to political ideologies that favor them but also to a variety of specific economic needs or problems. Some of these needs or problems include aiding economic development in areas where private entrepreneurs are either unwilling or unable to invest, capturing revenue from foreign-controlled companies, rescuing failing private enterprises, enhancing political or economic control by acting as a means of counterbalancing the economic power of private business groups or of political power blocks, and accomplishing social goals.[42] Raymond Vernon presented the following circumstances under which SOEs have been brought into existence:[43]

1. SOEs were used as fiscal agents—for example, levying taxes by selling at high monopoly prices, buying at low monopsony prices, or dispensing subsidies through sales at reduced prices. An interpretation of the results of the financial statements of SOEs is offered as follows:

> large profits may reflect nothing more than the taxing capabilities of the state, implemented by the grant of a monopoly to the state-owned enterprise, whereas large losses may conceivably be the expression of a conscious policy of grants from the public purse to some part of the national population. Where losses do occur, it is not easy for an outsider to distinguish between those that represent a planned policy of income redistribution and those that are rationalized after the fact in such terms.[44]

2. SOEs are charged with developing or maintaining an industry largely ignored by the private sector.

3. SOEs are used as a mobilizer of national monopoly and monopsony power, improving the terms of trade without resorting to the relatively clumsy device of taxes or tariffs. Export marketing boards in developing countries are clean examples of this role.
4. SOEs are used as official agents in bilateral trade arrangements to insure that neither party will have to pay foreign currency to the other in settlement of its transactions.
5. SOEs are used as agents of industrial policy to prevent certain industries from folding up too rapidly under the pressure of foreign competition.
6. SOEs are finally used to achieve a multiplicity of goals, which poses an intractable problem to managers of SOEs:

> In some circumstances, the multiplicity of goals would conceivably be manageable. If, for example, specific trade-off functions were laid down among competing goals, the manager might still be able to construct a strategy that was optimal when measured against the mandate of the firm. But governments are characteristically composed of a coalition of forces, each of which places rather different weights on conflicting goals. One ministry, therefore, may stress inflation goals, another employment goals, another budgetary goals; one politician will favor his area of the country, another politician his. And any of these elements in the coalition could easily have some voice in determining the rewards and punishments meted out to the manager.[45]

Similarly, Aharoni presented the following reasons used by governments to create SOEs:[46]

1. For strictly administrative reasons, to transfer a service from a government department to a more autonomous enterprise, and in the cases of LDCs to organize population control programs.
2. To boost the growth of a certain industry in fields where the size of the investment is deemed by the government to be too large and the short-run expected return is judged too low for private capital interests.
3. To influence the rate and direction of development in certain regions of the country and direct credit to projects deemed nationally important.
4. To control monopolies, ensuring that profit from a natural monopoly is gained by the government rather than some private citizens.
5. To promote competition by creating SOEs in monopolistic or oligopolistic industries.
6. To gain information on private business operations in areas previously foreign owned.
7. To promote exports through SOEs.
8. To establish equity between the public and private sectors. This is a difficult goal. Witness the following assessment:

> The cost of attracting private enterprise—in terms of subsidies, tax holidays, output guarantees and government financed loans—is often so high as to make some people wonder whether it is equitable to allow private investors to profit while letting the public bear most of the risks. The line of demarcation between "aid to the private sector" and "too much aid to the private sector" is often quite blurred.[47]

9. To achieve noneconomic national goals.

Finally Frederic Pryor hypothesized that the following economic influences give a certain degree of predictability to the creation of SOEs:

a. *Economies of scale.* One manifestation of economies of scale is the existence of "natural monopolies," industries in which an optimal scale enterprise produces a significant share of total industrial production. These may be common in certain utilities (water, sewage, electricity, gas), in communication (postal and telephone), and in transportation (possibly railroads).
b. *Externalities.* Examples of negative externalities leading to nationalization occur in industries in which pollution or destruction of collective resources cannot be easily controlled without government ownership. Examples of positive externalities leading to nationalization occur in instances such as education, multipurpose river projects, and "production" of "high culture" in which the benefits cannot be sufficiently captured by private owners to encourage private production.
c. *Public purchases.* Certain situations occur where a public agency is a large or sole buyer, and where vertical integration may yield appreciable economies. Examples include weapons production as well as certain health services.
d. *Large "unearned" income.* Certain production leads to larger incomes which are considered unearned. This occurs in some mineral mining, as well as in natural monopolies.
e. *Power and sovereignty.* Some industries involve economic power sufficiently great to compromise the independence of the political system. One prime example is weapons productions; other possible candidates include airlines and petroleum. In small, less developed economies, instances abound.[48]

Other Motives for SOEs

The conventional economic argument of market failure is usually used as an argument in favor of government intervention in production. The causes of market failure are generally attributed to economies of scale, public goods, externalities, and information asymmetries. As stated by Jonas Prager,

> When the limited size of the market precludes competition, when private producers will not enter a market because of the free-rider nature of the good, when others rather than the producing firms bear the costs or appropriate the benefits of production, or when the information needed to make rational decision is itself scarce, the market mechanism will not provide efficient results.[49]

In addition to the argument of market failure, other motives for government ownership include: ideology, economic sovereignty, income, finance, and employment.[50]

1. Ideology, especially socialist ideology, favors nationalization, hearing government as the representative of the people, and ownership of the means of production by the

people as way of reducing capitalistic exploitation and more fairly distribute the economic pie.

2. Economic sovereignty favors nationalization and SOEs as a condition for the effective functioning of the independent polity.
3. Income resulting from the profits of SOEs is a better alternative to taxing an already fiscally burdened population.
4. The financing of SOEs from internal and external funding is easier to get than if it was geared to a private sector plagued by the uncertainties of development.
5. Employment is improved by the creation of SOEs.

Vernon elaborated on the following international implications of SOEs:[51]

1st: SOEs are more vulnerable to the domestic political process, forcing them to use either more or less foreign inputs than others.

2nd: SOEs are generally expected by their governments to achieve a high level of exports, which may result in increased jobs or foreign exchange earnings. However the export drive may fail when SOEs tend to avoid elaborate commitments to the requirements of the foreign market.[52]

3rd: SOEs may favor trading with state enterprises in other countries rather than with their private counterparts, because governments like doing business with one another, and can enter in long-term commitments.

4th: SOEs can find themselves at a disadvantage compared with their private multinational competitors, because they may be unable to be involved in the global distribution of their products, and in high technology fields where economies of scale are important yet flexibility must be maintained. In the case of high technology fields, SOEs may find it preferable to enter into partnerships with multinational firms.[53]

Managers of SOEs

In most developing countries a career in the government sector and/or in an SOE is attributed to a lot of respect and status. As a result the SOEs can attract the best-educated and most-talented people in a society, especially those who can't find a position in the private sector because of a lack of ties to the ownership of private business.

The managers of SOEs face special political problems, especially when the SOEs are used to achieve a multiplicity of stated goals. The manager has to respond to different political coalitions with conflicting goals. The tenure of a government minister is short, leaving the manager of SOEs with different goals from one administration to another. The political intervention in the management of SOEs is generally done in the name of national interest. For example, management of SOEs in various countries has been required to keep their prices down, as part of an anti-inflationary program; to invest in economically unprofitable endeavors—against their own judgment; to purchase locally made products at high prices to help some "infant industry" or subsidize a certain sector; they have been used as employment "reservoirs" to avoid unemployment. They have been directed not to raise wages and salaries and thus have lost their competitive position for manpower; at the same time they are not allowed to fire, thus maintaining a corps of inefficient workers who could not be removed to other industries.[54]

Needless to say, the losses of SOEs are easily blamed on management putting them in a very delicate position of balancing the need for efficiency with the need for political compliance. One way out for the managers of SOEs is to excell in bargaining trade-offs. As stated by Vernon:

A process of unceasing bargaining appears to be going on between most state-owned enterprises and the government bureaus, ministers, and politicians to which the enterprises are presumed responsive. As noted earlier, the government side is in a position to offer a variety of benefits. It can provide subsidized capital, underwrite unusual risk, provide protection from imports, forgive direct and indirect taxes, and offer exemption from government regulations. In return, state-owned enterprises can take on high-risk projects, hire unwanted labor, place plants in backward areas, hold down prices and profits, and tax some selected classes of customers while subsidizing others. To be sure, using the same ingredients, governments have been known to make bargains with private enterprises as well, but the evidence seems to point to the general conclusion that the special relationships between state-owned enterprises and governments based upon such bargains are more extensive and intensive than those made with private enterprises. In some countries and some periods, as in Sweden today, the distinction may be slight; but in other times and places, the distinction is quite strong.[55]

Another strategy is for the managers to try to increase their independence from the government apparatus, and/or increase their bargaining power. An assessment of this strategy follows:

The manager's search for independence from government may appear to entail certain personal risks at times. But from the viewpoint of the firm as a whole, it represents a low-risk strategy. According to the record, state-owned enterprises that get into trouble as a result of an independent strategy are rarely allowed to founder; when the help of the government is needed again, that help is usually forthcoming. Numerous cases that support this generalization are to be found both in Europe and the developing world.[56]

It is still a more accurate assessment that the managers of SOEs are limited in their innovativeness. To pursue the unproven, the managers of SOEs will find closed doors. One alternative is to start one's own SOE, which is practically impossible, or exit the SOE and embrace the private sector.[57] Another more logical alternative is to focus on the economic goals of SOEs and give them more importance than social and political goals. This is done by an allocation of resources according to efficiency criteria, increasing their autonomy, and controlling their environment. One danger of this attribute of managers of SOEs is the potential of abuses that conflict with the national interest. A possible scenario follows:

> In many cases, governments have found themselves facing situations where managers of SOEs decided on investments and committed funds for such investments without prior approval of the board of directors or prior knowledge of the minister. In some cases it was learned at a later stage, after large sums of funds had already been invested, that the project would not be as profitable or as socially desirable as originally envisaged. In these cases, the government faced a difficult decision: either stop investing funds in the project and see the large past outlays as huge sunk costs or continue the investment, hoping to reduce the total loss in this manner. In some cases, the more government tried to control by adding more formal requirements, the less it controlled in practice.[58]

SOEs are sometimes forced to adopt managerial policies that ensure the interest of other persons at the expense of the national interest and conventional efficiency. As stated by Aharoni:

> SOEs are often asked—unofficially—to undertake activities that have very little to do with either the company's own operating objectives or the national interest, but are helpful to a government minister for other reasons. Carrying out such activities through an SOE has the dubious result of not subjecting these activities to rigid parliamentary scrutiny. These costs of those activities are buried as ostensibly inefficient operations of the firm. This state of affairs has led to loss of public money and has weakened initiative and morale within SOEs.[59]

SOEs in the Developing Countries

State-owned enterprises account for about 10 percent or more of the gross national product of developing economies. They are found in various industries, both in developed and developing countries. In the developing countries, there is even a trend consisting of using state-owned trading firms, charged with the sale or purchase of some specified product for a given country.[60] Both the left- and the right-wing regimes, as well as liberal and military administrations, create SOEs to enter new industries. The need for growth rather than merely ideology turned the state in the developing countries into the role of entrepreneur, with sometimes the encouragement and assistance of aid donors and Western advisors.[61]

The motives for SOEs in developing countries are economic and/or sociopolitical. The economic motives are related to the need for savings mobilization, the need to secure employment, and the need to undertake capital-intensive projects in many ''natural monopoly'' cases.[62] The sociopolitical motives are related to the ''commanding heights'' argument that the states of developing countries should control the industries at the heights, decolonialization efforts, and the social goals of income redistribution, correction of imbalances in regional growth, and reduction of unemployment.[63]

SOEs are basically the norm in the "modern" sector of many developing countries. They can be the only way to create strong development in a key sector, especially when there is a lack of financial markets of sufficient size and sophistication as well as managerial expertise. As stated by John Sheahan:

> Public enterprise can be a constructive complement to private enterprise in the developing countries for two main reasons. First, in purely economic terms, it can be used to improve response to opportunities whenever private enterprise is thinly developed, highly averse to risk, or just plain unimaginative. It is even more absurd in an underdeveloped economy than it is in the United States to consider private business managers as fully alert and ready to act on every possible opening. That is to say, confident and dynamic entrepreneurship is a scarce resource everywhere, but especially scarce in developing countries. If public enterprise is conceived as a complementary input, adding centers of decision in which incentives are not weighed down by fears of losing personal fortunes, the ability to respond to opportunities can be increased.[64]

The reasons for public ownership in the less developed countries can also be attributed mainly to the ideology that sees nationalization or the creation of SOEs as vital to development.[65]

The degree of public ownership of SOEs in the developing countries may be measured by the share of the labor force working in production facilities owned 50 percent or more by the government, or the share of government ownership in the tangible reproduceable wealth, a measure that avoids problems both in the evaluation of land and other types of nonreproduceable wealth, and in the evaluation of patents and other types of nontangible wealth.[66] The first measure of public ownership is justified by either the goal of SOEs to create employment and get rid of excess labor, especially in the developing countries, or the goal of giving workers control of SOEs. The control of SOEs by workers in some developing countries involved two very different conceptions: "(1) outright control of the firm by its own workers, subject only to general regulations applicable to all enterprise, and (2) participation by workers in limited spheres of decision, oriented toward open criticism and exchange of ideas rather than complete authority."[67]

The size of SOEs is generally measured in terms of their share in total investment and value added of the country. The market prices for products and factors of production in the developing countries is known to be universally biased toward demand for capital and skilled labor and biased against demand for unskilled labor.[68] These distortions acting against the demand for labor give the SOEs the opportunity to improve both resource allocation and employment, by using accounting prices based on opportunity costs.[69] The SOEs in the developing countries can become a means of getting rid of excess labor and reduce a known bias toward capital-intensive fields and techniques of production more prevalent in the private sector. They are generally developed in the so-called natural monopoly sector (decreasing-cost public utilities), small-scale monopoly producers of sumptuary products (liquor, beer, tobacco) and basic necessities (salt, matches), transportation (railroads, airlines), and even banking.[70] In most developing countries, they can also be found engaged in manufacturing, mining, steel-making, crude-oil refining, petrochemicals, shipbuilding, textiles, and construction.

SOEs in the developing countries are the only way for those countries to develop high technology industries. The SOE is used to acquire advanced technology, and to invest millions of dollars in the development of human capital to absorb foreign technology or develop it locally.[71] As stated by Ravi Ramamurti, the SOE

> is prepared to invest millions of dollars in building facilities and developing human capital to make sophisticated products for markets it isn't sure exist. Further, it does so not caring whether it will make huge profits or, alternatively, knowing full well that even if all projections were met, it would earn a low or negative return at market prices. Politicians and bureaucrats who sponsor such SOEs are driven less by profit ability than by strategic goals such as promoting technological development or attaining self-reliance in an industry regarded as critical for national security or long-term economic development.[72]

In most of these cases private investors are unwilling or unable to enter these fields because of the sheer size of the capital required or because of the riskiness of the projects. Both capital-intensive and risky projects became the subject of SOE investment in the developing countries. Unfortunately the result of this risk taking by SOEs is sometimes disastrous. Witness the following assessment:

> However, much of the risky investment undertaken by SOEs is risky primarily because of its capital intensive [*sic*] involving projects of large scale. And government decisions to invest in such activities are often made on the basis of distorted macro-economic signals, many erected by the government itself. Here the scope for significant mistakes that lead to major losses for society as a whole can become very large. The result is often the classic ''purple dog'' project (a more apt characterization than the traditional ''white elephant'' label applied to ruinous state-enterprise investments) that requires heavy government subsidies from beginning to distant end.[73]

The other side of the coin is that a lot of SOEs in the developing countries may be a ''purple dog'' from a cash flow point of view but also a savior to large segments of the poor, in particular the urban poor, by providing vital services such as food distribution, electric power transmission, water supply, and transportation. SOEs are also the best tool to advance income redistribution objectives through the subsidization of prices of necessary commodities.[74] If waste and inefficiency can be eliminated, SOEs in the developing countries are at the core of the objective of rectifying social and regional imbalances.

SOEs and Income Distribution

Income distribution is a major development objective of most developing countries. The target is high income growth coupled with equitable distribution of income and wealth. SOEs are used as the instrument for the implementation of national policies of income distribution. One way of implementing these policies is through employee incomes by providing high wages, carrying excessive staffs or surplus labor, providing generous incentives, and favoring liberal social expenditures.[75] These distributional benefits accruing to employees are not without adverse consequences.[76]

Another way of implementing income distribution objectives by SOEs is through pricing policies, offering lower prices to low-income consumers and/or to final consumers. Other consumers may be asked to offer the price benefits (a form of cross-subsidizations). The government may also be asked to offer subsidies, by identifying the deserving consumers, and providing funds to cover the distributional policies.[77]

A third way of implementing income distribution objectives by SOEs is through deficits. The deficits may be corrected by the SOEs through drawing on reserves, cutting in working capitals or borrowing, improving productivity, and relying on cross-subsidizations.[78] The government may also contribute by subsidizing the deficit by adopting any of the following measures: introducing new taxes, reducing expenditures, or borrowing additional funds.[79]

Evaluation of SOEs in the Developing Countries

In evaluating SOEs in developing countries, a distinction needs to made between two broad groups: those whose main concern is economic in the implementation of investment opportunities, and those whose main concern is social.[80] The first group needs to be evaluated using normal financial criteria of return on capital and cost recovery as well as the SOEs' contribution toward the national economy in terms of value added, savings and investment, employment creation, and foreign exchange earnings. The second group of SOEs needs to be evaluated by how effective they have been at delivering the needed product or service to the social target group, without neglecting financial control. Witness the following example:

> If the government could put a monetary value on the specified social target, such as a credit for the amount of use of the warehouses by small farmers in the Indian example, and then require a positive return on assets taking such a credit into account, this could create a set of pressures which could, while leaving it up to the firms as to where to cut costs, orient choices toward preserving the intended social function.[81]

Commercial profitability of SOEs may be a way for SOEs to reduce their financial dependence on government and increase their autonomy. Another powerful argument for commercial profitability stems from the expectations of key outsiders who view profit as the ultimate objective of SOEs. As stated by Ramamurti:

> In other words, commercial profitability seems to lend *legitimacy* to SOE management by creating the impression among some external groups that the SOE is well run, well managed, or playing a useful social role. It would seem that most outsiders lack the capacity or information to probe deeper into the causes of that profit (or loss), including such factors as noncommercial objectives and pricing policies.[82]

To measure the profit performance of SOEs in LDCs, A. Gantt and G. Dutto relied on performance ratios where the base was not the total assets because of measurement problems, but the "current activity" of the SOE defined as half of the current revenue plus current expenditures [(current revenue + current expenditures) / 2].[83] Using this base they relied on the following ratios: flow of funds as a percentage of activity, gross investment ratio as a percentage of activity, surplus after investment as a percentage of activity, and transfer excluding loans from government budget.

In examining the performance of a large number of private and SOEs existing in a number of different industries in Indonesia for 1971, R. Funkhouser and P. W. MacAvoy used a ratio of financial profitability measured as the difference between sales revenue and direct expenditures, excluding depreciation and interest, expressed as a percentage of sales revenue.[84]

Economic profitability of SOEs in developing countries is generally measured as the difference between benefits and costs at economic efficiency (shadow) prices.[85] The following indicators of profitability may be derived:

1. The economic benefit-cost ratio (EBC) where economic efficiency is obtained with EBC > 1.
2. The economic returns to capital ratio (ERC) where economic efficiency is obtained with ERC = economic opportunity cost of capital.
3. The unit economic benefit (UEB) where economic efficiency is obtained with UEB > 0.
4. The domestic resource cost ratio (DRC), measured as the ratio of economic opportunity cost of domestic resources to international value added, where economic efficiency is obtained with DRC < 1.
5. The effective protection rate (EPR), measured as the ratio of domestic value added to international value added, which indicates the extent of protection and incentives given to SOEs through trade control and promotional policy measure.[86]

P. M. Jackson and A. J. Palmer also suggest the following indicators of performance of SOEs:

1. *volume of activity:* mileage; number of customers or clients; number of buses, trains, aircraft, etc. . . ; passenger journeys; passenger miles; production tonnages;
2. *operational performance:* number of staff per customer or client; costs per unit of output;
3. *financial performance:* operating margins; sales per employee; sales related to costs; revenue support per bus;
4. *quality of service:* waiting time for services; percentage of late trains; first class postal delivery success rates.[87]

Physical indicators expressing the production efficiency of SOEs include machine efficiency, human efficiency, and materials efficiency. They are defined as follows:

Machine efficiency, which can be revealed by factors such as capacity utilization, percentage of downtime due to breakdowns, machines-hours required for given units of output.
Human efficiency, judged by factors such as the availability of the labour force during the year and losses due to absenteesim, strikes, lock-outs, or go-slows and man-hours required for a given unit of output.
Materials efficiency, which must bring out the factor of consumption coefficient, the amount of raw materials consumed for a given unit of output.[88]

Marketing indicators of SOEs include the following: ''Percentage share of the market; growth of sales; percentage of domestic sales to export sales; growth of export sales; unit value of sales.''[89] All these indicators can best be used by distinguishing between the following five components of control.

A_1 = objectives
A_2 = past actuals
A_3 = potential
B = actuals
C = performance evaluation

The evaluation of these is achieved from the computation of the following variances:

$A_1 - B$ = performance vis-à-vis targets
$A_2 - B$ = growth rate
$A_3 - B$ = productive efficiency vis-à-vis norms[90]

In addition to economic efficiency, X-efficiency as introduced by H. Leibenstein is important for the SOEs in developing countries.[91] X-efficiency refers to the efforts of firms to maximize profits and minimize costs, taking into account the internal management structure and the environment in which they operate. A failure to reduce cost, to introduce improvements, and to use available opportunities to operate efficiently results in X-inefficiency. X-inefficiency in SOEs of developing countries has been attributed to monopoly market conditions, poor organization, and sociocultural traditions. High protection and bureaucratic management structures can also aggravate the situation of social efficiency. The reasons for X-inefficiency in SOEs follow:

> But X-inefficiency in SOEs is not by any means exclusively due to any inherent inability or unwillingness of managers to minimize costs for a given level of output. Pressures for X-inefficiency also arise from the external environment in which SOEs operate. These include faulty incentive structures for workers and managers, established by government agencies (in the form of rigid limits on compensation), governmental insistence upon redundant labor, whether for patronage reasons or to relieve unemployment problems (or both), as well as such factors as government-imposed materials-procurement requirements geared to rewarding political favorites rather than control of costs.[92]

The inefficiency may also be related to the government requirements of price control and social responsibilities that increase costs and/or lower profits. The presence of X-inefficiency in the developing countries is evident in the enormous differences in productivity from country to country in particular industries using the same technology.

Meeting noncommercial objectives is another important goal of SOEs, resulting in a strong concern with social efficiency. Social efficiency can be related to the need for income distribution between different income groups and regions; and can be achieved through channels such as wages and material input policy, pricing of outputs, distribution of financial surplus, and enterprise location. Social efficiency can be measured by the provision of public profits, defined as follows:

> Public profit can be thought of as financial profits, adjusted for economic efficiency and other non-commercial objectives. Inputs and outputs are revalued at shadow prices to allow for the divergence between market and efficiency values; the costs of meeting non-commercial objectives are deduced before public profit is calculated and treated as implicit subsidies to the enterprise.[93]

The indicators for economic and social efficiencies of SOEs are best determined through a matching between national objectives and appropriate evaluation criteria. National objectives and evaluation criteria of SOEs are shown in Exhibit 5.1.

Exhibit 5.1
Objectives and Evaluation Criteria

CASE 1

National objective	To promote technological self-reliance.
Statement of enterprise objectives incorporated in corporate plan	While our enterprise will place high emphasis on increased production, improved productivity, reasonable prices and improved quality of our products, we recognize the broader national goal of achieving technological self-reliance. We therefore accept as a major objective the promotion of technological development through our enterprise, and we desire to make specific contributions to the country's pool of technological advancement.
Disaggregation of specific components of the corporate objective:	*Evaluation criteria:*
1. Creating a research and development department.	1. Was a research and development department actually set up and how many persons are working in it?
2. Allocating adequate funds for research and development.	2. What percentage of the enterprise's turnover has been allocated to research and development?
3. Developing technological skills through training programmes within the enterprise.	3. Which in-house training programmes for technological development have been introduced?
4. Sending managers or technicians for advanced training in technological development to outside institutions.	4. How many managers or technicians have been sent for advanced training outside?
5. Developing trouble-shooting units on the shop floor.	5. What contributions have the trouble-shooting units made?
6. Searching consciously for import substitution possibilities.	6. What are the specific contributions of the enterprise towards import substitution?
7. Examining the increased utilization of domestic raw materials.	7. What research has been done on domestic raw materials and has it resulted in increased use of national resources and consequent reduction of imports?
8. Unpackaging of imported technology.	8. Which technologies have been purchased from abroad and what is

	the manner in which they have been unpackaged?
9. Utilizing fully domestic skills through subcontracting.	9. What is the extent of use of local skills through subcontracting?
10. Fostering new ideas and methods of work to improve productivity.	10. Have research and development produced some new ideas or methods?

CASE 2

National objective	To develop backward regions. The corporate objectives of our enterprise are essentially to provide consumer goods needed by the general national objective of promoting the development of backward regions. We therefore accept as a corporate objective the task of making a specific contribution towards such regional development through our operations.
Statement of enterprise objectives incorporated in corporate plan	
Disaggregation of specific components of the corporate objective:	*Evaluation criteria:*
1. In selecting the location of our plants we will consciously give preference to location in backward regions.	1. How many plants has the enterprise set up? Which of them are located in a backward region? Are there any new investment proposals, and if so, are the proposed locations in a backward region?
2. While developing the infrastructure of supporting services needed in our plants, we will make available such services to the local region.	2. What infrastructural supporting services have been supplied by electric power, water supply, roads? Are such infrastructural services used solely by the plants, or is the surplus being made available to the locality? Quantify the extent of electric power and water so provided. Are the roads being used for purposes other than that of plant operations?
3. While promoting measures for the welfare of our workers, we will attempt to extend the facilities so created to the local region.	3. What welfare services have been set up for workers—schools, hospitals, health centers, birth control clinics, creches, entertainment? Are these facilities also being extended to persons of the locality? Quantify the

number of nonworkers admitted to enterprise schools, hospitals, clinics, etc.

4. Through our plants established in backward regions we will generate employment for local persons.

4. How many jobs have been created by the establishment of the plant? How many of these jobs have been filled by recruits from the local backward region and how many through "imported" labour?

5. We will consciously follow a system of procuring supplies from the local region to generate income.

5. State the extent of supplies of raw materials and other inputs purchased by the plant. State the specific amount of supplies procured from the backward region. Indicate percentage of supplies obtained from local region.

6. We will promote ancillary activities in small-scale industry around our plants in backward areas.

6. Have any ancillary small-scale industries been developed? How many? What is the employment and turnover generated through ancillaries?

7. We will make positive efforts to prevent any adverse impact of our operations on the local area and exercise in particular vigilance in combating pollution.

7. Describe potential pollution dangers caused by the installation of your plant. Indicate specific anti-pollution measures taken and the cost incurred.

8. We will take steps to improve the environment surrounding our plants.

8. Describe what specific contributions your plant has made to the improvement of the surrounding environment. Have you established any gardens, parks or play fields?

9. We will maintain a lively contact with local authorities and extend managerial and technical support in solving local problems.

9. What is the relationship developed with local authorities? What specific contributions has the enterprise made to the solution of local problems?

CASE 3

National objective

To promote the integration of women in development.

Statement of enterprise objectives incorporated in corporate plan	The primary objectives of our enterprise are to produce and distribute electronic equipment and telecommunications. While devoting our primary attention to the building up of technological capability and high standards of production at economic cost, we are conscious of the broader national objective of integrating women into development. Our enterprise therefore proposes to make a conscious effort to contribute towards this national goal and to provide a model to other enterprises by using women as useful input in our operations and as a necessary part of our human resources.
Disaggregation of specific components of the corporate objective:	*Evaluation criteria:*
1. In our recruitment we will not practice any form of discrimination against women and will provide them equal opportunities for employment.	1. What is the total number of employees in the enterprise? What is the number of women employees and what percentage does it represent? Has the recruitment of women during the past year raised the percentage of female employment?
2. In our wage and remuneration policy there shall be no discriminatory practices, and we shall introduce a system of equal pay for equal work.	2. Please confirm that wage scales and remuneration are identical for men and women and give satisfactory reasons where they are not. What is the percentage of the wage bill paid to women, and what relationship does this percentage bear to their percentage of employment?
3. Taking note of the special responsibilities of women towards the family and children, we shall consciously provide special facilities to women to enable them to meet responsibilities.	3. What are the special facilities created for women—creches, special maternity hospitals, maternity leave conditions?
4. We will provide special training arrangements for women to upgrade their skills.	4. What are the specific training schemes designed for women? What percentage of the in-house trainees are women? Have any women been sent for external training?

5. We shall encourage the advancement of women in our enterprise to higher levels of responsibility.	5. How many women have been promoted to managerial ranks? What is the highest position held by a woman in the enterprise?
6. The enterprise will take keen interest in the welfare of the families of our workers outside working hours.	6. Describe the enterprise's contribution to family welfare.
7. The enterprise will attempt to provide part-time employment wherever possible to women in the locality.	7. Describe efforts to provide part-time employment for women. How many? How much does the enterprise spend for this purpose?

Source: Prasley Fernandes, "An Approach to Evaluating the Performance of Public Industrial Enterprises," *Industry and Development* 7 (1983), pp. 31–34. The views expressed here are those of the author and do not necessarily reflect the views of the secretariat of UNIDO. Reprinted with permission from United Nations Industrial Development Organization.

Performance of SOEs in the Developing Countries

The enthusiasm about the role of SOEs in the economic development of developing countries is now waning. The interventionist policies of the 1950s and 1960s are losing ground in the 1990s to the neoclassical perspective that emphasizes the role of markets and price mechanism in the development process, and calls for the removal of all forms of government intervention in product and factor markets and a reduction of the public sector. The move is motivated by the recent dismal performance of most SOEs in the developing countries in terms of financial, economic, social, and macroeconomic performance.[94] Witness the following assessment by the World Bank: "Some state-owned enterprises have been able to operate as successful commercial ventures without burdening public finances. In most countries, however, many have drained budgetary resources, contributed to overall public sector deficits, weakened fiscal management, and made negative contribution to value added."[95]

The sheer size of the public sector in the developing countries may be at the core of the efficiency problems of SOEs. The World Bank's 1981 report on economic prospects in sub-Saharan Africa (the "Berg Report") concluded that "it is now widely evident that the public sector is overextended, given the present scarcities of financial resources, skilled manpower, and organizational capacity. This has resulted in slower growth than might have been achieved with available resources, and accounts for the present crisis."[96]

The degree of public ownership is not the main determinant of the performance of SOEs. The nature of the political environment is at the cause of the disastrous performances of SOEs in both developing and developed countries. Witness the following assessment by the World Bank:

The key factor determining the efficiency of an enterprise is not whether it is publicly or privately owned, but how it is managed. In theory it is possible to create the kind of incentives that will maximize efficiency under any type of ownership, but there is a great difference between what is theoretically feasible and what typically happens. As a commercial entity, a state-owned enterprise must sell in the marketplace. As a public organization, it is given other objectives and is exposed to pressure from politically powerful sectional interests. State-owned enterprises are often operated as public bureaucracies, with more attention to procedure than to results; and ready access to subsidies can erode the incentive for managers to minimize costs.[97]

Not all evidence about the performance of SOEs is negative. Attempts to prove that the public sector in developing countries is "overextended" and requires "rolling back" have not been successful. P. Nunnenkamp's testing of the hypothesis of an inverse relationship between macroeconomic performance and the size of the public sector provided inconclusive evidence.[98] C. Kirkpatrick's attempt at the same hypothesis yielded a negative but statistically insignificant correlation between the output of the public sector and the GNP.[99] Similarly there seems to be no strong evidence of a statistically satisfactory kind to indicate that SOEs in developing countries have a lower level of technical efficiency than private firms operating at the same scale of operations.[100]

The performance of SOEs can be drastically improved by strong measures taken by the government. Various possibilities exist. For example Austin et al. suggest the following requisite actions:

- Clarification of inter-governmental reporting structures (emphasizing both autonomy and accountability).
- Clarification and simplification of enterprise performance objectives (with the aim of reducing the incidence of conflicting objectives).
- Depoliticizing the appointment of senior SOE managers by having the chief executive officer appointed by state enterprise board rather than by the ministry or head of state.
- Creation of performance-based incentive reward systems, including the use of management bonuses and profit-sharing schemes.
- Improved procedures for appointing state enterprise boards, emphasizing greater professionalism and longer continuity.
- Improved management information systems focused on key performance indicators.
- Strengthened accounting and financial reporting practices including the use of annual outside audits for the larger enterprises.[101]

The investment in SOEs of developing countries is another way of raising the investment ratio to the level expected to achieve progress toward self-sustaining growth advocated by development planning models. As such they are instrumental to development planning and economic development in the developing countries.

The focus on economic efficiency of SOEs in the developing countries can be judged as misplaced and wrong given the complex objectives of SOEs in those countries. Witness the following assessment of the situation:

> Private firms, by and large, maximize profits, and if profit maximization were the right objective for the public sector also, there may remain no compelling reason for nationalizing industries and setting up a public sector. The decision to set up a public sector and then ask it to do what the private sector would have done is like going to a cinema to try to sleep rather than to see the movie.[102]

Sheahan suggested that the developing countries keep those SOEs that are successful, in the sense of prospering without special subsidies or government help, in the public sector, and privatize those that are losers, which would combine the advantages of lesser risk aversion by SOEs with those of greater consciousness by private owners.[103] It is an excellent idea to try to rejuvenate and help all those successful SOEs and those that are instrumental to the development policies of the developing countries, and to privatize all those that can best be handled by the private sector. It will create an optimal mixed economy for the developing countries. For the SOEs that are kept because of their vital role in economic development a sense of priorities among the possible gains from SOEs is needed. An example of their collective scale of priorities is as follows:

1. Some degree of improved efficiency. In this, the main gains are from structural changes in basic conditions and in the taking of certain kinds of major risks. These risks include innovation and social policies of various kinds, which private enterprise might not undertake. The efficiency gains are mainly not of the marginal, allocative sort. Those can result from rational operation of public enterprise, but their net benefits are relatively small, and they occur mainly as side effects of otherwise rational policies.
2. Some softening of social impacts from decisions by public enterprise, including possibly an improvement in the regional and urban balance of enterprise activities.
3. Some improvement of content and ''social relationships'' within the enterprise.
4. Some degree of improved equity by making output cheaper than it otherwise would be for needy citizens (but this effect is expected usually to be limited and short).[104]

PRIVATIZATION

Nature of Privatization

Any attempt to improve public-sector performance is often associated with privatization. Privatization involves basically the transfer of assets or activities from the public to the private sector, with the aim of improving the efficiency of public-sector enterprises through increased exposure to market forces.[105] Definitions abound. For Michael Beesley and Stephen Littlechild, privatization refers to the formation of a Companies Act company and the subsequent sale of at least 50 percent of the shares to private shareholders, with the idea of improving industry performance through increasing the role of market forces.[106] Privatization is viewed by J. A. Kay and D. J. Thompson as several distinct, and possibly alternative, means of changing the relationships between the government and the private sector through denationalization, deregulation, and contracting out.[107] It is a transfer of ownership where the government bows out and the private sector makes an entrance.[108] The private sector is assumed to provide a more efficient environment:

> The conclusion is also straight forward. An economy can become more efficient only if the profit motive and competition jointly drive its SOEs. Profitability provides the incentive, while competition acts to channel the profit motive to the efficiency goal rather than to profitability for its own sake. A corollary follows. The most direct manner to achieve efficiency in the public sector is to allow the private sector to take over. Today's catchword, of course, is privatization.[109]

Privatization is also an attempt at expanding the private property system. Advantages of the private property system include its ability to stimulate innovation and encourage entrepreneurship and risk taking, its strong incentive to use property in the most efficient way toward increasing output, its efficiency in allocating resources among individuals, its ability to attract savings, its ability to distribute income commensurate with the efforts extended by individuals, and its contribution to a pluralistic social structure.[110]

The threat of bankruptcy, following privatization, acts as the ultimate solution on inefficiency. However, privatization needs to be adapted to the cultural context of each country.[111]

The World Bank is nationally aware of the simple fact that the private sector does not necessarily outperform the public sector and vice-versa, and of the dangers of outright privatization in relation to simple deregulation of markets.[112] A 1983 World Bank report assessed this issue.[113]

Instruments of Privatization

Privatization instruments can best be described by three types: asset transfer from the public to the private sector, generally through sale; deregulation or liberalization of statutory monopolies (with or without asset sales) and with particular emphasis on removal of entry restrictions; and franchising or contracting out the provision of marketable goods and services to the private sector.[114] The objectives and instruments of privatization are shown in Exhibit 5.2. They are explicated next:

1. *Asset sale,* as a privatization instrument, involves disposals of assets in the public-sector firms and natural monopolies through offers for sales of shares. The sales of the shares may be at a set price or through share sale by tender. The allocative efficiency may not be possible if the privatized firm is a monopoly

Exhibit 5.2
Objectives and Instruments of Privatization

Objectives / Instruments	Allocative Efficiency	Productive Efficiency	Revenue Receipts	Remarks
1.1 Asset Sales (of monopolies)	No	Yes	Yes	Regulatory framework required to control monopoly abuse
1.2 Asset Sales (of companies in competitive product markets)	Yes	Yes	Yes	–
2. Deregulation (with asset sales)	Yes Provided market is competitive or contestable	Yes	Yes But less than in 1.1 if incumbent's dominance is expected to be short-lived.	–
2.2 Deregulation (without asset sales)	Yes Provided market is competitive or contestable	Yes Provided trading losses are not underwritten by the government	No	–
3.1 Franchising (Chadwick-Demsetz Auction)	Yes Provided bidding is competitive	Yes Subject to contract being incentive-compatible	No	))) Franchising) authority required) to monitor
3.2 Franchising (Monopoly Rents Auction)	No	Yes	Yes	) and enforce) contracts)

Source: S. Domberger and J. Piggott, "Privatization Policies and Public Enterprise: A Survey," *The Economic Record* (June 1986), p. 155. Reprinted with permission.

that still needs to be regulated. The productive efficiency is possible if capital market pressures force management to recontract with labor the best labor mix and to implement the best production techniques. Revenues receipts are naturally guaranteed by the sale itself.

The financial gain or loss from the sale depends, however, on whether the price paid is more or less than the present value of prospective earnings from the asset.[115] The cash obtained from the sale may be used by the government to meet budget deficits, offer tax cuts, undertake increased current expenditures, and reduce the public debt.[116]

2. *Deregulation* consists of liberalizing and removing entry restrictions in the market. Allocative efficiency is expected if the deregulated market is competitive or contestable. Productive efficiency is possible if deregulation is accompanied by asset sales. Without asset sales, it is still possible provided trading losses are not underwritten by the government.

3. *Franchising,* as a privatization instrument, consists of conferring rights in the supply or distribution of goods and services to a sole producer or operator over a period of time. The purpose of franchising is to introduce an element of competition for a market where competition within the market is neither feasible nor desirable as in natural monopolies. Both E. Chadwick[117] and H. Demsetz[118] suggest competition taking place through bidding for the franchise contract, and the award of the contract to the contestant bidding the minimum supply price. An alternative award mechanism is to grant the contract to the producer bidding the highest capital sum of the franchise. This last mechanism is evaluated as follows:

> Since the award of the franchise confers monopoly rights upon the producer, the values of bids under this scheme are likely to reflect contestants' expectation of the discounted stream of monopoly rents over the life of the contract. This scheme obviously provides revenue receipts to the government by transferring, at least in part, the expected future profits from the franchisee to the franchisor. However, unlike the Chadwick-Demsetz auction, it does so at the expense of allocative efficiency.[119]

Other instruments include (1) Transfer of management only, not of ownership to the private sector. Leases management as well as contracting with the private sector for the delivery of public services fall in this category. (2) Shifting the financing of publicly provided goods from taxpayers to consumers through user fees.[120] A continuum of possibilities in privatization is shown in Exhibit 5.3. The privatization implementation process is also shown in Exhibit 5.4.

Privatization, Productive Efficiency, and Allocative Efficiency

One central concern in privatizing nationalized industries is the effect it would have on both productive and allocative efficiency. Productive efficiency refers to the achievement of a minimum cost in the delivery of the product or service. Allocative efficiency refers to the fulfillment of consumer needs at prices that reflect the costs of provision. Both the product market and the capital market act as monitors of both forms of efficiency—the product market by providing consumers with alternative products and alternative firms, the capital market by providing threats of bankruptcy or takeover. If privatizing creates different competitive private firms, rather than just a smaller or larger private monopoly, there are great incentives for both productive and allocative efficiency in a capital market environment that can impose bankruptcy or takeover. In the absence of competition following privatization, as in the case of the creation of a large private monopoly, there are no incentives to both allocative and productive efficiency, as well as no threats of bankruptcy or takeover. As stated by Kay and Thompson,

Exhibit 5.3
Continuum of Possibilities in Privatization

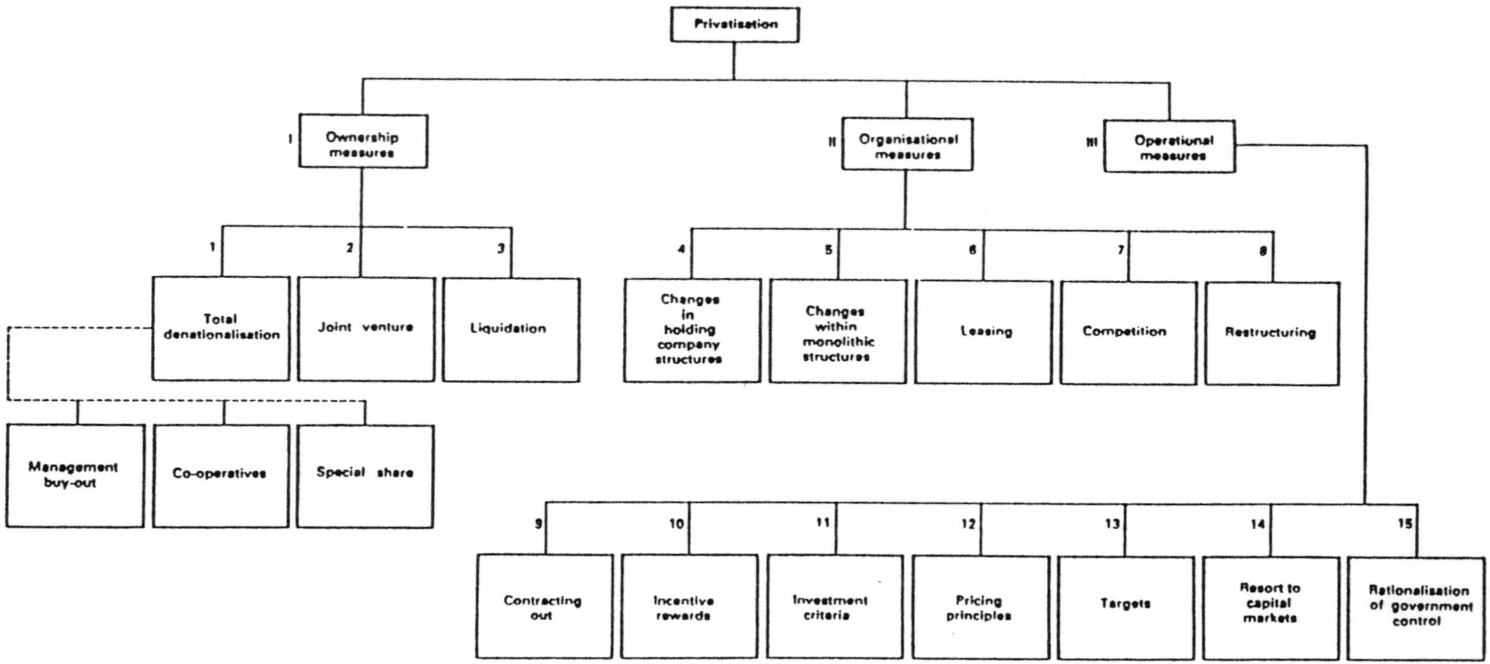

Source: V. V. Ramanadham "Privatisation: The UK Experience and the Developing Countries," in V. V. Ramanadham, ed., *Privatisation in Developing Countries* (London: Routledge, 1989), p. 5. Reprinted with permission.

Exhibit 5.4
The Privatization Implementation Process

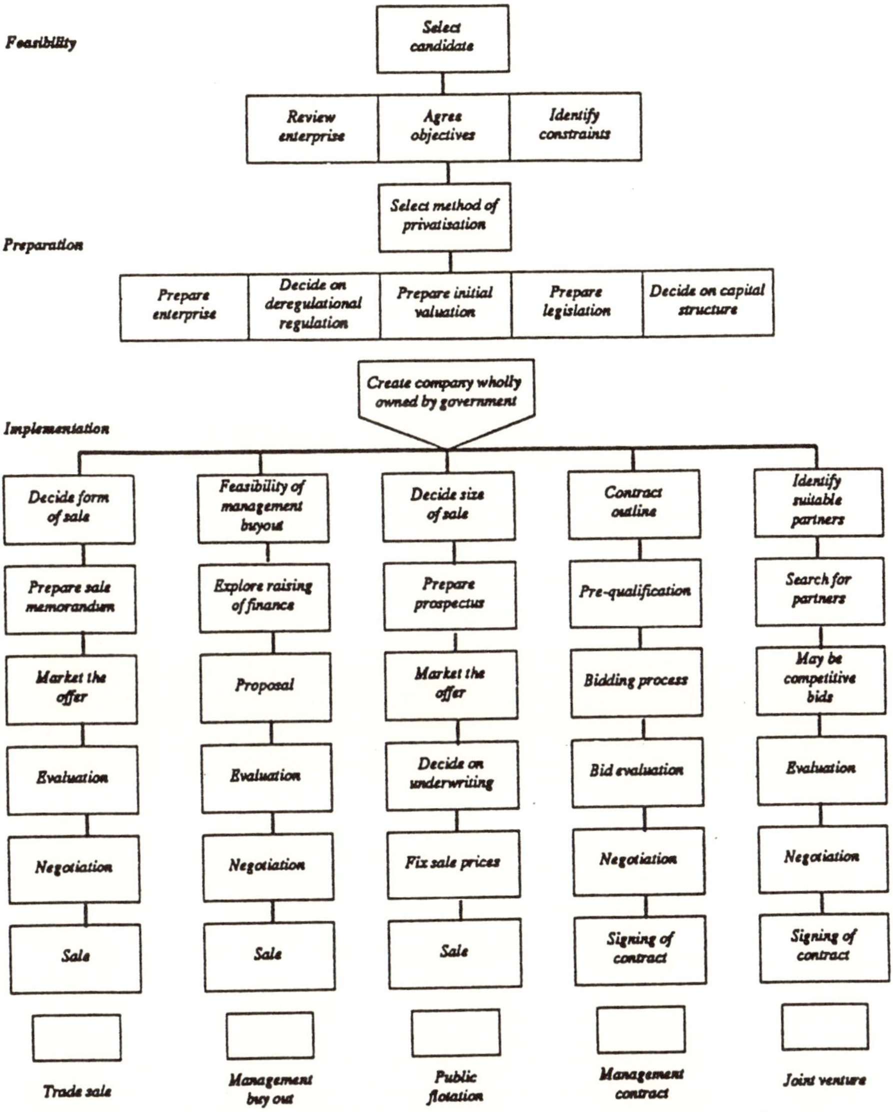

Source: Coopers & Lybrand, "Implementing Privatization," OECD East-West Accounting Issues Conference, Paris, September 25–27, 1990, p. 3. Reprinted with permission.

it is competitive, privately owned firms which have incentives to achieve both productive and allocative efficiency. Privatisation tends to promote productive efficiency, competition allocative efficiency. The incentive to productive efficiency comes from the requirement on private firms to achieve profits to stay in business in competitive product markets, to avert the threat of takeover from the market for corporate control. . . . If, however, there is little competition in the product market if the risk of bankruptcy is slight, and if the risk of takeover is minimal, the pressures of the market affect a private sector manager no more than his public sector counter part.[121]

Competition is therefore vital for privatization. It allows for the maximization of consumer benefits and the limitation of monopoly power. The absence of competition makes it hard to evaluate the performance of privatized firms.

But there is support for the view that the efficiency of all firms—public or private—is improved by a competitive environment. The regulation of private firms which do not face competition sometimes distorts incentives in ways which lead to higher cost levels than those of directly controlled public enterprises. The consequence is that under perfect competition private firms are likely to do better, but if there is little competition regulated private firms do not perform better than public firms and may do worse. It follows that privatization in an uncompetitive environment is likely to be positively harmful, in particular if the resulting firm is small enough to be at serious risk from takeover. Privatization will tend to improve performance in a company only if supported by liberalization; and if the two conflict, liberalization is decidedly to be preferred.[122]

It follows that the efficiency following privatization differs under the following circumstances: when a private monopoly replaces a public monopoly, when privatization occurs in the context of competitive markets, and when government privatizes the delivery of service but retains ownership and direction.[123]

1. In the case of the monopolistic private firm, a case for existence can be made in the developing countries where the market may be too small to support more than one single efficient firm.
2. In the case of the private firm in a competitive environment, efficiency can be achieved through the elimination of the various constraints on internal efficiency that may characterize some SOEs.
3. In the case of government ownership with private service delivery, efficiency is contingent on the characteristics of each contracting situation. As stated by Prager:

The conclusion seems apparent. The desirability of contracting out depends upon the relative inefficiencies in the entire package of costs, not production outlays alone. In certain cases, monitoring costs will be low and the advantages of contracting out substantial. In other instances, monitoring costs will be significant, offsetting the potential gains in efficiency of the contracting out. A case-by-case evaluation rather than a sweeping generalization appears the wiser course.[124]

Privatization and Public-Sector Failure

Privatization is mostly advocated as a better alternative given some evidence of public-sector failure. The evidence of public-sector failure is made on the basis of efficiency measures. Some may point to the fact that the consistent losses of SOEs may be due to the government-imposed low prices more than to inefficient operations.[125] It is still more plausible to argue that the absence of efficiency-promoting incentives better explains the poor performance of SOEs.

> Efficiency is one of many goals sought by political decision makers, and it is frequently a low-ranked priority at that. But even where profitability is a goal and efficiency is a means of achieving that goal, the state-owned enterprise is often not provided with the flexibility needed to accomplish its stated objective. Also, the reward structure in public enterprise often does not compensate efficient operation. Indeed, at times the system encourages inefficiency.[126]

The reward system, in the form of efficiency-promoting incentives provided by privatization, can rejuvenate the operations of former SOEs. The privatization drive assumes that the competitive market system, left to its own devices, without government intervention, will yield better economic results in terms of efficiency and social justice than other systems of economic organization. Higher production of resources is expected, as well as less inefficiency and corruption, which are generally viewed as direct results of the use of the state as a mechanism for import substituting industrialization and the excessive use of subsidies.[127]

A criterion for privatization is the present value of aggregate net benefits to consumers, employees, suppliers, exports, and taxpayers. Of these interest groups, consumers are generally rated first in evaluating the merits of privatization. More specifically two sets of consumers are considered: actual or potential consumers of the industry, and other consumers, who benefit from saving in resources following privatization.[128] Privately owned firms are expected to have a greater incentive to produce goods and services in the quantity and variety that consumers prefer. As stated by Beesley and Littlechild,

> companies which succeed in discovering and meeting consumer needs make profits and grow; the less successful wither and die. The discipline of the capital market accentuates this process: access to additional resources for growth depends on previously demonstrated ability. Selling a nationalized industry substitutes market discipline for public influence. Resources tend to be used as consumers dictate, rather than according to the wishes of government, which must necessarily reflect short-term political pressures and problems of managing the public sector's overall demands for capital.[129]

The logic of privatization is argued as follows:

1. Privatization could help raise revenues for Third World treasuries that were effectively bankrupted by their state-owned enterprises.
2. In the private sector only the fit can survive. Privatization, by pushing back the frontier of the state, could lead to innovative management and to promote economic efficiency.
3. By raising revenues for the public sector while transferring economic functions to the private sector, privatization can increase savings, investment and growth. This is especially true if there is a zero-sum relationship between the public and the private sector so that the larger the former and the more it spends, the smaller the latter and the less it saves,
4. Privatization could lead to further economic democratization through increasing participation in the ownership of national assets.
5. Finally, divestiture of national enterprises can take the form of reprivatizing firms. Two cases are prominent in this context. The first category is firms that have been nationalized essentially for noneconomic reasons, such as nationalism or attempts to promote a socialist economic structure. The second case is enterprises that failed in the market place and have been taken over by the state.[130]

An argument against the public sector in general and SOEs in particular is found in the "crowding out" hypothesis. It basically states that the public-sector investment reduces private investment if it relies on scarce resources that would otherwise be available to the private sector.[131]

Another argument against the SOEs in developing countries is the inevitable political interference and the resulting economic inefficiencies. As stated by Paul Cook and Colin Kirkpatrick,

> in many LDCs the public enterprise is an important instrument for political patronage. Senior staff are frequently political appointments with little industrial management experience; employment, purchasing and pricing decisions are subject to political intervention; the boundaries of government and enterprise control are ill-defined and continually shifting. The absence of clearly defined objectives and the limited operational autonomy given to public enterprises inevitably have an adverse impact on the efficient internal operations of the public enterprise sector.[132]

Privatization and Capital Markets

Privatization is difficult to implement in the absence of capital markets, which can act as a great motive for the transfer of SOEs to private ownership and also can help in the capital formation stage of privatization.[133]

The success of capital markets rests on convincing private and corporate savers to channel funds in the equity markets rather than the less formal, less restricted, and sometimes more native outlets. A reform of capital markets in the developing countries is needed to create a better climate for privatization. This reform should include at least an end to interest or dividend controls; a legal and administrative frame for the guarantee of investor protection; standards for accounting and disclosure; a developed accounting profession; reductions in the cost, complexity, and bureaucracy of equity issues; a fair tax system; and incentives for domestic and foreign investments.[134]

The capital market can also benefit from the privatization of large SOEs, leading new investors to enter the market and generating a higher volume of transactions. A deepening as well as a widening of the capital market is expected to follow privatization of large SOEs. Four reasons are suggested:

> First, the equity that is being sold is normally of good quality and represents an attractive investment opportunity. Purchasers gain comfort from the fact that the vendor is a government and have learnt by experience that governments are risk-averse when it comes to privatisations. Success is valued highly, which is no wonder, given privatisation's invariably high profile.
>
> Second, a government that is raising finance by selling equities will borrow less for a given public sector financial deficit than it would do otherwise. A government's total demand on the capital market may therefore be unchanged by a privatisation programme. . . .
>
> Third, and this point is often overlooked, even a single privatisation may create a company that is a material component of a stock market's index. . . .
>
> Fourth, it should also be remembered that governments who are selling equity become interested in the operations of the equity market and, implicitly or explicitly, take steps to strengthen the market. . . .[135]

Privatization and Management

The most effective and influential of interest groups is the senior management of the potentially privatized industry.[136] They are sometimes eager to get rid of government control as long as the organizational structure is not changed and the new environment is not too competitive. However, privatization without competition can be pointless and even harmful.

The managers of SOEs are civil servants who constitute a constituency in their own right, and form a kind of privileged urban elite. Privatization offers them both new opportunities and new anxieties. On the one hand, with privatization, they can hope for higher salaries and incentive schemes that may not have been permissible in the public sector. On the other hand, they now have to deal with the harsh realities of competition, profit objectives, and most of the time hard work. As a result one may argue that truly imaginative managers will find conditions in the private sector more congenial, leaving to the SOEs those more comfortable with the status.[137] As a result, "The outcome is that the private sector becomes ever more dynamic as it receives an influx of the more aggressive and imaginative men and women, while the public sector tends to stagnate."[138] These managers join a private sector to face both the carrot of reward and the stick of unemployment. In spite of the new realities of facing a hard-budget constraint, rather than the soft-budget constraint of SOEs, these managers find themselves better motivated to achieve their objective of self-improvement in a more rewarding climate, better conducive to the efficient production of goods and services.

Privatization in the Developing Countries

Privatization in the developing countries occurs largely through the external pressures from international aid donors and banking agencies, such as the World Bank, the International Monetary Fund, and the U.S. Agency for International Development (USAID). It is also used as a new development mechanism to shore up the sometimes dismal performance of SOEs in the developing countries. The debate about privatization in the developing countries centers on the merits of the market model versus the bureaucratic model, articulated as follows:

1. Whereas the market model stresses financial autonomy with emphasis on profitability, the bureaucratic model relies on the national budget for financing SOEs, and losses are accepted for social reasons.
2. Whereas the market model stresses clean commercial and social objectives, the bureaucratic model suffers from confusion about objectives and political interference in decisions.
3. Whereas the market model stresses operating independence, the bureaucratic model stresses close scrutiny of input decisions.
4. Whereas the market model stresses performance monitored by outputs, the bureaucratic model stresses attention to politically sensitive output (prices), and shows lack of concern with overall enterprise efficiency.
5. Whereas the market model stresses political competition from domestic rivals and imports, the bureaucratic model imposes tariff barriers and licensing to limit competition and legal restrictions to prevent market entry by potential domestic competitors.[139]

Here is a clear indictment of the bureaucratic model:

> The bureaucratic framework offers scope for political interference and nepotism. Integration of state enterprise accounts into national budgets reduces the likelihood of independent financial control. Absence of clear financial responsibilities diminishes the incentive to use scarce funds efficiently. There is more opportunity for corruption or straightforward looting as it is harder for employees to monitor their subordinates or superiors. Outside auditors find it harder to get to grips with what is going on. The inevitable government monopoly also attenuates pressures to allocate resources efficiently in the product market where inflated costs can be passed on in full.[140]

There is also the perception that development planning has not succeeded. The other alternative available to the developing countries is a shift to the neoclassical market-oriented view of the development process and policy. Neoclassical economics can be defined as "a paradigm that tells one to investigate markets and prices, perhaps expecting them often to work well, but also to be on the watch for aberrations and ways of correcting them. Perhaps the single best touchstone is a concern for prices and their role."[141]

The neoclassical school calls for a liberalization of the economy, a reduction in the role of the public sector and the number of government regulation and controls, and a heavier reliance on the market and price mechanisms.

The rise of a managerial class in most developing countries has accelerated the turning of SOEs to the private sector. In addition, changes in the structure of international markets, with easier access to needed technology in many fields of industry and agriculture; lower costs of transportation and communication; better education of indigenous engineers, agronomists, private managers, and public officials; reduced costs of transportation and communication, followed by reduced costs in the search for foreign sources of technology; and better access to the international capital markets, have also encouraged governments of developing countries to reconsider the role of SOEs in favor of privatization.[142] The eternal cash squeeze faced by developing countries made the process inevitable.

The World Bank and the IMF provided the strongest external stimulus for privatization in the developing countries, putting much of the blame for the lackluster performance of these countries on excessive government intervention. As the report of one of the World Bank's first economic missions to a developing country put it, "to date, none of man's efforts to repeal the law of supply and demand have been successful."[143] The position of both institutions is for a role of government limited to the provision of institutions that would allow the private sector to function effectively, and to the investment in economic infrastructure such as power complexes, transportation networks, port installations, and telecommunications facilities.[144]

There are definitively barriers to privatization in the developing countries. These barriers arise at both policy and administrative levels.[145] At the policy level, these obstacles include political and ideological barriers, held by proponents of state-owned enterprises; economic barriers, when there is a belief in the superior efficiency of state enterprises; and social barriers, when the activities and assets of public enterprises are viewed as social goods. At the administrative level, these obstacles include buyer willingness, when buyers prefer to use their funds in more profitable ventures; buyer capacity, when the buyer's funds are limited; enterprise size, when the size of the state-owned enterprises exceeds the capital available to private buyers; administrative mechanisms, when competitive bidding is difficult to implement; institutional resistance, when political pressure works against privatization; and the press of other agenda items, when other political agendas have primacy.[146]

There are various ways of overcoming the barriers to privatization. First: when the privatization barrier involves the questionable economic capacity of private capital markets to absorb the huge offering of shares, foreign placement could be considered. Other options involve debt financing with the government providing a local currency loan to allow for a highly leveraged layout, or an installment plan whereby the new owners pay for the stock net of the profits generated by the new enterprises.[147]

Second: when the privatization barrier involves the political accusations and backlash of selling to the few, the government could target buyers with the greatest vested interest in running the firm, such as employees, suppliers, clients, or even foreign multinationals.[148]

There is definitely a need for a planned approach to privatization in the developing countries. Examples of issues that need to be addressed include the following:

- Over what period of time will the divestment program be conducted?
- Since for financial and other reasons the companies cannot be sold all at once, in which order should they be sold?
- How much of the equity in each SOE should be offered for sale?
- What form of decision-making and approval process should be followed in carrying out the divestment program?
- Who will manage the process once it is established?
- How will the divestment effort be financed?[149]

Privatization can succeed best sometimes when ownership rights are offered to foreign investors. Limiting ownership to domestic investors can sometimes hinder the success of privatization, especially in cases where the foreign investors and/or firms can offer production management skills, marketing and technical support, as well as the capital modernization most needed in the developing countries.[150] Excessive trade protection and government intervention coupled with restrictions to foreign ownership can be harmful to privatization efforts in fields where both foreign capital and expertise are vital.

An interesting strategy for privatization calls for starting with the easiest solutions; starting with situations where privatization is likely to be able to demonstrate success; creating a competitive situation; ensuring that the leadership of the privatized firm, especially the personal qualities of higher management, is of the best; avoiding being too ambitious; and creating policies to improve the performance of SOEs that are not suitable for privatization.[151] The following considerations should guide any privatization policy:

1. Privatization schemes should be designed to maximize net consumer benefits, measured primarily by lower prices and improved quality of service, rather than stock market proceeds. A futures market for shares would facilitate flotation.
2. The promotion of competition—by removing artificial restrictions on entry, making resources equally available to potential entrants, and restructuring the existing indus-

tries—is the most effective means of maximizing consumer benefits and curbing monopoly power.

3. Stricter competition policy is preferable to rate-of-return regulation, efficiency audits and related forms of government "nannying."
4. Clear ground rules should be laid down concerning the criteria for providing uneconomic services and the sources of finance for these.
5. Compensation should be paid for serious transitional unemployment, though in the longer run employees' prospects will be enhanced by privatization.
6. Priority should be given to privatizing those industries where consumer benefits are likely to be greatest. Potential benefits will depend upon the size of the industry, whether it has already received attention, and whether competition rather than monopoly is likely to ensue.[152]

CONCLUSIONS

A mixed economy is definitely vital to the economic growth of developing countries. Both public and private sectors have roles to play. The public sector, through state-owned enterprises, is needed in all those areas where national interests and basic needs of the population demand it. The private sector is needed in all those areas where incentive systems provided by the price mechanism, capital markets, and a degree of competition lead to a better economic performance than those provided by SOEs. In some of these cases the discipline of the private sector is more conducive to efficiency than any regulation imposed by a government.

NOTES

1. Milton Friedman, *Capitalism and Freedom* (Chicago: University of Chicago Press, 1962), p. 15.
2. John Kenneth Galbraith, *The Affluent Society* (Boston: Houghton Mifflin, 1958), pp. 251–253.
3. Robert H. Haveman, *The Economics of the Public Sector* (New York: Wiley, 1976), p. 49.
4. R. Musgrave, *The Theory of Public Finance* (New York: McGraw-Hill, 1959), pp. 3–27.
5. Burton A. Weisbrod, "Collective Action and the Distribution of Income: A Conceptual Approach," in R. H. Haveman and Julius Margolis, eds., *Public Expenditures and Policy Analysis,* 2d ed. (Chicago: Rand McNally, 1977), p. 105.
6. Ibid., p. 113.
7. Ibid., p. 114–123.
8. Ibid., p. 129–130.
9. Robert Dorfman, "General Equilibrium with Public Goods," Paper presented to International Economics Association conference on Public Economics, September 1966, p. 4.

10. Peter O. Steiner, "The Public Sector and the Public Interest," in Haveman and Margolis, *Public Expenditures and Policy Analysis,* p. 31.

11. Ibid., p. 33.

12. Ibid.

13. Albert O. Hirschman, *Exit, Voice and Loyalty* (Cambridge, Mass.: Harvard University Press, 1970). In this book, Hirschman introduced two options for expressing individual preferences: either through an entry or exit option, or through a voice option.

14. Dennis C. Mueller, "Public Choice: A Survey," *Journal of Economic Literature* (June 1976), pp. 412–415; and Dennis C. Mueller, *Public Choice* (Cambridge: Cambridge University Press, 1979), pp. 125–147.

15. This strategy was first noted by Charles M. Tiebout, "A Pure Theory of Local Expenditures," *Journal of Political Economy* (October 1965), pp. 416–424. The strategy rests on important and questionable assumptions, namely, the full mobility of all citizens.

16. J. H. Buchanan, "An Economic Theory of Clubs," *Economia* (February 1965), pp. 1–14.

17. Mueller, "Public Choice," p. 414.

18. Ibid.

19. Gordon Tullock, "The Paradox of Revolution," *Public Choice* (Fall 1971), pp. 88–99.

20. Steiner, "The Public Sector and the Public Interest," p. 41.

21. Ibid., p. 45.

22. H. R. Bowles, "The Interpretation of Voting in the Allocation of Economic Resources," *Quarterly Journal of Economics* 58 (November 1943), pp. 350–356.

23. Steiner, "The Public Sector and the Public Interest," p. 46.

24. J. C. Harsanyi, "Cardinal Welfare, Individualistic Ethics, and Interpersonal Comparisons of Utility," *Journal of Political Economy* 63 (August 1955), pp. 309–321.

25. A. Bergson, "A Reformulation of Certain Aspects of Welfare Economics," *Quarterly Journal of Economics* 52 (February 1938), pp. 310–334.

26. K. Arrow, *Social Choice and Individual Values* (New York: Wiley, 1951; rev. ed. New Haven, Conn.: Yale University Press, 1963), pp. 104–105.

27. Bergson, "A Reformulation," pp. 310–340; A. Bergson, "On the Concept of Social Welfare," *Quarterly Journal of Economics* 68 (May 1954), pp. 233–252; C. Hildreth, "Alternative Conditions for Social Orderings," *Econometrica* 21 (January 1953), pp. 81–94; M. C. Kemp and A. Asimakopulos, "A Note of 'Social Welfare Functions' and Cardinal Utility," *Canadian Journal of Economics and Political Science* 18 (May 1952), pp. 195–200; A. K. Sen, *Collective Choice and Social Welfare* (San Francisco: Holder-Day, 1970), pp. 123–125.

28. Mueller, "Public Choice," pp. 421–422.

29. A. Downs, *An Economic Theory of Democracy* (New York: Harper & Row, 1957).

30. Ibid., p. 295.

31. M. Olson, *The Logic of Collective Action* (Cambridge, Mass.: Harvard University Press, 1965), chs. 5 and 6.

32. Yair Aharoni, *Markets, Planning and Development* (Cambridge, Mass: Ballinger Publishing Company, 1977), p. 247.

33. Malcolm Gillis, "The Role of State Enterprises in Economic Development," *Social Research* (Summer 1980), p. 252.

34. W. G. Shepherd, "Objectives, Types, and Accountability," in W. G. Shepherd,

Public Enterprise: Economic Analysis of Theory and Practice (Lexington, Mass: Lexington Books, 1976), pp. 38–40.

35. Ibid., pp. 38–39.

36. Ibid., pp. 39–40.

37. Ibid., p. 37.

38. Ibid.

39. Jonathan Aylen, "Privatization in Developing Countries," *Lloyds Bank Review* (January 1987), p. 20.

40. V. V. Ramanadham, *Public Enterprise: Studies in Organizational Structure* (London: Frank Cass, 1986), p. 1.

41. Ibid., p. 2.

42. James Austin, Lawrence H. Wortzel, and John F. Colum, "Privatizing State-Owned Enterprises: Hopes and Realities," *Columbia Journal of World Business* (Fall 1986), pp. 52–53.

43. Raymond Vernon, "The International Aspects of State-Owned Enterprises," *Journal of International Business Studies* (Winter 1979), pp. 7–15.

44. Ibid, p. 8.

45. Ibid, p. 10.

46. Aharoni, *Markets, Planning and Development,* pp. 252–255.

47. Ibid.

48. Frederic L. Pryor, "Public Ownership: Some Quantitative Dimensions," in Shepherd, *Public Enterprise,* p. 9.

49. Jonas Prager, "Is Privatization a Panacea for LDCs? Market Failure versus Public Sector Failure," *The Journal of Developing Areas* (April 1992), pp. 302–303.

50. Ibid., p. 303.

51. Vernon, "The International Aspects of State-Owned Enterprises," p. 11.

52. Ibid., p. 12.

53. Ibid., p. 14.

54. Aharoni, *Markets, Planning and Development,* p. 263.

55. Vernon, "The International Aspects of State-Owned Enterprises," p. 10.

56. Ibid., p. 11.

57. Prager, "Is Privatization a Panacea for LDCs?" p. 309.

58. Aharoni, *Markets, Planning and Development,* p. 276.

59. Ibid., p. 263.

60. M. M. Kostecki, "State Trading in Industrialized and Developing Countries," *Journal of World Trade Law* (May/June 1978), pp. 187–207.

61. Aylen, "Privatization in Developing Countries," p. 17.

62. Gillis, "The Role of State Enterprises," pp. 260–261.

63. Ibid., pp. 262–263.

64. John B. Sheahan, "Public Enterprise in Developing Countries," in Shepherd, *Public Enterprise,* p. 229.

65. Aharoni, *Markets, Planning and Development,* pp. 250–251.

66. Pryor, "Public Ownership: Some Quantitative Dimensions," pp. 3–4.

67. Sheahan, "Public Enterprise in Developing Countries," p. 220.

68. Henry Burton, "Economic Development and Labor Use: A Review," *World Development* (December 1973), pp. 1–22.

69. Sheahan, "Public Enterprise in Developing Countries," p. 216.

70. Gillis, "The Role of State Enterprises in Economic Development," p. 253.

71. Ravi Ramamurti, *State-Owned Enterprises in High Technology Industries* (Westport, Conn.: Praeger, 1987), p. 267.

72. Ibid., p. 258.

73. Ibid., p. 278.

74. Ibid., p. 283.

75. V. V. Ramanadham, *Public Enterprise and Income Distribution* (London: Routledge, 1988), p. 13.

76. Ibid., pp. 28–29.

77. Ibid., p. 54.

78. Ibid., p. 84.

79. Ibid., p. 86.

80. Sheahan, ''Public Enterprise in Developing Countries,'' p. 223.

81. Ibid., p. 226.

82. Ravi Ramamurti, ''Performance Evaluation of State-Owned Enterprises in Theory and Practice,'' *Management Science* (July 1987), p. 890.

83. A. Gantt, II, and G. Dutto, ''Financial Performance of Government-Owned Corporations in Less Developed Countries,'' *International Monetary Fund Staff Papers XV* (March 1968), pp. 102–142.

84. R. Funkhouser and P. W. MacAvoy, ''A Sample of Observations on Comparative Prices in Public and Private Enterprise,'' *Journal of Public Economics* 2 (1979), pp. 353–368.

85. Ramesh Adhiraki and Colin Kirkpatrick, ''Public Enterprise in Less Developed Countries: An Empirical Review,'' in John Heath, ed., *Public Enterprises at the Crossroads* (London: Routledge, 1990), pp. 35–36.

86. Ibid., p. 36.

87. P. M. Jackson and A. J. Palmer, ''The Economics of Internal Organisation: The Efficiency of Parastatals in LDCs,'' in Paul Cook and Colin Kirkpatrick, eds., *Privatisation in Less Developed Countries* (New York: St. Martin's Press, 1988), p. 207.

88. Prasky Fernandes, ''An Approach to Evaluating the Performance of Public Industrial Enterprises,'' *Industry and Development* 7, (1983), p. 26.

89. Ibid., p. 27.

90. Ibid., p. 25.

91. H. Leibenstein, *General X-Efficiency Theory and Economic Development* (Oxford: Oxford University Press, 1978).

92. Gillis, ''The Roles of State Enterprises in Economic Development,'' p. 271.

93. Adhikari, and Kirkpatrick, ''Public Enterprise in Less Developed Countries,'' p. 41.

94. Ibid., p. 25.

95. World Bank, *World Development Report* (Washington, D.C.: Oxford University Press, 1988), p. 180.

96. World Bank, *Accelerated Development in Sub-Saharan Africa: An Agenda for Action* (Washington, D.C.: World Bank, 1981), p. 5.

97. World Bank, *World Development Report 1983* (Washington, D.C.: Oxford University Press for the World Bank, 1983), p. 50.

98. P. Nunnenkamp, ''State Enterprises in Developing Countries,'' *Intereconomics* (July/August 1986), pp. 186–193.

99. C. Kirkpatrick, ''The World Bank's Views on State-Owned Enterprises in Less Developed Countries: A Critical Comment,'' *Rivista Internationale di Scienze Economiche e Commerciali* 33 (1986), pp. 685–696.

100. R. Millward and D. M. Parker, "Public and Private Enterprise: Comparative Behaviour and Relative Efficiency," in R. Millward, *Public Sector Economics* (London: Longman, 1983).

101. Austin, Wortzel, and Coburn, "Privatizing State-Owned Enterprises," pp. 59–60.

102. A. Sen, "Profit Maximization and the Public Sector," John Matthai Memorial Lecture, Kerala University, India, Mimeo, 1975, p. 16.

103. Sheahan, "Public Enterprise in Developing Countries," p. 215.

104. Shepherd, *Public Enterprise,* p. xii.

105. Ibid., pp. 145–146.

106. Michael Beesley and Stephen Littlechild, "Privatization: Principles, Problems and Priorities," *Lloyds Bank Review* (July 1983), p. 1.

107. J.A. Kay and D.J. Thompson, "Privatisation: A Policy in Search of a Rationale," *The Economic Journal* (March 1986), p. 18.

108. Prager, "Is Privatization a Panacea for LDCs?" p. 301.

109. Ibid, p. 311.

110. Aharoni, *Markets, Planning and Development,* p. 14.

111. Woodward, Nick, "Public Enterprise, Privatization, and Cultural Adaption," in Heath, *Public Enterprise at the Crossroads,* p. 282.

112. Paul Mosley, "Privatization, Policy-Based Lending and World Bank Behavior," in Cook and Kirkpatrick, *Privatization in Less Developed Countries,* p. 128.

113. World Bank, *World Development Report 1983,* p. 50 and 86.

114. Simon Domberger and John Piggott, "Privatization Policies and Public Enterprise: A Survey," p. 154.

115. Kay, and Thompson, "Privatisation: A Policy in Search of Rationale," p. 28.

116. Ramanadham, *Public Enterprise and Income Distribution,* pp. 100–101.

117. E. Chadwick, "Research of Different Principles of Legislation and Administration in Europe of Competition within the Field of Science," *Journal of the Royal Statistical Society, Series A* 22, (1959), pp. 381–420.

118. H. Demsetz, "Why Regulate Utilities," *Journal of Law and Economics* 11 (1968), pp. 55–56.

119. Dombergh and Piggott, "Privatization Policies and Public Enterprise," p. 136.

120. Pan A. Yotopoulos, "The (Rip) Tide of Privatization: Lessons from Chile," *World Development* 17, 5, (1989), p. 684.

121. Kay, and Thompson, "Privatization: A Policy in Search of a Rationale," p. 22.

122. Ibid., p. 25.

123. Prager, "Is Privatization a Panacea for LDCs?" p. 302.

124. Ibid., p. 316.

125. Ibid. p. 305.

126. Ibid., p. 307.

127. E. A. Brett, "States, Markets and Private Power: Problems and Possibilities," in Cook and Kirkpatrick, *Privatisation in Less Developed Countries,* p. 49.

128. Beesley and Littlechild, "Privatization: Principles, Problems and Priorities," p. 3.

129. Ibid., p. 4.

130. Yotopoulos, "The (Rip) Tide of Privatization," p. 684.

131. M. Blyer and M. S. Khan, "Government Policy and Private Investment in the Developing Countries," *IMF Staff Papers* (31, 1984), pp. 379–403.

132. Paul Cook and Colin Kirkpatrick, ''Privatisation in Less Developed Countries: An Overview,'' in Cook and Kirkpatrick, *Privatisation in Less Developed Countries,* p. 12.

133. Aylen, ''Privatization in Developing Countries,'' p. 23.

134. Ibid., p. 25.

135. Gerry Grimstone, ''Privatisation: Macroeconomics and Modalities,'' in V. V. Ramanadham,'' *Privatisation in Developing Countries* (London: Routledge, 1989), p. 114.

136. Kay and Thompson, ''Privatisation: A Policy in Search of a Rationale,'' p. 29.

137. Prager, ''Is Privatization a Panacea for LDCs?'' p. 308.

138. Ibid., p. 308.

139. Aylen, ''Privatization in Developing Countries,'' p. 19.

140. Ibid., p. 21.

141. Little, I.M.D. *Economic Development: Theory, Policy and International Relations* (NY: Basic Books, 1982), pp. 25–26.

142. Raymond Vernon, *The Promise of Privatization* (NY: Council on Foreign Relations, 1988), p. 8.

143. Report on Cuba—Findings and Recommendations of an Economic and Technical Mission Organized by the IBRD in collaboration with the Government of Cuba in 1950, p. 158, quoted in J. H. Adler, ''The World Bank's Concept of Development—An In-House Dogmengeschichte,'' in Jagdish Bhagwati and Richard Eckaus, eds., *Development Planning* (Cambridge, Mass.: MIT Press, 1973), p. 34.

144. Bon Babai, ''The World Bank and The IMF: Rolling Back the State or Backing its Role?,'' in Vernon, *The Promise of Privatization,* p. 256.

145. Austin, Wortzel, and Coburn, ''Privatizing State-Owned Enterprises,'' pp. 54–55.

146. Ibid., pp. 55–56.

147. Ibid., p. 58.

148. Ibid.

149. Ibid., p. 56.

150. Aylen, ''Privatization in Developing Countries,'' p. 26.

151. John Heath, ''Privatisation: Modalities and Strategies,'' in V. V. Ramanadham, *Privatisation in Developing Countries* (London: Routledge, 1989), pp. 123–124.

152. Beesley, and Littlechild, ''Privatisation: Principles, Problems and Priorities,'' pp. 17–18.

SELECTED READINGS

Aharoni, Yair. *Markets, Planning and Development.* Cambridge, Mass: Ballinger Publishing Company, 1977.

Austin, James, Lawrence H. Wortzel, and John F. Coburn. ''Privatizing State-Owned Enterprises: Hopes and Realities.'' *Columbia Journal of World Business* (Fall 1986), pp. 51–60.

Aylen, Jonathan. ''Privatization in Developing Countries.'' *Lloyds Bank Review* (January 1987), pp. 15–30.

Beesley, Michael and Stephen Littlechild. ''Privatization: Principles, Problems and Priorities.'' *Lloyds Bank Review* (July 1983), pp. 1–20.

Blyes, M. and M. S. Khan. "Government Policy and Private Investment in the Developing Countries." *IMF Staff Papers* 31 (1984), pp. 379–403.

Burton, Henry. "Economic Development and Labor Use: A Review." *World Development* (December 1973), pp. 1–22.

Cook, Paul and Colin Kirkpatrick, eds., *Privatisation in Less Developed Countries.* New York: St. Martin's Press, 1988.

Domberger, Simon and John Piggott, "Privatization Policies and Public Enterprise: A Survey." *The Economic Record* (June 1986), pp. 145–162.

Funkhouser, R. and P. W. MacAvoy. "A Sample of Observations on Comparative Prices in Public and Private Enterprise." *Journal of Public Economics* 2 (1979), pp. 353–368.

Gantt II, A. and G. Dutto. "Financial Performance of Government-Owned Corporations in Less Developed Countries." *International Monetary Fund Staff Papers XV* (March 1968), pp. 102–142.

Hatherly, David J. "Privatisation and the Social Role of Audit." *Financial Accountability and Management* (Autumn 1987), pp. 249–266.

Heath, John, ed. *Public Enterprises at the Crossroads.* London: Routledge, 1990.

Kay, J. A. and D. J. Thompson. "Privatisation: A Policy in Search of A Rationale." *The Economic Journal* (March 1986), pp. 18–32.

Kirkpatrick, C. "The World Bank's Views on State-Owned Enterprises in Less Developed Countries: A Critical Comment." *Rivista Internationale di Scienze Economiche e Commerciali* 33 (1986), pp. 685–696.

Prager, Jonas. "Is Privatization a Panacea for LDCs? Market Failure versus Public Sector Failure." *The Journal of Developing Areas* (April 1992), pp. 301–321.

Ramanadham, V. V. *Privatisation in Developing Countries.* London: Routledge, 1989.

———. *Public Enterprise and Income Distribution.* London: Routledge, 1988.

———. *Public Enterprise: Studies in Organizational Structure.* London: Frank Cass, 1986.

Ramamurti, Ravi. "Performance Evaluation of State-Owned Enterprises in Theory and Practice." *Management Science* (July 1987), pp. 876–893.

———. *State-Owned Enterprises in High Technology Industries.* Westport, Conn.: Praeger, 1987.

Shepherd, W. G. *Public Enterprise: Economic Analysis of Theory and Practice.* Lexington, Mass.: Lexington Books, 1976.

Vernon, R. "The International Aspects of State-Owned Enterprises." *Journal of International Business Studies* (Winter 1979), pp. 7–15.

———. *The Promise of Privatization.* New York: Council on Foreign Relations, 1988.

Index

About the Author

AHMED RIAHI-BELKAOUI is Professor of Accounting at the College of Business Administration, the University of Illinois at Chicago, and Chairman of the Cultural Studies and Accounting Research Committee, American Accounting Association (Internal Accounting Section). Riahi-Belkaoui is also a member of the editorial board of several professional journals and is author of 19 previous Quorum Books and co-author of two more.